The Long Road to Baghdad, Volume 2

Edmund Candler

Nabu Public Domain Reprints:

You are holding a reproduction of an original work published before 1923 that is in the public domain in the United States of America, and possibly other countries. You may freely copy and distribute this work as no entity (individual or corporate) has a copyright on the body of the work. This book may contain prior copyright references, and library stamps (as most of these works were scanned from library copies). These have been scanned and retained as part of the historical artifact.

This book may have occasional imperfections such as missing or blurred pages, poor pictures, errant marks, etc. that were either part of the original artifact, or were introduced by the scanning process. We believe this work is culturally important, and despite the imperfections, have elected to bring it back into print as part of our continuing commitment to the preservation of printed works worldwide. We appreciate your understanding of the imperfections in the preservation process, and hope you enjoy this valuable book.

Photo: *Maull & Fox, Ltd.*

GENERAL MAUDE.

The
Long Road to Baghdad

By
EDMUND CANDLER
Late Official "Eye-Witness" in Mesopotamia

With 19 Maps and Plans and 16 Half-tone Plates

In Two Volumes
VOLUME II

Cassell and Company, Ltd
London, New York, Toronto and Melbourne
1919

CONTENTS OF VOL. II

CHAPTER	PAGE
25. The Advance	1
26. Mahomed Abdul Hassan	17
27. The Hai Salient and the Dahra Bend	29
28. The Crossing	49
29. The Forcing of Sannaiyat	57
30. The Pursuit	65
31. To Baghdad	80
32. The First Days in Baghdad	97
33. The Turk in Baghdad	114
34. After Baghdad—The Meeting with the Russians	130
35. The Shatt-el-Adhaim	151
36. Samarrah	165
37. The Blossoming of the Desert	179
38. The Bible and Babel	194
39. Najaf	208
40. The New Offensive: Ramadi	221
41. Jebel Hamrin and Tekrit	236

THE LONG ROAD TO BAGHDAD

CHAPTER XXV

THE ADVANCE

THERE was nothing very memorable in the first days of the advance, but it was a relief to be breaking new ground. There was an exhilaration in moving on. We seemed to have spent interminable years cooped up at El Orah, Falahiyeh, and Arab Village. Each of these camps repeated the other so exactly that time came to be reckoned, not by locality so much as by phases of emotion, or absence of emotion—the anxiety and depression of the long months before the fall of Kut, the dead monotonous resignation of the hot weather afterwards, when the sun and flies contributed the physical element to our mental Avernus, and then the relief of being cool and comfortable again and the prospect of becoming something, or doing something, and ceasing to be an altogether derelict army.

Was it to be Baghdad or Kut? Nobody knew. Most of us thought Kut, though the Tigris was very broad, and the defences at Sannaiyat so indefinitely repeated in the rear of the position that unless we could turn the place by a crossing upstream the breaking through would cost more than it was worth. After all, the value of Kut now was more sentimental than strategical, and whatever shape our policy or strategy took, the immediate and ultimate objective was to contain, or kill, as many Turks as we could, or in current metaphor "to pull our weight."

We were conscious during the lull before the advance that the two Army Corps on the Tigris, with a bare 18,000 Turkish rifles opposed to them, were not pulling their weight. The cold weather was advancing, and the rainy season, which, if severe, might be almost equivalent to immobilisation. There were signs of impatience at home, uneasiness in India. In the public eye Mesopotamia had become a sink, a backwater; our troops had lost moral, we were for ever marking time. But it is the proof of a strong commander not to be hustled by impatience or the mistrust that grows out of long inaction. Many a campaign has been lost by concession to the spirit of restlessness. But Maude chose his own time; nor did he communicate it. If Force D was not pulling its weight, it was because it was still in the training stage. Sinews were being developed. We had to create the staying-power that would carry us on after the first lap or two of the advance. This in the form of material and supplies; for the Army Commander had decided that no move should be made until we had accumulated a seven days' reserve at Sinn.

For the moment an organiser was needed more than a strategist or tactician; Maude was all three. In this connection I may quote a Staff Officer whose opinion carries weight everywhere in the Army. "There are three things necessary for carrying on a campaign," he said. "You want the fighting man whose genius is strategy and tactics; and you want the man who understands everything about Staff work; but these may be wasted without the brain for organisation and the interior economy of the army. I don't think I had ever struck a man who combined two of these qualities, certainly not three, until I met Maude."

The Advance

One's first impression of the Army Commander was modesty, repose, confidence, strength. One gradually realised the thoroughness and single-mindedness of the man, the far vision, the minute application to detail. He was a master of detail. He had his eye all the while on the ultimate end and on everything that concerned the immediate means to it—supply, transport, operations, intelligence, the psychological factors. In every branch of Staff work he was the inspirer and director. The reconstruction of the fighting machine, the breaking up of the Turk's force on the Tigris, called for qualities which when found in combination amount to genius. In the dark days we prayed for a great man; and he was on the spot. General Maude might have been born for the task. His whole life was a preparation for it. The large vision was a gift; the discipline, method and single-mindedness were the outcome of the training his character had imposed on himself. I have heard his quiet strength compared to a flood, but it was a flood canalised. He had the concentration that is the first essential of greatness. He was not to be diverted by side issues. His one thought was to crush the Turk.

When we occupied Sinn on May 20th, after the Turks had evacuated it, our forward posts at Magasis, The Pentagon, and Imam Ali Mansur on the right bank were eleven miles upstream of the Sannaiyat position on the left, where the Turkish lines intercepted navigation on the river. Consequently, to supply our troops in the Sinn area a light narrow gauge (2 ft. 6 in.) railway was built from the advance base at Sheikh Saad to a point within the Sinn position lying between the Dujaila and Sinn Aftar Redoubts. This line was afterwards carried on to Imam Ali Mansur, though it was not opened for traffic until we were securely established on the Hai. It was then pushed on to Atab. A glance at the skeleton map will suggest what would have been gained in mobility and

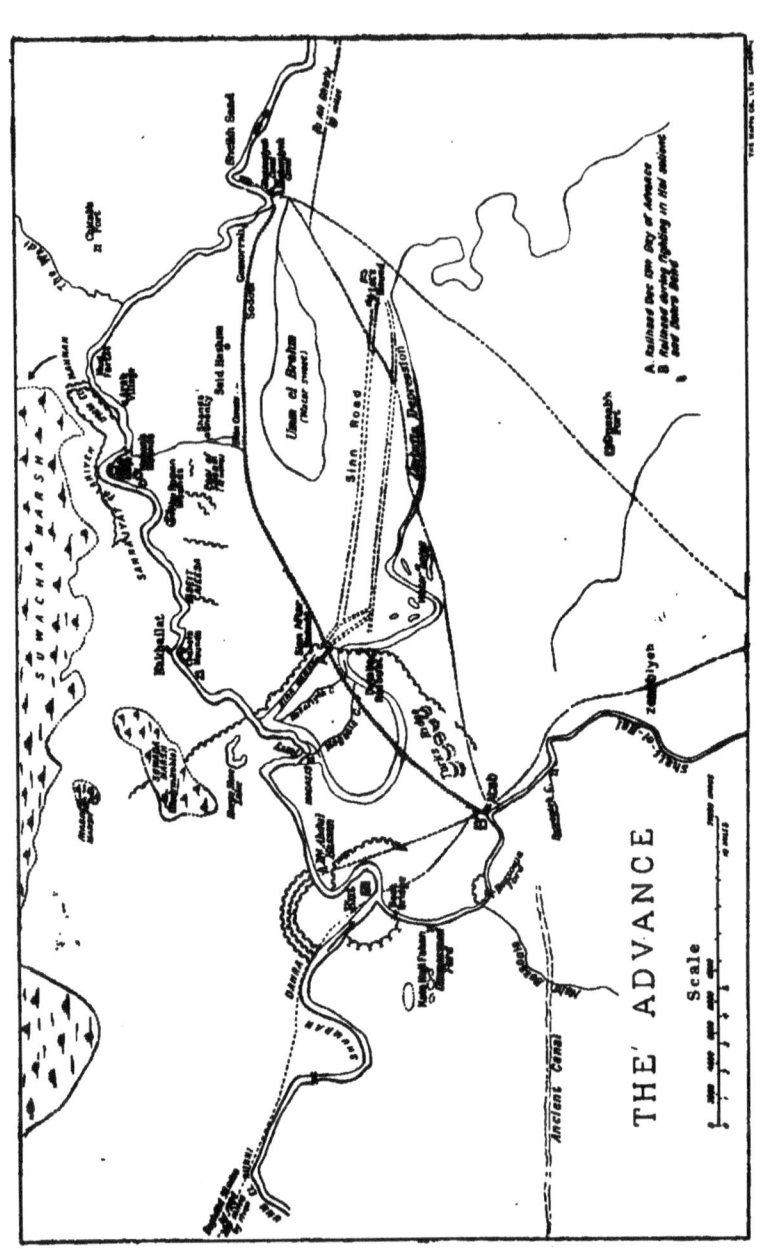

in the saving of transport if we could have established river communication up to Magasis. Sinn railway station was only three and a half miles from the river; Magasis Fort was on the river bank; yet freight was discharged from steamers at Sheikh Saad, twenty miles distant by rail. This entailed the upkeep of thousands of horses, mules, carts and Ford vans. It doubled our land transport in a country where there was no grazing, no local purchase to depend on, no fuel, and where everything, even the water for the blockhouses on the line of communications, had to be carried up from Sheikh Saad. For this makeshift single line did not suffice to feed the troops at Sinn, much less to deliver the seven days' supplies which had to be accumulated there before the army could advance with any certainty of being fed.

In the vexed months between December, 1915, and December, 1916, the ups and downs of the Mesopotamian Force depended very largely upon the organisation of transport, and it may be as well before entering upon the narrative of the advance to give some account of the preparations which made it possible. It was officially stated that the number of ships on the river in January, 1916, when the Relieving Force left Ali Gharbi, was practically the same as in June, 1915, when the first advance was made up the Tigris from Qurna. Yet in December, 1915, Force D had been doubled by a stroke of the pen; before the advance from Sinn it was nearly doubled again. But this multiplication on paper was not easy to translate into fact. It is one thing to import an army; it is another thing to move, feed and equip it. Before anything could be done it was necessary to create river transport. In the emergency caused by the investment of Kut, every variety of river craft was collected in India, Burma, Egypt and elsewhere, and dispatched in tow or under its own steam to Basra. Many of these sank on the way. Of a consignment of twenty-one stern-wheelers, mostly from the Irrawaddy and Brahmaputra, four only reached port. Some of the vessels which made the journey safely were found unsuitable for the river. In the meanwhile shipping specially designed for Tigris navigation was being built at home. Mistakes were made, for the vessel which can be adapted to all the vagaries of the Tigris is hard to find. From the end of March to the beginning of July there is flood water, and a steamer has to make head against a 5-knot current. Then in the late summer and autumn the channel is only 5 ft. deep, and nothing drawing over 4 ft. 6 in. is any good. The channel is constantly changing; the sharp twists and turns complicate navigation; and, as a rule, vessels have to tie up at night. Different types of craft are serviceable at different seasons and in different sections of the river. Square or punt-shaped bows were a peril in the narrows, as were the long 175-ft. lighters, which almost spanned the channel. Short bull-nosed vessels, which could run into the bank, slide off, and turn sharp bends became the approved patterns here. And every steamer had two barges abreast. These were necessary—even if they carried no cargo or troops—to protect the paddle-wheels, which would otherwise be stripped of their floats by collision with the banks. For the through voyage the early type of paddle steamer designed by Messrs. Lynch & Co., which carries a cargo of 400 tons on a 4-ft. draught, has hardly been improved upon. Modifications of this were introduced, and the P-50 class was evolved. These ships were built in Glasgow, and came out under their own steam. Then there were the tugs and barges. A whole fleet of them were sent out and put together at Abadan on the Shatt-el-Arab. By the time we reached Baghdad we had nearly 600 transport vessels, steamers, tugs and barges on the river. No sacrifice was made to economy; a single vessel of the P-50 class cost £75,000.

The Advance

I explained in an earlier chapter how the scope of the Tigris as a line of communication was limited to the number of vessels that could move at one time up and down stream through the narrows. This stretch of eleven miles between Ezra's Tomb and Amara is only 5 ft. deep at low flood, and up-bound vessels had to bank it. But the congestion here was removed by the railway [1] with its terminus at Qurna, whereby freight could be pushed through from Qurna and Amara and loaded again in steamers and barges above the narrows. Qurna became a port for sea-going steamers. The bar at the mouth of the old channel of the Euphrates was dredged, and vessels from Bombay drawing 14 ft. could moor by the Tree of the Knowledge of Good and Evil. At the same time the transmitting capacity of the narrows was doubled. Electric light was installed, and a new system of control by telephone was introduced between Ezra's Tomb and the Mecheriyeh Canal. Hence ships were able to work upstream by night, and from sixteen to twenty vessels could pass up and down within the twenty-four hours. At Basra there was a model like a war game showing the position of every ship on the river with its peculiar distinguishing flag; and the controller of navigation at the end of the wire with this kindergarten map in front of him regulated the movements of the fleet. An anxious eye was cast on the oil and coal barges with the red and yellow flags; for they were the crux of everything. If they failed the whole fleet failed. And in spite of all provision one never felt sure about the narrows; a large boat or barge foundering in a bad spot might hold up river transport for days.

The low flood season was an anxious time, and one admired the ingenuity by which the Inland Water Transport were able to get the maximum carrying capacity out of all the craft on the river. By the middle of June

[1] This was converted into a metre gauge in the autumn (1916).

the sea-tugs of over 5-ft. draught were falling back below Ezra's Tomb. The deeper-draught paddlers plied between Amara and Kut; the lighter-draught vessels between Kut and Baghdad, or above Baghdad, or in the narrows, while the P-50 class and the Lynch Brothers boats made the through journey all the year. The record ton-mileage by the middle of May, 1917, was six and a quarter millions. I am anticipating here, but the whole question of the river transport is bound up with the advance, and it is better to deal with it once for all at a point in our narrative where its uses are most evident. For without the I.W.T. we could never have reached Baghdad.

It should be understood, too, how the inland arteries of supply were organically connected with the development of Basra. For the requirements of the I.W.T. could not be satisfied until the mouth of the river had been converted, in substance as well as in name, into a port. By July, 1916, the military imports into the Shatt-el-Arab had reached two-thirds of the average tonnage which is landed at Karachi or Rangoon, and this without the embarkation facilities or the trained port staff which is essential for technical work of the kind. For in the early days we did not look ahead, but muddled on from day to day, uncertain how far our policy would carry us. Mesopotamia was only a side show, and there was no one immediately concerned who was ready to spend £6,000 on a pier or to import 10,000 men in Labour Corps for construction work alone. Dry docks and dredgers and repairing workshops were expensive luxuries which were not considered in the budget. There were no jetties for ocean-going steamers; and boats that had been moored in midstream for weeks, costing £250 demurrage a day, were unloaded by *mahailas* which could only put into shore at full tide. When the vitals of the Empire were crying out for tonnage there was a great fleet of merchant ships lying idly at anchor on the Shatt-el-Arab. As many as forty might be seen waiting for discharge extended in a line eight miles long up and down the river. In July, 1916, thirty-nine days was the average period passed in port by a vessel bringing in supplies. Yet it was clear that money put into Basra Port was no mere war expenditure, but a permanent investment. The congestion of the river front, with the land reclamation involved, the building of wharves, jetties and pontoon-landing stages, the clearing of ocean-going steamers and loading of river craft by inadequate and untrained labour, the establishment of coolie corps—all this called for the god-out-of-the-machine-like qualities demanded in the creation of river transport. In the end the price was paid ungrudgingly, the god-in-the-machine was found; competent agents were provided him. But it was a slow business; and the ordinary man, as he knocked his shins against one obstacle after another, noted defects and swore profanely when he could put a finger on a spot where Cosmos was not being evolved out of Chaos with the same spontaneous ease as in the first chapter of the Book of Genesis.

Thus when we advanced in December the force was organically sound and complete, and provision had been made for its continued nourishment and equipment. No physical need was forgotten, and those who spoke of its broken moral had soon to eat their words. In our new offensive we had two Army Corps, four full divisions, to throw into the field all at once, if there were occasion, in a concerted action, and not in detail as when we advanced to relieve Townshend, one division following the other upstream at intervals to make up the wastage as the troops in the firing line were destroyed piecemeal. Even the blunders, incompetence and bad luck of those early days helped us, for the Turk was filled with such contempt for our arms that he had left

18,000 rifles at the most to oppose the British on the Tigris and to safeguard the capital of his Eastern Empire. The remainder of his army was too dispersed for any considerable reinforcement to be called up in time in case of reverse. On January 4th, 1917, three weeks after the advance, and before we had inflicted any serious loss on the Turks, their total strength on the Tigris front was estimated at 80 battalions, or 20,500 rifles.

As for ourselves, our Force was complete, and it was understood that we were to have no reinforcements. Losses would be made good by new drafts, but we had to carry our offensive through with the troops we had already in the country. During the summer the 7th Division held Sannaiyat on the left bank, the 13th and 14th Divisions held the right bank, garrisoning Falahiyeh, Highland Nullah, Twin Canals, the Sinn positions, and the blockhouse line along the railway from Sheikh Saad to Sinn. The 13th Division put in some hard months' training at Amara. In the first week of September they were on the march to the front, and we knew that the long-expected hour had struck. But it seemed that the elements had been reserving their malice for us since our last offensive. On December 6th the first rain fell since the surrender of Kut; on December 8th it poured all day, and from the railway at Twin Canals we surveyed our mud-bound motor convoys and ambulances and watched the slow-moving caterpillars churning through the mire with their heavy guns. But it was only a threat. The next morning the skies were clear and the wind soon dried up the mud. The day's rain had done us a service in laying the dust which for months had shrouded horse, foot and wheels on the march.

The offensive opened on the night of December 13th with a surprise march on the Shatt-el-Hai by the Cavalry Division and 3rd Corps (13th and 14th Divisions). Simultaneously our artillery was very active at Sannaiyat, and intense bombardments kept the enemy in their trenches and drew up reinforcements to meet our threatened attack. In the march on the Hai I joined the 40th Brigade, and I remained with them for three months save for a spell or two in the hospital and some brief intervals when they were left behind in reserve. The Brigade had its stomachful of fighting, and one could not have been with a better unit if one wanted to see how good troops should be handled, and how they go into the attack. They never failed in the assault of a single position all through the advance.

The night march on the Hai was not one of the thrilling incidents of the campaign, though its success meant much to us. Once more I was part of the long, slow, sleepy, rhythmic wave of men which oozed out over the land like a dark flood that has found a breach in an embankment. We ran against no outposts in the dark, but I remembered Dujaila and wondered what the morning would bring forth. The night march across perfectly flat country without landmarks was carried out smoothly without a hitch. The infantry and cavalry reached their objectives at the exact time. The cavalry crossed at Basrugiyeh, the 8rd Corps at three fords farther upstream in the neighbourhood of Atab. In our column the South Wales Borderers were first across, the Cheshires followed. Within an hour the Welsh Pioneers were building a ramp; two pontoon bridges were thrown across; and the enemy outposts melted away mysteriously into the open desert.

The Hai, which is an effluent, not an affluent of the Tigris, is a hidden river bordered by low scrub. There is nothing in the landscape to reveal the stream's sinuous course. It was nearly stagnant in December, and in places dry. Fords were numerous, but treacherous. One or two transport carts were swallowed in the quicksands, and I nearly lost my horse when my orderly took him down to water the next morning. The stream was only 6 in. deep when we crossed, but before we had moved our camp many miles it was running bank high, a swirling flood.

The cavalry, after crossing, swept the west bank of the Hai clear of the enemy as far as Kala Haji Fahan, within two miles of the Tigris. The Turks held this position until the cavalry were within two hundred yards, but were driven out of their trenches. The 88th Brigade on the east bank were thus protected from enfilade fire, and they advanced and consolidated the ground gained. The main body of the cavalry then pushed on to the Shumran bridge on the Tigris, six miles upstream from Kut. The advanced patrols reached to within 800 yards of the bridge. We watched them returning in the dark silhouetted against a flaming background. For the Turk had fired a long strip of brushwood against which our horses could be seen from the Turkish camp coming in towards the Hai—a clever device for night observation.

In the meanwhile our aeroplanes were active. On the night of December 14th one of our pilots flew over Kut by moonlight and dropped bombs on the Turkish gunboat as she was towing the pontoon bridge in sections upstream from Shumran. He bombed the vessel from 100 ft., and caused her to run aground and slip her tow. He returned to the aerodrome for more bombs and again drove her into the bank. He repeated this a third time, and the three journeys kept him in the air from midnight to 6 A.M. The pontoons were cast adrift and scattered, and during the next day the Turks were unable to transfer troops across the river except by ferrying.

On December 15th the 88th and 89th Brigades pushed on to within 600 yards of the enemy's position on the Hai bridgehead and dug in. We had linked up our old front-line defences with the new position. It was necessary now to throw out posts west of the Hai—

this as a safeguard against sniping, to prevent the enemy bringing their guns close in, and to serve as a pivot for a further offensive. Hence our demonstration on the east bank on the 16th. Every available gun was turned on the Turks in their trenches opposite Kut, and their wire entanglements were broken up as if we were preparing for an assault. In the meanwhile two brigades, the 35th and 40th, were pushed out some two miles west of the Hai. The Arabs chose this day for a demonstration. An interminable procession of them came trekking up from Hai town in the direction of Shumran, spanning the distant horizon. We turned our machine guns on, but they were out of range. One body, far away from Bessouia, where we were watching, passed near a hidden outpost of the South Wales Borderers, who laid out fifty of them at 900 yards with their Lewis guns. An old man with a red banner and an escort of scimitars came through the fatal zone unscathed. These "Buddoos" were useful to the Turk in containing our troops; for we could not ignore them. On this particular day they would have made a splendid target for our guns. Unfortunately we could not release a single battery from the bombardment of the Turkish trenches on the Hai.

The first few days of the advance saw us firmly established in our position outside the Hai, seven miles beyond our farthest outpost at Imam Ali Mansur. Incidentally this *coup* deprived the Turk of supplies from Hai town, and gave us the command of the one waterway between the Tigris and the Euphrates along which an advance could be made upon Nasiriyeh. But these were side issues. Our first objective was to occupy a zone beyond the Shatt-el-Hai. Once established here, we were in a position to deal with the Turkish detachments on the right bank in the Mahomed Abdul Hassan loop and at the Hai bridgehead, and to operate against the Turkish communications along the river upstream of Kut. We gained our objective very cheaply at the cost of some 500 casualties.

On December 20th the 40th Brigade and the cavalry made a cast upstream in the hope of being able to effect a surprise crossing at the bend by the brick kilns four miles west of Shumran. The bridging train was brought up in readiness; the cavalry were to seize the brick kilns and the two sides of the neck of the peninsula, while the infantry crossed in pontoons at the apex. This move was purely tentative. If the Turks were surprised it was to be carried through; if they were in readiness, it was to be abandoned. The orders were that the troops were on no account to risk the losses of a stubbornly contested crossing. From the beginning the venture offered little hope. The attempt was made in daylight. Snipers held the bank opposite the point of crossing, and our machine guns failed to keep down the fire. The crew of the first boat that pushed off were immediately put out of action; two men of the South Wales Borderers were killed and three wounded as they left the bank. And the opposition on the flanks, or the neck of the bottlehead, was more serious. The brick kilns were held by an enemy force reckoned at some 150 rifles, supported by two guns on the other bank. As the element of surprise was eliminated, the forcing of the passage was not attempted.

It was perhaps as well that the passage was not effected, for during the next few days it rained heavily and the Turks would have had us at a disadvantage. The whole country became a swamp, and we could not have kept up our communications so far from railhead. Trains were only now running to Imam; the line had not yet been pushed on to Atab. As it was, we had the greatest difficulty in feeding our troops on the Hai; and to relieve the congestion the cavalry had to be sent back to Arab Village. But this was all part of the day's work in Meso-

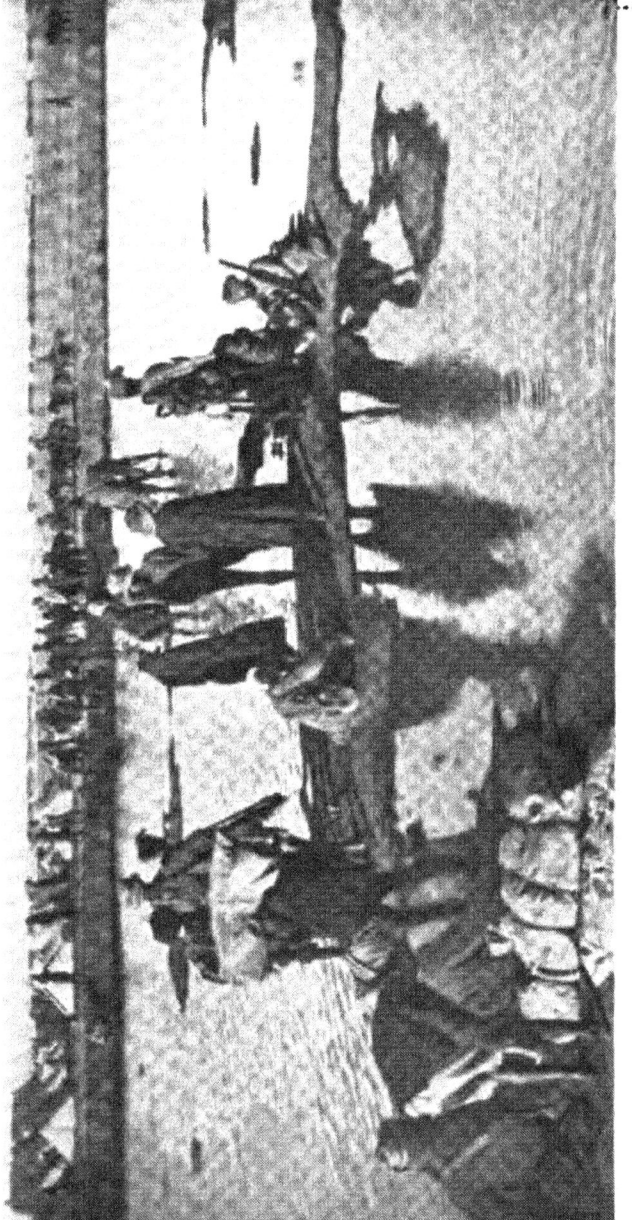

FLOODS.

potamia, where an army may be immobilised in the rainy season by the mud, in the spring by inundations, in the summer by heat, and in the early autumn by the sickness and exhaustion consequent upon the heat. With the exception, perhaps, of October and November, there is no month in which one may move with any certainty of a clear month's uninterrupted operations.

For the next ten days the mud held up carts and pack animals; it was not safe for a camel to start on a day's journey lest he should split and die, and the permanent way sank down to strata in which wheels were jammed off the track. A company of infantry crossing the line would hold up an engine with the oily mud left behind by their boots. Carts carried less; trains, when they ran at all and then it was with half loads, took double the time between the stations; animals made fewer journeys; the camel and the motor lorry, the most primitive and evolved agents of supply, were alike immobilised; and the railway broke down for thirty-six hours. Yet transport, taxed to its limits before, rose to the new demand. By lightening loads and staging convoys some sort of mobility was evoked under conditions in which the elements conspired to clog all movement. One man in authority with the ear of "Q." sat by the telephone wires and so juggled with the Brigade Supply and Transport Companies and the Divisional Supply and Baggage Columns that every unit contributed its quota of mobility and was fed in spite of itself. Every regulation save the unwritten one—to use one's common sense—was swept aside for the exigencies of the hour.

During the next fortnight, on account of the mud and rain, operations carried us no farther. But roads and bridges were constructed, and the railway was extended to Atab on the Hai. Constant raids and reconnaissances harassed the enemy's communications on the right bank as far as Baghailah. On the left bank an attempt was made to move the Cavalry Division round north of the Suwacha Marsh to operate against the enemy's communications, but this too failed on account of the flood. Still, in spite of the temporary *impasse*, everyone was in good spirits now that we were doing something after the long summer and autumn halt. The mere change of scene was a relief. We were able to observe Kut now from the west and to watch the people gazing at us from their roofs. The town, seen from our camp across the Hai, had a compact and solid appearance like a bluff rock in the sea. The white houses against the dark background of palms resembled a chalk cliff, and the one tall minaret standing out like a lighthouse completed the illusion. We could have reduced the place to a heap of mud and bricks any day we liked.

At the end of the first week in January the position at Sannaiyat, where we and the Turks faced each other on the left bank, was unchanged. For the rest, the general dispositions were that we held the right bank, the Turks the left—with the two exceptions of Mahomed Abdul Hassan and the Hai bridgehead. So long as the enemy held these positions, which constituted a threat of a counter-offensive against us, any forward movement on our part was impossible; and for the next six weeks he clung to his footing on the right bank with the most dogged persistency and determination. But the obstinacy with which he held on proved his undoing. It enabled us with our greatly superior artillery little by little so to eat away his strength that by the time we had evicted him from the right bank he was too weak to counter our stroke across the Tigris. Had he withdrawn his forces from Mahomed Abdul Hassan and the Hai bridgehead at an earlier stage, and waited for us to attack by forcing a passage over the river, we should have been faced by a much more difficult proposition.

CHAPTER XXVI

MAHOMED ABDUL HASSAN

At the beginning of the December operations the enemy held two main trench systems on the right bank. The first of these was the loop of Mahomed Abdul Hassan, or the Khaderi bend, opposite Khaderi Fort, where the Tigris takes a bend almost due north of Kut; the second, a rough triangle south and south-west of the Kut peninsula with its apex nearly two miles down the Shatt-el-Hai from the point where it leaves the Tigris, and the ends of its base resting on the river upstream and downstream of Kut. Mahomed Abdul Hassan, the first of these positions, was in the nature of an outwork of the Hai defences. So long as the Turks held it we were denied positions from which our guns might enfilade the bridgehead; it also covered the enemy defences in the Kut peninsula which supported the trench system on the Hai. Accordingly we dealt with Mahomed Abdul Hassan first.

Though there was no actual fighting at Mahomed Abdul Hassan during the first three weeks of the advance, the struggle for the bend may be said to date from December 18th, when we began to throw our net of trenches round the Turks on a wide front. The first stroke was dealt on the night of December 22nd, when the North Lancashires and the H.L.I. occupied a point on the Tigris opposite the south-east end of the Kut peninsula, driving a wedge in between the two enemy trench systems on the right bank. We extended our position here on the 28rd and gradually advanced our lines to Kut East Mounds, the northerly point of which was held by the enemy.

Thus we were established side by side with the Turks, holding alternate positions on the same bank of the river. One of us had to turn the other out, and the odds were against the Turk, with his inferior artillery and precarious communications.

Our infantry, which by this time had pushed forward to within 300 yards of the enemy, attacked in the mist on the morning of January 9th, 1917. On the night of the 8th and 9th demonstrations had been made on all fronts to prevent the Turks reinforcing the garrison of Mahomed Abdul Hassan. The enemy's position on the Hai was heavily bombarded; the cavalry were dispatched on a raid to Baghailah; while at Sannaiyat four raiding parties entered the Turkish trenches. The Baghailah demonstration availed us nothing, as the cavalry got lost in the mist, but the action at Sannaiyat was a singularly bloody and desperate affair. Three of the raiding parties were drawn from the 28th Brigade, the Leicesters, the 53rd Sikhs, and the 56th Rifles; each battalion supplied two officers and thirty men. The fourth party was drawn from the Sappers, one officer and ten men. All the officers were lost, killed or missing, and a large proportion of the rank and file. Whether the loss was made good in the diversion I will not presume to judge; but the sacrifice demanded of the raiders was one of that devoted kind in which the men who give their lives see nothing of the reward, which is reaped elsewhere.

The Turkish front line at Mahomed Abdul Hassan lay across the bend some 2,400 yards, with both flanks resting on the river. We assaulted on a 600 yards front, leaving some 1,800 yards of hostile position on our right flank, while the left flank rested on the river bank and was protected. On the left the 9th Brigade went in and cleared Kut East Mounds and some 600 yards of the river front. Here there was some desperate hand-to-hand fighting with bayonet and bombs. The 1/1st Gurkhas carried the

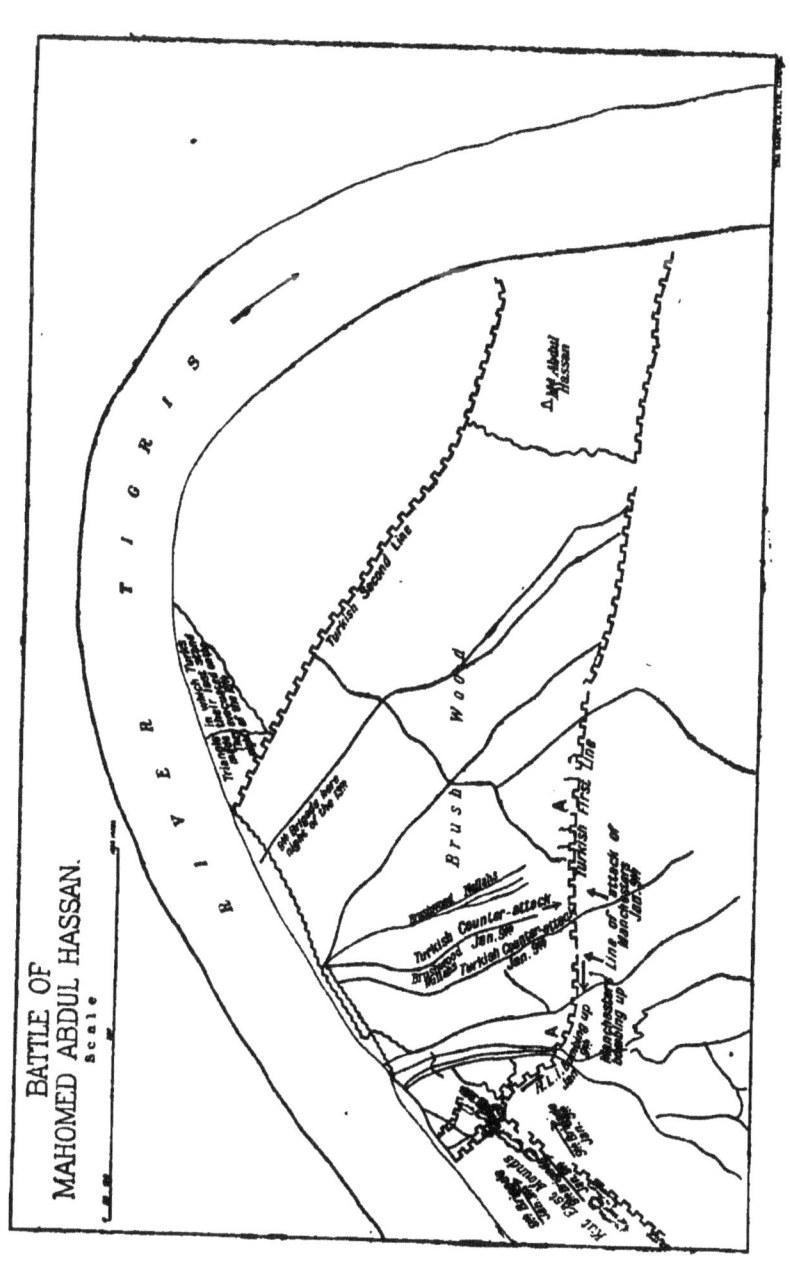

redoubt on the mounds, pushed along the sandhills, and bombed down the river bank as far as the fourth nullah. The Gurkhas saw red and translated their vision into fact; two hundred Turkish dead were found within a radius of 800 yards the next morning. The 105th Mahratta Light Infantry took 200 yards of Turkish trenches and bombed up the four nullahs to the position along the river bank which the Gurkhas had taken, then wheeled to the right and dug themselves in in the fourth nullah. The 93rd Burma Infantry bore away to the north and cleared another hundred and fifty yards of the Turkish line. There was some confusion in the mist, but the work was all cleanly done, and each of the three regiments bore its part in it. To complete our objective on the left flank, it only remained for the Highland Light Infantry to bomb up and gain touch with the Manchesters, who, according to plan, would be working down from the captured portion of the Turkish line 400 yards on the right. This was accomplished, and the two British regiments joined hands soon after the assault.

The Manchesters had attacked on a 200 yards front and got in with few casualties, close up to our barrage, before an enemy head had emerged from behind the parapet. The Turkish trenches had been subjected to more than one intense bombardment during the previous days, and were battered out of shape. They were lightly held, and, I believe, not by the pick of their troops. These we were to meet later in the action. The garrison of the first line were broken by the tons of metal poured in before the assault. Most of them surrendered.

Once in the enemy's first lines, the bombing parties of the Manchesters worked along the trench on both flanks, on the left to join up with the H.L.I., who were bombing up from the river; on the right to extend the position gained another 800 yards and there to form a block, while other parties worked up to points in the brushwood nullahs between the first and second Turkish lines, which were to be converted into communication trenches by our sappers and pioneers. It was down these nullahs that the enemy counter-attacked in overwhelming force and enveloped a party of the Manchesters. There was a thick fog, very favourable to a surprise, and the Turks who had been lying up in the scrub suddenly loomed out of the mist like a football crowd. The Manchesters were pinned into a trench from which it was difficult to use their rifles, their Lewis gun jammed with dirt, but the small party hung on, cut off from all support, and fought to a finish with bomb and bayonet, until they were practically exterminated; the Turkish dead found on the spot the next morning outnumbered ours. The wave swept on and caught a second party of the same regiment on the flank, driving them back to the trench we had captured, where it was held up.

In the meanwhile the Turks were pressing down the trench on our right. It was here that a small working party of Pioneers, a mere platoon, under a young subaltern, Lieut. Gordon, of the 84th Sikh Pioneers, found themselves with a handful of the Manchesters in the crisis of the action. They held the breach, built up a block, and bombed the Turks lustily for hours. Other Manchesters joined them. Captain Close-Brooks was killed as he stood on the parapet and directed the bombing. Pembroke (Sec.-Lieut.) took over from him and fell badly wounded. Yates (Sec.-Lieut.) succeeded him and was killed in the trench. Hardman (Sec.-Lieut.) and Walker (Sec.-Lieut.) took over in turn and were both killed. Henderson survived. He was given a clasp to the D.S.O. he won at Dujaila, where he was one of the two officers who came out of the redoubt unwounded. Here, too, he and one other officer of the Manchesters, Major Brown, returned unwounded. In France Henderson bore the same charmed life; and I saw him twice afterwards, once at a critical moment in the fight on Jebel Hamrin, and again at Tekrit holding a forward trench with a handful of his men and his right flank in the air.

In the evening we still held this ground, and had driven the Turks out of the section of the trench they had recaptured. The day's work had given us the whole of Kut East Mounds, part of the west side of the Mahomed Abdul Hassan loop, extending by 600 yards the gap we held between the two Turkish positions on the right bank of the river, and 1,000 yards of the first-line trench (A), which lay astride the bend. We captured 7 officers, 155 other ranks, one machine gun, and buried a trench full of Turkish dead.

January 10th was a comparatively quiet day. We advanced our line with little opposition, and it seemed that the back of the Turkish resistance was broken. Before evening we had them pinned in a narrow triangle on the river bank, and most of us thought it was all over. Two regiments of the 40th Brigade which had come up in reserve were sent back to the Hai. But the Turk was far from beaten. The gallant remnants of the battalions who fought on the 9th had been withdrawn, and fresh troops had been ferried over at night to take their place. But owing to the scrub and nullahs and the steep river banks it was difficult to estimate with what force the position was held, and the misty mornings made aeroplane reconnaissance impossible. At two on the afternoon of the 11th we were preparing for the final scene when the Turks counter-attacked on both flanks and penetrated our line. They were held up on our right by the steady fire of the 47th Sikhs and the 182nd Machine-gun Company; on our left the wave spent itself and was rolled back. As they broke they became a target for our guns. They lost heavily, but it was one of the most gallant sorties ever seen.

After this there was more tentative and sticky fighting. Turkish and Arab prisoners said, "The English are not so brave as the Turk. They will only advance under cover of a thousand guns." And feeling this, the Turks were heartened, and from their last foothold made most desperate sallies.

I remember a slim Jew advocate of Constantinople, dug out of the Gehenna of Mahomed Abdul Hassan after the third bombardment, and moralising on the inequality of things in fluent Parisian French. Chance had herded him somehow with a battalion of tough Anatolian peasants, hard, and simple in their wants as cattle—a piece of china amid rude earthenware. He complained bitterly of being "thrown into this desert of savage men with the manners of children."

While he was holding forth an ammunition wagon drew up and a stack of braziers was unloaded for the men in the trenches. "You have everything," he said, "the guns, the ammunition, the comforts, the food."

He was too excited to notice a convoy of 200 Ford motor vans crawling slowly through the mud on the horizon, on the road between Atab and Arab Village. Each car contained three bundles of chopped straw for the cavalry, consumed four gallons of petrol a day, and engaged the whole-time services of an able-bodied man who might have been in the firing-line.

It was quite true. We had everything Science could devise; they the scantiest provision. On January 8th, 8,000 lb. of fresh meat from the Argentine were delivered at Sinn. I thought of their hard round ration biscuits of the consistency of brick, ferried over in coracles to their dug-outs at night. And we had the transport, the guns, the shells. We must have put in 100 lb. of metal in those days to 1 lb. of theirs; we must have spent fifty pounds of English money where they spent a lira. Yet no troops could have fought more doggedly.

It was borne in on me that we are undoubtedly a

hyper-materialised race; and our dependence on our commercial and scientific developments was never so apparent as in these months. The Turkish sortie from their last battered foothold at Mahomed Abdul Hassan with the river at their back seemed to fling this in our face. The Arab's contempt for us increased. The more the forward area became congested with our troops the more he raided and looted at night, cutting the wire between the block-houses, evading our bomb traps, and getting off with our rifles, horses, and ammunition, generally untouched. The Briton is as brave as a lion when he is challenged, and as devoted as a samurai. But when there is no clear spiritual call, no palpable limb to be hewn off some Monster of Evil, living close to Nature has its advantages; and it often seemed that the nearer one is to nakedness, the better one is armed.

We had a whole Cavalry Division, a thing rarely seen, scouring an enemy's country in war. When it moved forward, the Arabs receded into the mirage; when it retired they harassed its flank and rear. On January 11th the cavalry rode on a raid to Hai town. They camped three days in the place and the attitude of the people seemed friendly. Supplies were brought in freely. Officers patronised the Turkish baths and spent hours curio-hunting in the bazaar. Shops were emptied of rugs, samovars, and antiquated arms, and everything was paid for in good coin and sold in good humour. On the morning of the 14th, when the cavalry were clearing up camp before moving off, the usual crowd collected and stood about in their long cloaks, searching the ground for empty tins and rubbish. These scavengers had concealed arms in their clothes, and as soon as the rearguard disappeared behind a long bund a mile outside Hai town, they followed up and opened fire on them. At the same time clouds of ragged horse and foot emerged out of the nullahs and villages on both flanks. All day the

"Buddoo" pursued his habitual desert tactics, hanging on our skirts and firing at us at extreme range, while the Cavalry Division fought a rearguard action from eight in the morning till four in the afternoon. But the ground is broken between Sinn and Hai, and there was detached fighting. The Arabs killed and stripped a British officer and left his naked body on the ground to be recovered by us; there was skirmishing in which our cavalry charged with the lance. They were burning to attack, but the orders never came. We ought to have wheeled back the whole Division and swept the desert with these scallywags, sparing none, and then ridden again into Hai. A proclamation was posted on the walls of the town announcing an Arab victory, telling how thousands of the British had been slain and how their cavalry had scattered and fled. Certain proof was forthcoming in the shape of arms and loot. And we never returned in our might and destroyed the place as we should have done if we had not been afraid—or so it must have seemed to the people of Hai. Instead we sent aeroplanes, dropping bombs, and lending colour to the Arab boast that he and the Turk were better men-at-arms than we, and that we were only brave under cover of our engines and machines.

However, the Staff College and the drill book prevailed in the end, and brought us into positions in which the Turk met his betters at the end of the bayonet. The Arab, of course, does not stand against odds where loot is problematical. The great difficulty of the Mahomed Abdul Hassan peninsula was that, lying within a narrow loop of the river, it was enfiladed by the enemy's artillery and machine guns from across the Tigris on both flanks. Hence our unwillingness to mass troops and rush the position. The Turks with the river behind them might perhaps have thrown in their hand if they had seen the best part of a division descending on them in irresistible waves, but they held their ground against a battalion on each flank. When the H.L.I. advanced to attack the position on the 11th, they were so thinned out by this enfilade fire that they were too weak to withstand the counter-attack. The Turks were keenly alive to this advantage, and turned it to account. They also realised that the capture of the loop would enable our artillery to enfilade the Kut peninsula in the same way, as well as both banks of the Hai, and to control the inundation. Such was the strategic importance of the Mahomed Abdul Hassan bend. The Ottoman troops were ordered to hold on, and they held on with their backs to the wall in a manner that compelled our admiration. Their position was hopeless; we had them cornered. The end was only a question of patience and guns. War is not sport, and it was not worth while wasting troops on frontal attacks. Instead of rushing the position we threw forward our trenches gradually until the area they held became so cramped that our concentrated gun fire made it untenable. Even so there were sorties and counter-attacks, and our infantry had to go in with the bayonet again before the Turk quitted.

The remnants of the force slipped away in their boats and coracles on the night of the 18th-19th. They kept up the ruse of digging until the small hours. We thought they were digging themselves in deeper against our artillery fire. As a matter of fact, they were burying their dead. And in doing so they filled up their trench, preparing their cemetery and a strategical line of retreat at the same time, so that our infantry had to advance in the morning without cover exposed to their fire from the other bank.

An intense bombardment was timed for 6.80, but a patrol of the 59th Rifles working up the river bank discovered that the post was evacuated and got the message through just in time to save the bombardment of the empty triangle, the expenditure of 21,000 shells, and the face of the Staff and the gunners. For there is nothing the Turks would have enjoyed better than to have lain snug in their dug-outs across the Tigris and watched us shelling their abandoned trenches.

At Mahomed Abdul Hassan the Turk showed some of the old Plevna spirit. With his back to the swollen Tigris, no bridge, and only a few coracles and pontoons to depend upon for communications, he held his ground stubbornly; gradually forced back into a narrower area in which our barrage became more and more concentrated, his trenches pounded into a confused shambles by our guns, he emerged and counter-attacked with the utmost gallantry. And he did not quit until we had driven him into his last ditch.

We can afford to bear witness to our enemy's grit; it would be a poor compliment to our fighting men if we did not. These were the best Ottoman troops, and the dogged tenacity of the Turk behind the parapet is proverbial. As a private in the Wiltshires put it, " Until he's got a crump on his —— cokernut the ole Turk doesn't know when he's beat." The Turkish Commander sent a message to the O.C. at Mahomed Abdul Hassan congratulating the troops upon the "steadfastness in holding their ground in spite of bloody losses during to-day's bombardment in the mist." The document was found on one of their dead. " The Corps Commander kisses the eyes of all ranks and thanks them " was the expressive Eastern phrase. " I too kiss all their eyes and thank them."

We dealt the Turk some heavy blows at Mahomed Abdul Hassan, but the hard unmalleable concrete of the man received few visible dints. So far we had only driven in one outwork of his defences on the right bank. Our losses were probably about equal. So far as mere attrition went it was the case of the hammer and the anvil, and there did not seem much prospect of wearing him down before reinforcements arrived. Or so it seemed to the ordinary man. But General Maude, the weapons of offence once in his hand, was confident of the issue all through. He saw the advance in its true perspective, and recognised how the momentum he was applying must gather force. It was a calculation in the limits of human endurance by a Commander who had reduced the psychology of war to a science. Each hundred yards of trench captured was an integral part in the sum of victory. The carrying of the section K21A to K21B on a front of 800 and a depth of 150 yards was worth twenty miles on the road to Baghdad. An acre or two of ground, barely appreciable on a large scale map, marked one degree more in the gradient down which the Turk was being rolled inevitably to his collapse.

CHAPTER XXVII

THE HAI SALIENT AND THE DAHRA BEND

THE fighting on the Tigris was almost continuous from the day we began our offensive on December 18th, 1916, to the capture of Samarrah on April 28rd, 1917. The Mahomed Abdul Hassan Bend was the first enemy stronghold to fall to us. The second, the elaborate trench system enclosing the Hai bridgehead, fell with the capture of the liquorice factory on February 10th. The third, a continuation of this system thrown from east to west across the Dahra Bend, was finally cleared in the assault on February 15th. In this fighting we gained eighteen miles of the Tigris bank, following the bends of the river. Viewed in the old perspective, each series of operations, taken by itself, would amount to a considerable campaign. The expenditure was large in life and munitions; but if we spent more in metal than the Turk, he paid more dearly in blood.

Our advance on the right bank was slow, but each step was sure and deliberate, and owing to our ascendancy in artillery almost inevitable. The Turk could not afford to hold his first line in strength under the intensity of our barrage. We got in every time, and to regain his ground he was compelled to counter-attack. Thus, so long as we were content with nibbling away at his defences and did not overshoot our objective, the costliness of the offensive was thrown on him. We flung our net of trenches round him in one bend of the Tigris after another, where with the river behind him he was in a position that did not admit of indefinite withdrawal.

He was faced with the inevitability of being forced back into a gradually dwindling area in which our barrage became more and more concentrated. For two months we advanced our line step by step, established ourselves within easy jumping-off distance, battered the enemy's trenches, went in and cleared them with the bayonet, and broke up

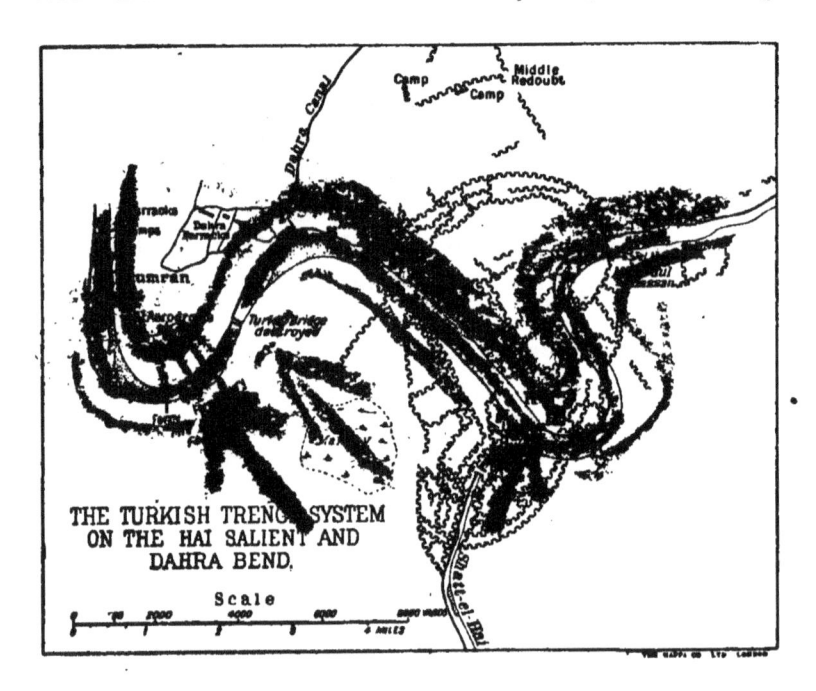

THE TURKISH TRENCH SYSTEM ON THE HAI SALIENT AND DAHRA BEND.

his counter-attacks with our rifle fire and guns. But it was far from being a walk-over for our infantry. I have borne witness to the fine fighting qualities of the enemy at Mahomed Abdul Hassan. He put up a great defence here against odds. In the Hai salient he yielded ground with equal stubbornness. It was only, in the last day's struggle for the Dahra Bend, that his moral, or resistance, was broken.

Praise of the Turk is by inference eulogy of our own men. War in Mesopotamia demanded an ever greater staunchness from them. The Turk was resisting the invasion of his own soil, whereas for the last three months the only palpable objective to our men in the trenches had been to kill as many of the enemy as they could.

They had done this cheerfully—in many cases through a campaign of over two years. And there was little stimulus in his environment for the fighting man. The Turk was an enemy against whom few of us felt any bitterness of spirit, and, as an accomplice of the Hun, a mere accident in the system we were sworn to destroy. The barren acres in front of us, often strewn with more debris of munitions than blades of grass, were only a weariness to us when we possessed them. It is hard to conceive the staleness of this kind of fighting, and the dead monotony of Mesopotamia as a field of war. There was no longer the incentive of the garrison at Kut. This year it was only a series of ditches in a mud flat, furrows in an infinity of caked clay leading nowhere as far as the man in the trench could see, for we had forgotten the hope of Baghdad. Each day we attacked a new ditch and each ditch became the grave of the inheritors of the green fields of England—buried in this barren alkaline soil. One could not keep depression at arm's length sometimes when the glamour of war had faded. One knew how tired of it all the men were. It was the accursed country more than anything else that weighed down one's spirit. Yet one was always reading about the keenness of our troops, as if they were burning " to be up and at " the Turk again. If one were fighting at home it would be easier to keep the flame of sacrifice and idealism and generous impulse always burning. Fighting the Hun in the cornfields of dear old England one would see red till one dropped; the dullest clod would " hop the parapet " with a holy glee. But the soldier man got a little tired of it in Mesopotamia. Out there with toil and dirt and death and wounds as one's daily companions, and with rare intervals of refreshment, one had to draw upon deeper and more austere sources of inspiration.

As the old crowd is exhausted, new drafts succeed; the younger generation is drawn in. The tired veteran of the firing line after nearly three years of tedious communion with death is standing-to, ready for another assault. In an hour or two the battalion is going in again. Those who get across will hold 800 yards of Turkish front, an extension of Golgotha, R.19.A to R.19.B perhaps, or some such cabalistic symbol on the map. The new drafts will fill the place of the men in the battalion who have fallen—young blood to whom the whole thing is a supreme adventure, the test of manhood, or at least a consecration which ranges them with men whose good associates they wish to be. But it was of the tired men I thought most, whom tradition, or a sense of decency, kept slogging on in spite of weariness.

These are obvious reflections, unspeakable by a soldier, yet natural in a civilian who has watched and marvelled at the endurance of spirit in the fighting man.

There were few signs of tiredness, none of collective tiredness, among the troops who fought in the Hai salient. We began our offensive here on both banks on January 25th. On the east bank the 40th Brigade were attacking. I was going round the trenches with the Brigadier (General Lewin) the evening before the assault. He wanted to make sure that his men knew exactly what they were going to do. We had suffered at Mahomed Abdul Hassan by units who were carried beyond the objective in the flush of victory, but the orders for the coming attack were clear. Four hundred yards of the enemy's trenches in front of our firing line had to be taken, held, and consolidated, and no one save the bombing parties was to go one step beyond. But the General's visit to the trenches preceded the issue of regimental orders. He stopped at every second bay and asked the men how far they were going and what they were going to do. None of them knew, but none erred on the side of caution. The General explained tersely what was expected of them, threatening anathema to the heedless, and extinction from our own guns, and he rubbed it in in his half-amused Irish way that it would be their own fault. As we progressed, the cumulative uninstructedness of two battalions lent emphasis to a sufficiently emphatic tongue. At last we came to a small Irishman with clear steady eyes and the true Hibernian smile. "Well? How far are you going to-morrow?" the General asked him. "Bedad, sir," he answered, "I am going as far as I can. Eight or nine miles if they'll let me."

"You will stay in the enemy's firing line," the General said quietly and sternly. But the Irishman took this as an imputation upon his spirit. "Not I, sir," he protested. "It is into Kut that I will be going." The General repeated the order. But as he spoke this mettlesome Celt interrupted, protesting that one trench was not enough, and that he was "not going to let them say that he was afraid," and I knew that he meant it, that if by any accident his Company Officer failed to instruct him, he would go straight on, beyond the enemy's captured trench, alone or accompanied, without looking round until he fell.

However, nothing was left to chance. I saw him the next morning contentedly cutting a firestep in the enemy's first line, converting a parados into a parapet, and waiting for the Turk to come on.

I was with the Wiltshires in the trench when they went over. They looked thoughtful and a little strung up, but there was no tiredness about them. When the yellow flags were hoisted to show that they had got in, I crossed over and found the enemy's firing trench broken up by our artillery and heaped with dead, the parapets fallen in on a debris of rifles and ammunition and litter of all kinds. We captured two officer prisoners, 186 rank and file, three trench mortars and a machine gun. During the day the Turks made repeated attempts to bomb us out of the ground gained, both on our flanks and in attacks directed down our communication trenches on to our centre. The Wiltshires and Royal Welsh Fusiliers stood their ground and out-bombed them every time. In the morning we attacked on a 600 yards front; before dawn we had bombed out on both flanks and held 1,200 yards of the enemy's first line and a strong position in the second. At two in the morning the Turks put in another counter-attack and were repulsed with loss. Thus their defensive was more costly than our attack. We counted 400 of their dead in the position, apart from the barricade of corpses they put up in a communication trench to serve as a block. Thus little by little the 40th Brigade crept forward on the east bank of the Hai under the barrage of our guns, consolidating the ground we had gained, until on February 10th we had driven the Turk across the river. The waves of infantry, sweeping on forty or fifty yards behind the artillery screen, carried the enemy's first line every time, killing or capturing the garrison.

Then we had to look out for counter-attacks. The parados was rapidly broken down, firesteps cut in the wall of the trench, Lewis guns brought into place, and double blocks built up under the cover of bombing parties at the points where the captured trench ran into the enemy's position. Then when the Turk counter-attacked over the open he was delivered into our hands. Afterwards the ground we gained was extended by our bombers on both flanks and generally to strong points in advance of our line. We dug communication trenches back to our old position, and at night threw wire across our new front.

The Hai Salient and Dahra Bend

But on the west of the Hai the Turks' resistance was stronger, their trench system more elaborate, and held in greater force. On the morning of January 25th the 89th Brigade attacked on the west bank simultaneously with the assault of the 40th Brigade on the east bank. All went well at first. The 9th Worcesters and 7th North Staffords rushed the trench directly the artillery screen had lifted, and the North Stafford grenadiers began clearing the communication trench on the left. This was the danger point. The three officers commanding the bombing parties had fallen during the advance; the bombers themselves had lost heavily. An hour after the attack the Turkish grenadiers were massing and pressing down the trench. Just then a heavy *Minenwerfer* came into action from a concealed position on the left and dropped shells with deadly accuracy into the rear of the Staffords, who were already being attacked on three sides. Under cover of a trench howitzer and a barrage of heavy fire the Turkish bombers, who carried no weapon or equipment save their grenades, dashed over the open and bombed our men in the trench. All the battalion grenadiers were killed or wounded. The Turks' advance was checked several times by the accurate fire of our artillery and of G Battery Stokes Mortar; and on each occasion the Stafford riflemen made a gallant stand fighting with bombs. But the fire of the enemy *Minenwerfer* was crushing. Four or five shells were seen in the air at the same time.

At 11.80 the enemy bombers had established their ascendancy and were closing in on the flank of the trench we had taken. The greater part of the line now gave, as the Turks counter-attacked across the open under cover of a barrage of artillery and machine-gun fire from the west. The whole position was in danger of being rolled up, but small parties of Worcesters and Staffords still held on. Then the order was given for the

Warwicks to attack. They came on over the open in a wave led by their commanding officer, Colonel Henderson (killed), and drove the Turks out of the trench. At three the Turks counter-attacked again. The bloody struggle was repeated. The bombing party of the Warwicks was broken by the trench mortar on the left, as the Staffords had been; and the enemy flooded into our line. The Turks, who in the first counter-attack had captured our signalling flags and the screens which served to mark our advance, used them to confuse our observers. The intense bombardment of the enemy's line of attack down the communication trench from the north-west was delayed. The infantry, believing that they were being shelled by our own gunners, left the trench, and the line was not recaptured that night.

Thus the first attack west of the Hai ended in failure, but great gallantry was shown in the Brigade. For it was a day of stubborn fighting, as is witnessed by the cost of it. The Brigade lost 85 officers and 900 rank and file; all three commanding officers fell. Seven out of eight of the guns of the Stokes Mortar Battery were put out of action. Three out of four machine guns in the trench were destroyed by the enemy's fire. A fifth which did not reach the line but came into action thirty yards behind, engaging the enemy bombers on the left, was fought with great gallantry until Sec.-Lieut. Green (M.G.C.) and team, almost to a man, were killed. The sergeant of the machine-gun company who saved the gun (Sergeant Cartwright, late 2nd Worcesters) died of heart failure as he carried it into our lines. Failure as a rule calls out finer and higher qualities than success. These machine-gunners, the Stafford bombers who fell to a man, the Warwicks who broke the counter-attack and rallied our wavering line, the Staffords and Worcesters who stayed in the trench side by side with the Turk, will not soon be forgotten.

The Hai Salient and Dahra Bend

During the night the 14th Division relieved the 18th on the west bank, and on the morning of January 26th the 82nd Punjabis and 26th Punjabis attacked and took the first line. The fateful *Minenwerfer* was put out of action by the bombers of the 82nd. During the advance a company of the 26th went out too much to the left, overshot their objective, and swung in again on a point in the enemy's communication trench. The mistake was turned to brilliant account and probably decided the action. This company wiped out the team of an enfilading machine gun on their way; and, once established in their precarious and unauthorised post, held on all day, entirely cut off, got their Lewis guns into position, and kept the Turks' heads down in the trenches from which they would have counter-attacked. The advance position they held on the enemy's flank saved the rest of the battalion and the 82nd in the captured trench from a pressure which might have been overwhelming. Both regiments lost heavily. Of the 82nd two British officers were killed and three wounded out of the eight who went over the parapet, and 240 rank and file out of 500. The 26th lost their Commanding Officer, Colonel Thompson —his body was found in the communication trench—and half their effectives. Under this punishment part of the line gave way, but the trench was never abandoned. At three in the afternoon a company of the Hants reinforced the garrison. After dark the whole battalion took over the line, relieving the two Punjabi regiments.

In the meanwhile the 40th Brigade on the east bank were closing the Turks in, extending and consolidating their front night and day, creeping up to the enemy's new line of resistance, preparatory to the next concerted attack on both banks, which was to be delivered on February 1st. On the right the 88th Brigade were advancing with their flank on the Tigris; on the morning of January 28th they occupied the Turks' old trenches;

the two brigades joined hands, and the net was completed behind the enemy from the Tigris to the Hai.

On February 1st the 87th Brigade attacked on the west bank, the 40th Brigade on the east bank of the Hai. On the east bank the Cheshires were in the firing line. The assault was driven in on a salient in the centre of the enemy's line. As on January 25th, the whole garrison was killed or captured; 165 prisoners were taken; the Turks were driven back on their rearmost trenches. The position once secured, the Cheshire grenadiers bombed out on both flanks until we had taken the whole line between the Tigris and the Hai. A third party worked along the enemy's communication trench and carried a strong point in advance. The objective was as cleanly won as on January 25th. The Brigade War Diary for the day reads like a repetition of orders, only with a change of tense.

Unhappily the parallel of January 25th held on the west bank of the Hai as well as on the east. Once more we failed here, while our objective on the east bank was carried without a hitch. The two battalions engaged fought with the most desperate gallantry; but the Turk had concentrated in this salient, which was the most vital point in his system of defence, and the initial attack of the 87th Brigade, like that of the 89th on January 25th, was rolled back.

The assault was delivered by the 86th Sikhs on the left and the 45th Sikhs on the right; both regiments went over the parapet in full strength and were practically annihilated. Only one British officer returned unwounded. The 86th Sikhs lost five British officers killed, one missing, three wounded; the 45th Sikhs lost two killed, four missing, one wounded. Of the two battalions, only 190 effectives came out of the assault. The exact nature of the dispositions which defeated us is not likely to be revealed, as the officers who might have thrown a

The Hai Salient and Dahra Bend

light upon them were killed or captured by the Turks, but the main causes of the repulse were these:

In the first place the communication trench (K1—K8) was believed to be open, but the Turks had filled in the greater part of it in the night, leaving a devoted garrison of bombers (at K2) in the air with all retreat cut off. Our own bombers who were to work along the trench to the

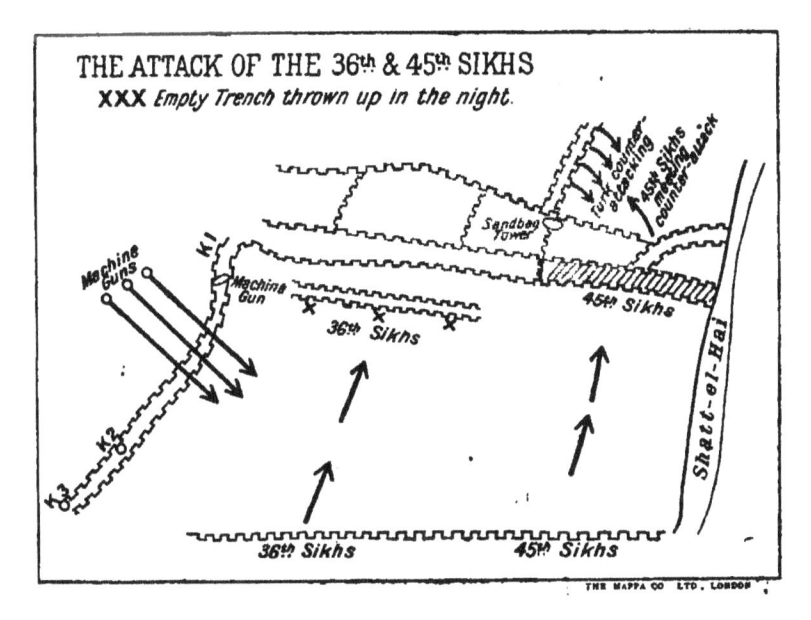

![The Attack of the 36th & 45th Sikhs. XXX Empty Trench thrown up in the night.]

Turkish position were held up by these, and it was naturally concluded that the whole trench was occupied. The Turks brought their machine guns up at close range, and swept the area of our attack directly over the trench (K1—K8) which they had filled in. The moment the 86th Sikhs emerged from the trench they came under a raking enfilade fire from this machine-gun battery on their left, and from the sandbag tower on their right. Our artillery barrage playing on their left flank was wide of the concealed guns, which had a clear target at close range.

Some of the 86th were hit before they had left the parapet, nevertheless they went across gallantly, leaving their trail of dead, until they found themselves in an empty trench (X) which they took to be the Turks' first line. It was a new and shallow trench dug by the enemy in the night. The second trap laid by the Turk, a stratagem as disastrous as the first. From this position the Sikhs fired into what they believed to be the Turks' second line, and they were mown down by a machine gun which had been brought up on the left and swept the trench as inevitably as a gust of wind. The regiment was wiped out. Only 92 returned. One gallant fellow, who found a scrap of cover, held on with his Lewis gun, which he worked until it jammed. He came back alone forty minutes after the attack was repulsed, with four wounds, but his gun intact.

The 45th Sikhs on the right carried the enemy's first and second line, and even penetrated to the third, but as soon as the attack of the 86th had been rolled up they were left in the air. The machine guns in the sandbag tower were switched on to them, and the Turks developed a strong counter-attack on their left. A British officer was seen to collect his men and close in on them in the open; he and his gallant band were enveloped and overwhelmed.

On the morning of February 3rd the 87th Brigade attacked, the 4th Devons on the right, the 1/9th Gurkhas on the left, the 62nd Punjabis (86th Brigade) in close support. This time our artillery barrage on the flank was drawn in closer and the enemy machine-gun fire was less formidable, but there was enough metal flying about to make it a rough crossing. The Devons and Gurkhas had seen the extinction of the Sikhs forty-eight hours before; the dead were heaped on the ground over which they advanced; they were glad of the cover. They crept up to within twenty-five yards of the Turkish fire trench before the bombardment lifted. The Turks, who were sheltering in the labyrinth of dug-outs behind, emerged just in time to receive their *coup de grâce*. The wave swept on to the second line. The Gurkhas' wild lust of hunting carried them blindly and irresistibly through. The Devons, who were on their left, are full of stories of their *élan*. To follow up the barrage and finish off the work of the guns is to "the Gurk" a kind of sublimated shikar. They seemed hardly conscious that they were dropping fast. In the third trench they had the Turk beat and were on him like terriers. "Here, here, Sahib!" one of them called, and pointed to a bay where the enemy still cowered, pitched his bomb on a Turk's head with a grin of delight and looked round at a paternal officer for approval. One little fellow was so excited that he followed his grenade into the trench before it had burst, and he and his Turk were blown up together.

I saw their gallant dead on the field next day lying in the stiff posture of offence in which they had fallen. But I did not see the attack on February 3rd. The 40th Brigade, with whom I was quartered, had been relieved by the 8th Brigade on the east bank of the Hai, after the action of February 1st, and on the night of the 2nd were ordered out on a flanking movement on the extreme left of our position. This promised to be exciting, so I stuck to the brigade; but as events proved, the affair offered little compensation for a second night without sleep. The diversion should have had a disquieting effect on the Turk. The appearance of four new battalions digging in on his right, while the cavalry were fetching an even wider circle, ought to have given him some moments of uneasiness and relieved the pressure he was able to throw in against our real objective. We were vigorously shelled at dawn; the Royal Welsh Fusiliers ran up against some strong enemy posts and lost their Commanding Officer, Colonel Hay, and another officer killed, and a score of men. But it is doubtful if the threatened encircling movement helped much. All day reinforcements were being brought up to meet our main thrust; counter-attack after counter-attack was delivered; but all were repulsed.

An hour and a half after we had taken their third line they came on in masses from the left of their position on the Hai, but were held up by our rifle, machine-gun and artillery fire. At 1.50 a second counter-attack was checked before it developed. At 2.50 another large assembly preparing to close in was scattered by our artillery. At 4.80 our artillery and machine guns swept the area over which the Turkish reinforcements were advancing in support, probably causing the heaviest casualties of the day. At the same time the enemy attempted a bombing attack which was checked and driven back on the flank. At six they made their last desperate thrust, closing in on both flanks, but this, too, was dispersed with heavy loss.

February 3rd was the biggest day in the salient; in a way it was decisive. It cost the Turk in dead more than any action since Beit Aieesa. His magnificent resolution in defence was broken. In the next fortnight's fighting his infantry was crumpled up by our guns. And the effect of the action was immediate on the east bank of the Hai. There was no more attacking here. Three artillery bombardments and the losing battle across the channel determined the enemy's retirement. Our infantry found the position evacuated after dawn. The pontoons at the mouth of the Hai were destroyed by our guns, and the whole right bank of the Tigris east of this point was clear of the enemy.

A description in detail of the operations on the Hai area between January 25th and February 15th would exhaust the reader's patience. After February 3rd two days stand out as distinct and salient. For the rest there are a hundred small affairs of outposts, patrols, pickets, skirmishes, countless individual acts of gallantry and endurance which must go unrecorded. The mere digging up towards the enemy's position, the wiring and consolidating of our line, meant a certain toll of lives. Even during the quietest phases the advance dressing stations would have their dozen or more cases to send in to the ambulance every morning; the Padre would have his burial service to read over the dead. Between January 12th and January 31st the 40th Brigade dug seven and a half miles of fire and communication trenches besides wiring and consolidating four miles of the enemy's captured line. And it was all done in the open, generally at night under a dropping fire. There was no time for sap work. But every man who fell digging saved many; every yard we approached nearer the enemy gave our infantry less open ground to cover in the attack.

Then there was the extension of our line by bombing up trenches after the assault, a thousand yards of ground gained here without the firing of a shot; fifty yards gained there at the cost of many lives. All through, the co-operation of the guns was perfect. A bombing party found themselves in a hot corner swept by fire from a strong point. The forward observation officer advised a halt. "If you get your men back fifty yards," he said to the subaltern in command, "I'll put the Hows on," and telephoned through to his battery. In a few seconds five high-explosive shells dropped on the redoubt with a shattering detonation. Then the white flag was hoisted.

This bombing work grew easier as the Turks' moral became depressed. Ground was covered more rapidly. Between February 9th and February 18th the South Lancashire bombers cleared over 5,500 yards of enemy communication trench and three strong points. There are many battalions who could quote a parallel record. But whole pages of statistics would be tedious. The story of the minor actions of six brigades must be crowded into as many paragraphs.

On February 9th we made another thrust at the enemy's main line. The King's Own went in this time after the usual bombardment, while the Gloucesters attacked a strong point on the extreme left. Both assaults were driven home. I watched the main thrust from a gunner's observation ladder a thousand yards behind the firing line. Here we had a clear view in almost insolent security. The Turks had not much ammunition to spare at this period, and were too much occupied with the attack and with countering our guns to spare much shrapnel for the nerve and intelligence of the machine. Not a shell dropped within fifty yards of the ladder.

I learnt a great deal by listening to the subaltern in the look-out above, and began to understand the intimate and essential connection of each gun with its own particular phase in the assault. "Why doesn't No. 4 gun fire?" he shouted through the din. "What the h—— has happened to No. 4? Tell No. 4 to go on."

A whole minute passed and many objurgations before the gunner at the telephone called up.

"No. 4 is out of action, sir. Case heated." Another minute passed. Numbers 1, 2 and 8 guns were instructed to lift and drop. Then I heard, "No. 4 gun in action, sir. Fired." The subaltern above called down, "That's O.K. Repeat. Tell them they are killing Turks."

Then, "Lift fifty."

I gathered that No. 4 was registered on a communication trench and was playing ninepins with the enemy reinforcements as they came up. It was the projector of some of those rustling Hows which were passing overhead and sweeping the zigzag scar in the clay 2,000 yards to our front. Soon Nos. 1 and 8 were put out of action for the same cause, temporarily disabled through overwork.

The Hai Salient and Dahra Bend

It was a hot fight, and no walk-over. An hour or two later in the firing line the bullets were pelting over like hail. But the Turks did not counter-attack till dark. Then they came bombing in four times on our centre and were driven back each time. After their last repulse they retired fighting a rearguard action all night, falling back towards the river. We threw in fresh troops and followed them up. As a result of the day's fighting we advanced on a front of 4,000 yards with a depth of almost a mile.

The action on the 9th may be regarded as the conclusion of the long series of engagements by which we ejected the Turk from the Hai salient. The next morning, February 10th, two companies of the 62nd Punjabis entered the Kut liquorice factory, the walled village on the right bank which had been held by Townshend's garrison during the siege. The position had been abandoned during the night, and the 62nd were only opposed by snipers from across the Tigris. The capture of the liquorice factory gave us command of the mouth of the Hai on both banks. But the end of one objective was the beginning of the next. The enemy's elaborate trench system was carried further west. He brought reinforcements over from the north bank. Blow after blow was dealt him; and there was no break or respite in these operations for the fighting man.

The loop of the Tigris north-west of Kut, known as the Dahra Bend, had to be cleared. On the morning of February 10th the 85th Brigade took over from the 86th and advanced our line on the right on the river bank. The 86th Brigade pushed forward in the centre and joined hands with them. The 39th Brigade threw out a line of pickets behind the 88th as a flank defence towards the south-west. The Gloucesters lost heavily in this advance, but dislodged the enemy's outposts. When on the morning of the 11th the North Lancashires took a point on the river bank, we held a continuous trench and picket line of 8,000 yards from the liquorice factory closing in the loop, within which the enemy were strongly entrenched. On this front we developed a big drive, forcing the Turks back on the Tigris as at Mahomed Abdul Hassan and on the Hai salient. In the meanwhile the 89th Brigade, who had also worked down the river nearer the neck of the loop, were gradually extending our line west. But there were strong positions to force before we were ready for another general attack. On the 11th the 102nd Grenadiers on the right rushed a strong Turkish redoubt. Their advance across the open was enfiladed by machine-gun fire, and they lost three British officers killed and three wounded out of eight who left the trench, and 250 rank and file. But they took the position. A company of the 37th Dogras followed in support to strengthen the garrison. All the officers of the company, British and Indian, were hit, and sixty-six of the rank and file. This was the first action in which the 102nd had been engaged since the fighting in January, 1916, when the battalion, reduced by casualties to a bare 100 effectives, was relieved to garrison the lines of communication.

On February 15th we were in a position to strike, but there was a strong point on our left, "the Ruins," on the river bank, which it was necessary to capture first, as the post enfiladed our advance. The Loyal North Lancashires rushed the place soon after dawn and dislodged the Turks. An hour afterwards the main assault was delivered, and the blow was struck with the most crushing and dramatic effect. Something in the Turk's spirit gave way. His resistance collapsed. The enemy, driven back on the Tigris, surrendered *en masse*. Not that we cleared the Bend without fighting. The 40th Brigade lost 380 in the day. But the Turkish prisoners taken by them and the 85th Brigade, who attacked in

The Hai Salient and Dahra Bend

the afternoon, amounted to an eighth part of Khalil Bey's whole army.

The South Wales Borderers, attacking on the left, the Royal Welsh Fusiliers on the right, went over in a wave. They had 650 yards of open ground to cover. Just as they reached the enemy's trench a body of Turks issued from the centre of the position and gave themselves up. This first surrender was infectious; it was repeated all along the line. The prisoners came forward in a stream waving white rags; for nearly an hour the procession was continuous; the Turks turned their shrapnel on them, only quickening the current.

"We do not wish to counter-attack," one of them explained; and after being close up to our barrage one could understand the disinclination. Whether these regiments were inferior to the troops we had been fighting at Mahomed Abdul Hassan and on the Hai, or whether the limits of endurance had been reached by the same brave men, it is not easy to judge. But we pushed our advantage home.

In the afternoon the 85th Brigade, the 87th Dogras (left) and Hants (right), delivered another attack on the right flank of the position we had taken. The garrison here had witnessed the morning's surrender, and the issue was the same. As our infantry advanced at a slow walk the Turks threw down their rifles and broke out of the trenches, an unarmed horde. The stream of prisoners who came out to meet the regiments attacking almost outnumbered them. Our troops walked through them, as they doubled passed running the gauntlet of their own guns. It was a most pacific-looking crowd that jumped our trenches, and quite unattended. They kept up their white rag flapping until they were out of sight. Some of them showed their gladness at being safely captured by signs and cheerful gestures, breaking into a kind of tripping step not unlike a dance.

Having carried these trenches, the 35th and 40th Brigades pushed through to the Tigris bank. The Turkish extreme left, cut off and left in the air by this movement, also surrendered. At six in the evening the enemy were holding a trench on the river bank. After dark this last foothold was rushed by the 4th Gurkhas, and the remnants of the garrison left in the loop were captured. Their boats had been insufficient to ferry troops and material across, and the points of crossing were swept by our shrapnel day and night.

During the previous week the Turks seem to have recognised that the battle for the right bank of the Tigris west of Kut was being lost. On February 10th they flooded ground to the west of the Massag nullah to oppose our advance. On the 12th they withdrew their bridge at Shumran.

The almost general surrender on the 15th appeared to be premeditated; but whatever the troops had decided, the Staff meant to hold the Bend. Two brigadiers were taken; the Divisional Commander escaped in a boat just in time; 2,200 prisoners were captured, including officers, between 2,000 and 8,000 rifles, 5 machine guns, vast quantities of ammunition, hand grenades, medical equipment, telephone wire and other plant.

At night the clear weather broke. Rain fell in torrents, flooding the trenches. For the last month the climate of Mesopotamia had favoured the invader, and the fickle elements were on our side. A captive officer gave us the Turks' point of view:

"We have been praying for this rain," he said, "for two months to hinder your advance; now it has come too late."

CHAPTER XXVIII

THE CROSSING

THE Turks must have been very much in the dark as to what our next move would be when we had cleared the Dahra Bend. We held the right bank of the Tigris, they the left for thirty miles from Sannaiyat to Shumran, and their position at Sannaiyat, with its left flank on the marsh, closed the river to us for navigation. If a cadet at a military college had put up such a tactical proposition a year or two before, he would have been rated for his ignorance of the first principles of war. And judging by newspaper criticism, the old Staff College tradition is not dead. "Why," it was asked, "if we are in a position to enfilade Sannaiyat, do we allow the Turks to hold on?" But the Turks, too, were in a position to enfilade us, and one of the things we have both learnt in this war is that strongly traversed and consolidated trenches cannot be reduced by enfilade artillery fire unless heavy guns are brought to bear on them. And if one has heavy guns there is no need to enfilade.

Neither of us had guns of sufficient calibre for this kind of work; and there were better ways of taking Sannaiyat than by costly frontal attacks. If we could cross the river some distance higher up and cut the enemy's line of communications the garrison would be left in the air without supplies. By pushing on with our offensive on the right bank we lengthened our own line and the Turks' at the same time; but we could stand this thinning out better than they. They had a trench and picket line all along the river bank, but they could not afford to be in force everywhere. It was open to us to concentrate and cross at any given point, provided the Turk was unprepared, and to seize a footing for our bridgehead. The passage would have to be made at night. If daylight saw us on the north bank the Turks would have a poor time bringing up their reinforcements in the open under our machine-gun and artillery fire.

Surprise was essential. Everything depended on the mystification of the Turk. He was kept intrigued all along the bank. There was a night raid across the river here, the splashing of pontoons lower down, the creaking of carts higher up, signs of movement everywhere. At Magasis, four miles by river downstream of Kut, a party of the 27th Punjabis landed, drove off a picket, and returned with a captured trench mortar. Forty of them landed and bombed along the bank both ways. They carried hand grenades and rifles with fixed bayonets, but no ammunition. It was a daring stroke. In the morning an air reconnaissance had reported a platoon and two machine guns at the point of the peninsula and a battalion inland; the machine guns had been removed. The river here is 800 yards wide, and was half in flood. The crossing took twenty minutes, but the swirling rush of water drowned the splashing of oars and the noise of embarkation, and the extreme distance of the crossing left the Turk unsuspicious and unprepared. As the party were pulling back across the Tigris the darkness was illumined by two beacon flares, the enemy's signal that we had crossed. A signal, too, to the Punjabis that the stroke had told. There was no doubt confusion in the Turkish camp, hurrying to and fro, and massing of armed men to oppose emptiness and shadows.

Also the enemy discovered much secret activity at the mouth of the Hai. A hostile Fokker evading our aerial guard observed that our sentries were being withdrawn from Shumran, and that a number of pontoons were being towed upstream under cover of the bank in the direction of the liquorice factory. At this spot there was much dumping of timber at night—all the inevitable noises of preparation exaggerated, all the natural precautions of secrecy religiously observed. No lights were shown; no human voices heard; only the clatter of planks and cables; while higher up, where the crossing was to be, the sound of unoiled wheels had become a nightly and familiar occurrence. When the Turk woke up on the morning of the 23rd he saw a forest of observation ladders which had grown up in the night, all facing Kut. His suspicions were confirmed. It was here that he concentrated his reserves to oppose our landing. On the evening of the 22nd three battalions were marched from Kut to reinforce Sannaiyat; on the morning of the 24th they were countermarched towards Shumran, and were thus lost to both battlefields.

It was decided to cross at three different points in the Shumran bend, and to throw the bridge across at the apex of the peninsula. I visited No. 1 Ferry, the highest point of crossing, two days before the event. It seemed a hopeless business. A swollen yellow stream in flood, 400 yards wide, with a current running five knots; and if you raised your head an inch above the scrub you drew a sniper's bullet. The Norfolks were to make the passage here. They had to get enough men over in ten pontoons to seize the other bank, ferry the boats back, cross again after the alarm, and continue the passage until the whole battalion was over, then to rush the trenches and dug-outs, scupper the riflemen and machine-gun teams, and throw their thin line across the bend, while the bridge was building, before the Turks could bring up their reserves.

Yet somehow on the morning there seemed more chance. I slept in a nullah close by, and crept up before it was light. The Norfolks had come up quietly in the dark, a cool and confident crowd. The Pioneers had been preparing the ground for embarkation. At 5.15 the pontoons were lifted over the embankment and placed silently in the water, each crew of four men with their own boat. When the last pontoon was lowered there was just light enough to see the other bank, but not figures, if there were any there, alert, and waiting for us. At 5.30 word was passed along to push off. And it was all done with so little noise that the sentries on the other side did not discover what was happening until the first boat was within fifty yards of the shore. Then a single rifle shot rang out. Then a fusillade in which a machine gun joined from upstream. One could not quite see what was going on across the river, but soon the first returning pontoon loomed into sight 300 yards downstream. They were quickly towed up to the ferry, manned again, the wounded rowers relieved, the wounded Norfolks carried to the ambulance dug-outs under the bund. The surface of the stream was churned with bullets. Then they began to shell us. But the pontoons threaded the fountain-like spray with surprising immunity. There were many casualties from bullets, but only one direct hit by a shell; the pontoon sank, but the crew were saved. The Norfolks pushed along under the bund, and dispersed the enemy's pickets. The first Turks we saw emerged from their dug-outs and surrendered. Within an hour we had got most of the rifle fire under. The machine gun was silenced. There were only shells now and the bullets of a few persistent snipers. Our machine guns sweeping the ground on both flanks, a trench howitzer pounding the enemy's dug-out 600 yards upstream, the barrage of our guns lifting and dropping behind, did good service. Not a Turk dared raise his head on the neck of land we were disputing.

The Crossing

In the meantime the 2/9th Gurkhas were forcing a passage 1,000 yards downstream, the 1/2nd Gurkhas 500 yards below them. The distant sound of musketry heard between the bursting of shells told us they were not having an easy time. In both cases the river was swept by machine-gun fire; both regiments ran up against strong points; the Turks lined the banks, threw grenades at the crews as they landed, and the fight developed into a bombing match between boats and shore.

At No. 2 Ferry the first three boats came in well together in echelon. Major George Wheeler[1] was the first on land. He jumped into the mud and water, followed by a handful of men, and charged the enemy across the foreshore on to the bund. A Turk, whose head appeared over it just as Wheeler reached the foot, hurled his rifle and fixed bayonet at him and lifted the top of his scalp. But he was soon on his feet again. With one other officer and four men he scattered a bombing party of forty who threatened to overwhelm the small band of Gurkhas who were manning the bund. Then he charged a group of Turks who had closed in on Lieut. Russell, who was down, and dispatched the man who was on the point of bayoneting him. When they had carried the bund and cleared the Turks out of the trench under it, the Gurkhas followed up a communication trench and took up a position 200 yards inland. This was a happy inspiration, as the enemy, when they turned their guns on, shelled the bund all the morning.

The 1/2nd Gurkhas at No. 3 Ferry had an even hotter crossing. At this point the top of the bund was swept by a machine gun from a house on the right, and the enemy had better cover.

To realise the nature of the assault, one should think

---

[1] Major Wheeler was granted the Victoria Cross for his gallantry in this action.

of the bund as the parapet of the enemy's trench: it was loopholed, and had head cover. The Gurkhas had to land within from fifteen to fifty yards of this and attack it; the gallant rowers—Hants men, most of them, with a section of the Burma Sappers—had to land their draft and push off. The boats made the shore at set distances apart. There was no quick shoulder-to-shoulder rush to stimulate *élan*. Each landing was an individual piece of initiative and heroism, gallantry in cold blood. Judged by any other standard than that of mere bulk, it was as great a thing as the landing at Helles, and it will be as historic.

One could read the story afterwards in the mud. Wherever a keel had scored the Turkish shore there were Gurkha dead and dead Hants rowers who had been lifted from the boats. Many of the pontoons still lay stranded in the mud. One had a hole in its side, a direct hit by a shell, and nine dead in it. And dead Gurkhas lay tumbled about the parapet; some had pitched forward and lay sprawling over it with the impetus of the fall. Beyond were dead Turks who had counter-attacked from inland.

In the face of all opposition the two regiments established a footing on the north bank. But as one by one the rowers were killed or wounded and the boats stranded or drifted downstream, Ferries 2 and 3 had to be abandoned. Before 7 A.M. 110 out of 280 of the Hants rowers had been hit, and there were only four pontoons available on the right bank. A company and a half of the two battalions had got across, and they hung on in spite of rifle, machine-gun, and intense artillery fire. The others, who were waiting to cross, moved upstream, when the boats were lost to No. 1 Ferry, and reinforced them from the point where the Norfolks had crossed. Later on they formed part of the line that swept the Turks from the bend.

The Crossing

To return to No. 1 Ferry. At eight o'clock six galloping mules brought up the first wagon of the bridging train. Chesses, buoys, ropes, anchors, cables, were flung on the ground, and a party of sappers rushed up and drove in the stakes of the first land anchorage. Then the pontoons came up one by one on carts, at a swinging canter, landmarks for miles. Most of the drivers sat nonchalantly on high. One or two, using their pontoons as dug-outs, kept their heads low, peeping over. Two or three were hit. An officer was killed, shot in the head. A mule fell limply in the traces and paddled the air with his feet. An hour passed, and the Turkish gunners had not discovered the bridgehead. They had registered on the head of the nullah 150 yards downstream, where the Norfolks had crossed, and they kept on shelling it till evening. Apparently they had no forward observation officer, no telephone wire. At ten o'clock one could stand on the fifteenth pontoon well advanced in the stream as secure as one ever is at the edge of a small scrap. There was one solitary rifleman hidden in some shell crater who continued to snipe us long after all other rifle fire had died down. Where he was nobody knew, but the man deserved a decoration. A few more of his kidney would have held up the bridgehead for hours. I had imagined a tornado of shells, pictured one relay of sappers relieving another as it was shot down, believed that so many pontoons must be paid for with so much blood. Each one as it was driven into place sounded the doom of the Turkish Army. Yet this crossing, the most vital thing in the campaign, was carried through as smoothly almost as if we were on manœuvres. Later on their howitzers swept the bank and the stream in their search for the bridge. But it was too late; they were beginning to think of saving their own guns. At four o'clock in the afternoon, eight hours after driving in the first land anchorage, the bridge was complete and our troops and transport were pouring over. It was a great feat. The stream here at the narrowest point in the bund was 295 yards wide, with a current running five knots.

In the meantime the infantry had advanced to a ridge astride the bend, sweeping the enemy before them. Six hundred prisoners were taken. The main artery of their system was severed. Our Sannaiyat troops, who had carried the first three lines of trenches, followed up without further opposition. Kut, for so many months the lodestar of the British and Indian soldier, became a mere incident in the advance.

CHAPTER XXIX

THE FORCING OF SANNAIYAT

SANNAIYAT, or Falahiyeh, as the position was called in Baghdad, had become a familiar name all over the world for more than a year. There was no village there, not even a mud hut; but the Arabs attach place-names to featureless stretches of country where they graze their herds by the river bank. For generations travellers have passed the spot on their journey up and down the Tigris without marking its possibilities for defence. Maps were vague and sketchy; lakes or marshes might mean nothing at all; it was not realised that in this apparently open plain there was one point that had the natural advantages of a Thermopylæ. The Turks neglected to hold it during Townshend's advance, and entrenched a few miles back in the inferior and more extended position at Sinn. But in the interval between Ctesiphon and our advance from Ali Gharbi in January, 1916, someone, possibly old von der Goltz himself, recognised Sannaiyat as the only strong position between Basra and Baghdad. Nowhere else could he have held up the Kut Relieving Force. The place was like a gate to a fortress with a moat on each side. The Turk held it against the British for over a year, and he might have held it until the end of the war if we had not scaled the wall behind and threatened to turn the key from inside.

The troops who made the original attack on April 6th, 1916, carried the first two lines of the position ten months afterwards and never moved from the trenches in the meanwhile. The 7th Division garrisoned the position all through the hot weather and winter, and during the fighting on the right bank which culminated in the crossing at Shumran they kept a constant pressure on the Turk in the narrow neck between the marsh and the river and pinned him to his ground. The two battalions, the Seaforths and 92nd Punjabis, which swept the Turks from their trenches on February 22nd, were the same that led the desperately gallant but ill-fated assault on April 22nd, 1916. But the beginning of the siege was three months earlier than that. It dates from the day of the first attack on El Hannah—January 21st, 1916—and everyone who was in Mesopotamia thinks of this ground as consecrated to the division which bled and sweated here for thirteen months, and which,. in the fighting between January 7th and April 22nd, 1916, suffered something like a complete reincarnation, losing upwards of 12,000 men. For El Hannah and Sannaiyat, though five miles apart, were only successive lines in the defence of the same fortress, the bottle-neck between the Suwacha Marsh and the Tigris. One position was almost an exact replica of the other, and the withdrawal of the Turk on the night of April 4th, 1916, from his first to his second line of defences was a masterly manœuvre.

Directly the news of the capture of Sannaiyat reached Baghdad the German families began to pack. Khalil Pasha had staked everything on the position, and he did not believe that it could be turned. To say that the crossing at Shumran gave us the key to the fortress is only a part of the truth. The metaphor is misleading if it suggests a picture of troops entering a door that has been opened from behind. Nothing could be farther from the facts. The crossing at Shumran and the forcing of Sannaiyat were concerted actions, the success of one being dependent on the other. The whole point of our tactics was to draw Turkish troops away from the Shumran area, where the crossing was to take place, by inducing them to reinforce the already considerable garrison at Sannaiyat. And no feint here would meet the purpose. The Turk was not to be bluffed. Nothing but a genuine assault driven home in real earnest would pin him to the position while his flank was in danger of being turned upstream. The capture of these trenches was as gallant in its way as the passage of the river, and more costly in life; but as it was only one of our repeated hammer strokes at the enemy's front, and had not the same elements of drama and adventure, one heard less about it.

The Turkish first and second lines at Sannaiyat were forty yards apart; the third, two hundred yards behind the second. These trenches were very lightly held on the day of the attack, but the enemy occupied a succession of lines behind with a clear field of fire from which they could sweep the ground over which we advanced. We might possibly have taken Sannaiyat by a succession of direct frontal attacks unaided by the passage of the river by which we cut the Turk off from his base of supplies; but it would have been at a tremendous cost. And behind Sannaiyat lay the Nakhailat and Suwada positions, which would have to be forced in turn before we could enter Kut.

For weeks before the attack the Turks had suffered many bombardments which had not been followed up by an assault. These Chinese bombardments, as they are called, must have been particularly annoying to him. While the storm lasted the enemy would keep their heads under and stick to their dug-outs; the moment it lifted their heads would be up and they would be manning the parapets. But the wave of infantry they were expecting did not appear. Instead, the guns opened again with devastating havoc on the garrison. It is a very ancient kind of bluff, but one which seldom fails to be effective; for the enemy cannot afford to take a bombardment as a feint, and must be ready every time. Also the uncertainty and mystification involved in these dummy bombardments, alternating with genuine artillery preparation for assault, tend to diminish the enemy's moral.

An obvious counter-move, and one which has been generally adopted in trench warfare, is to leave the first and second lines empty or thinly held, to retire to a third or fourth line, and thence to drive in a counter-attack before the assaulting party have time to dig themselves in and consolidate their position. At Sannaiyat the Turks had a covered tunnel in advance of their first line. This was probably for sentry groups, for it would be too dangerous a post to garrison.

When the 19th Brigade attacked on the morning of February 22nd all our wire was standing in front of our trenches. The supports of the *chevaux de frise* were loose, and could be easily swung round to give the infantry a passage. This was to lull the suspicion of the Turk. For all he knew the terrific commotion of our guns and trench mortars might have been a bluff, as so often happened, to tempt him to emerge, or to shake his nerves. The 2-in. 60-lb. mortar bombs sailed slowly overhead and fell in the trenches with devastating precision, and their heavy sticks, which came cracking back through the air, added a new noise to the din. The cloud of smoke and dust hung so thick that he could not possibly tell whether we were attacking or not until the curtain lifted and disclosed us in his second line.

At 10 A.M., when our bombardment lifted on to the third line, the dirty-grey cloud still rose, swelling and bellying, 40 ft. high in front of our trenches. One could not see an inch through this veil. Once over the parapet and in the open, the stretch of No Man's Land which had seemed such a long field for a sprint in the day of waiting was dwarfed to nothing. In a few

The Forcing of Sannaiyat 61

seconds the Seaforths and the 92nd were in the Turks' first line. There was no sign of a Turk in the trench. It was, in fact, no longer a trench, but an irregular fosse twice its original width, half filled in with broken revetments, wood, thatch and reeds. Very few of our infantry fell going across. They heard the regular tap of machine guns from the trench in the Turkish rear, but the comforting sound of bullets going high told them that the crews were rattled by our guns, as well they might be.

The orders were to wait in the first line one minute until the bombardment lifted from the second line; but when they went forward they could find no second line. In the centre of the front they were attacking the trench had been filled in by the Turks. There was no sign of it among the shell craters—only a series of immense molehills with the earth lying in powder on them. They looked for the trench, overshot it, and formed their line in an old irrigation cut, $1\frac{1}{2}$ ft. deep and 3 ft. wide, beyond. The Turkish position was intersected by a network of these, which, with the shell craters and confused labyrinth of broken trenches, made it impossible to tell where you were. However, the Highlanders and the Indian regiment found something like a definite edge to this erupted surface, offering a field of fire, and began to dig in as one digs when one knows that the enemy must be forming for a counter-attack across the open.

The Turks' third line was held by a few snipers. The enemy were mostly in the fourth line, a newly dug trench which had not, up to this time, been damaged much by our artillery. As soon as the bombardment lifted they were seen preparing for a counter-attack. They came on and were crumpled up by our guns. They came on again and were again blotted out. A third and heavier mass was seen, this time on our left, gathering for attack. They came on stoutly, and it was the only time during the day that our position was seriously threatened. But they suffered terrible losses. Enfiladed by a battery of machine guns from across the river, swept by artillery fire in flank, front and rear, they were almost exterminated. Our forward observation officers were busy on the wires, and the gunners never failed us.

Then, at one o'clock, the 28th Brigade went in on the right under cover of a similar bombardment; they had come in for heavy artillery fire all the morning, and the 51st Sikhs lost eighty men in the trenches before the advance. The remainder of the day was spent in digging in and joining up, no easy matter in this undulating, warren-like confusion of pits and mounds. Between 4 and 5 P.M. the battalion was hard pressed, but the Leicesters and two platoons of the 53rd Sikhs came up in support, and with these reinforcements it held its own. By evening we had dug a respectable trench, and at night we put up wire across the new front.

The Turks were sniping all the morning of the 23rd from their fourth line or from isolated dug-outs. Soon after midday it was discovered by taking bearings that certain points of the trench we had dug were within thirty or forty yards of the Turks' third line. Patrols were sent up communication trenches, and, pushing out on both flanks, found the line unoccupied save for the wounded and dead. At 8 P.M. our pickets were holding this new line. At 7 P.M. a bombing party was sent forward on our left to discover whether the Turkish fourth line was occupied. This party was counter-attacked in force and driven back, but at midnight the patrols went out again and found that the Turks had quitted. Their fourth line and communication trenches were a fearful shambles, choked with the dead and dying, many of them buried up to their waists and crying out for help. The Shumran crossing had been effected, the whole of the Sannaiyat position was in our hands. On the 24th the 7th Division advanced. The fifth and sixth lines at Sannaiyat and the Nakhailat and Suwada positions fell to them with barely a casualty. Kut was empty. And the 14th Division, that had forced the passage of the river thirty miles upstream, were sweeping through the barracks at Dahra and opening the road to Baghdad. The dead counted at Sannaiyat numbered 516, besides those the Turks had buried and those who had been buried in their trenches by our shells. Our casualties in the two days' fighting were 1,414. The division did not expect to go through at the cost of less than two or three thousand. But the Staff work during the long preparations had been as thorough as it could be. The plan of the enemy's trenches had been reproduced months beforehand, and every platoon, company, regiment and brigade knew its co-ordinate part. There were almost daily rehearsals; and they bombed and blocked and consolidated until they knew the lie of the enemy's trenches almost as well as their own. When the real attack came it was the repetition of a routine.

The rapidity of the enemy's retreat was remarkable. They were bombing us in the trenches at eleven on the night of the 23rd, and at 7.30 on the morning of the 24th they had covered the twenty miles to Shumran. They were so tired and helpless that they let our aeroplanes descend to a thousand feet and empty their Lewis guns on them without firing a shot. Nevertheless the conduct of the retirement at this stage was very creditable. In the face of disaster the Turkish Commander kept his head and held up our 3rd Corps and cavalry all through the 24th while the Sannaiyat troops were getting away.

Early on the morning of the 25th I was with the 40th Brigade at Shumran, when we saw our gunboats steaming up the river with their decks cleared for action. The infantry lined the bank and cheered them. It was the first time for months that the Navy and the troops in the firing line had met. And it was the first news many of us had that the 7th Division had unlocked the river at Sannaiyat, opening it once more to navigation. At last, after a year or two of incredulity, we began to think about Baghdad.

CHAPTER XXX

THE PURSUIT

WHEN Khalil Pasha realised that we were firmly established across the river at Shumran, while downstream his left wing was in danger of being cut off at Sannaiyat, he ordered a retreat towards Baghdad. And he formed a strong flank guard to hold the northern end of the Shumran peninsula, and to contain our 3rd Corps until his forces had passed upstream of the bend.

The crossing of the Tigris at Shumran was so dramatic in its achievement and so vital in its bearings on the whole campaign that the gallant part played by the 14th Division the next morning is in danger of being overshadowed. We were quick to follow up the crushing blow of February 23rd. That night we held a line right across the bend from bank to bank a thousand yards inland from the bridgehead. The 36th Brigade took up the right of the line, the Hants and 62nd Punjabis relieving the two Gurkha battalions, while the Norfolks and 67th Punjabis were on the left, and the 26th and 82nd Punjabis in close support. Soon after six the next morning the whole body of infantry swept forward and advanced 3,000 yards without a halt, clearing a Turkish trench on the way. The enemy had left picked troops in this position to cover the retreat. They were mostly bayoneted or shot; few surrendered. This cool and apparently careless advance in force was a most gallant affair and cost us nearly a thousand casualties. A blow like this was needed just then. Hesitation or caution would have encouraged the Turk to stand and been more expensive in the end. As it was, the sight of two brigades advancing steadily in full strength, inevitable as a wave, took the heart out of the garrison in the nullah behind, and before we could come up with them they were retreating in the direction of Imam Mahdi. But the machine guns in the Turkish barracks which had kept up a raking fire on the flank were still in action. Three were captured in the buildings with the support of the brigade machine-gun companies and the artillery on the right bank; two which had been withdrawn into the nullah were rushed by the patrols of the 26th Punjabis sent up to clear the barracks, as they were being brought into action again. On the right three field guns and 400 prisoners were added to the spoil; 1,660 prisoners were taken in the two days. This unfaltering advance over 8,000 yards of open exposed to heavy artillery fire and machine-gun fire on the front and on both flanks was made by troops who had been engaged in severe and continuous fighting for over a month.

I passed the field guns abandoned by the Turk three hours afterwards when with the cavalry in pursuit. The General of the leading brigade swung round to the rear of them, calling out to us not to mask the guns. It was only as we passed that we noticed that the pieces were unmanned and palpably Turkish. The gun horses were found in the barracks together with the limbers.

It was good to be riding through the enemy's barracks, his deserted aerodrome and stables, with the promise of the rarest thing in modern war—to be with a cavalry division in pursuit of an army in rout across an open plain. It is an experience which every cavalryman has prayed for but which not one in a thousand has known. As a matter of fact the promise once more proved vain. It was one of the dullest and most disappointing days I have spent in my life. Nothing was done. We lost a few horses and a few men, but barely sighted a Turk.

Other arms as a rule expect too much of the cavalry, though the limitations imposed on them by the evolution of the modern rifle and machine gun have been impressed on military students for years. But it is particularly in pursuit that the effectiveness of the rôle they can play has been exaggerated. "It appears to be anticipated," Colonel Henderson wrote in 1902, "that the cavalry, if led with sufficient boldness, and thundering forward in a close succession of steel-tipped lines, will have the supreme satisfaction of riding down a mob of panic-stricken fugitives whose bandoliers are empty, or who are so paralysed by terror as to be incapable of using their rifles." But, as he explains, men are not cattle. It is only exceedingly bad troops that have ever been reduced to such a prostrate condition as, for the application of their theory, the advocates of the cavalry torrent are compelled to postulate; and even bad troops possess in the present firearm a power of resistance against which the flood will break in vain. It is common experience that small bodies of defeated infantry have enough confidence in their magazine rifles to hold up large bodies of mounted men. But the forces we were fighting were not panic-stricken; their moral was still good; they were superior to our cavalry in numbers; and they were singularly well handled. The Turk put up a stubborn rearguard action in the deep nullahs that lay across his line of retirement. Our cavalry sent out feelers to the right, but the enemy's flanks were flung much farther to the north than was anticipated, and he kept us employed in dismounted action until dark. Much time was wasted, and the troops had to walk a mile before coming into action. At one o'clock in the morning they were back into camp. At five they were in the saddle again, and a second fruitless day was spent.

I was with the cavalry again the next morning (February 25th) when they were engaging a superior infantry force four miles north of the main rearguard action south-east of Imam Mahdi.

This time it seemed there was nothing to prevent them making a flanking movement and getting behind the Turks, who were compelled to follow the line of the river. But all through the pursuit the mobility of the cavalry was discounted by the lack of initiative in command, though there was keenness enough in the fine regiments that made up the division. Again nothing was accomplished. The enemy shelled us all day with a reckless expenditure of ammunition, though, happily, through the intervention of a providential mirage, their artillery was not as effective as it might have been. In the evening the division returned twelve miles into camp only to cover the ground again the next day. Men and horses were exhausted, but owing to the absence of water they could not stay where they were. They had to go on or go back. There is no doubt that they should have gone on and occupied a position on the river that would have blocked the enemy's line of retreat. A whole cavalry division, dismounted and dug in twenty miles in the rear of the tired and footsore Turkish infantry, would have left the enemy small hope of escape.

During the rearguard action of the 24th and 25th the Turks probably suffered more loss from the fire of our light armoured cars than the whole of the Cavalry Division were able to inflict. In a pursuit like this, in which the enemy have little time to dig in and consolidate successive positions, the "Lambs,"[1] as they were euphemistically called, discovered their most effectual rôle. They were equally good in scouting and skirmishing. On the 24th two cars were ordered to discover the position and strength of a flanking party of the enemy's rearguard. They advanced and found the Turks holding a series of shallow, newly dug fire bays in continuation

[1] Light Armoured Motor Batteries.

of a deep nullah. The first car crossed through to the Turkish side between these pits, leaving the second to work along our side. They first cleared the bays on the right and left of the point crossed, then travelled up the line, one car on each side, keeping ten yards out to give them the sweep of their guns, and too near the enemy infantry for their artillery to play on them. The Turks stuck to their rifles and machine guns with great boldness, pouring in a terrific fire. One car had eleven bullets through the port, and the foresight of the machine gun knocked off. The lead flattened like mud against the chromo-nickel plating. There was no ricochet inside, only the paint of the eye shield spattered and half blinded the man at the gun. A Turk hit the other car with a bomb, blew in the crank case and inspection plate, cut the steering rod in half, punctured the oil-feed, and was shot before his bomb had exploded. But it was an unequal fight, and the garrison of this shallow line of incomplete dug-outs was practically annihilated.

On the 25th five armoured cars approached the enemy's position on a reconnaissance. The Turks were found to be lying up under the crest of an undulating ridge. One car passed through a gap in the defences to within 800 yards of an enemy battery and opened fire on the team with great execution. All five passed along in calm and deliberate file to the end of the line, like a procession threading London traffic, then returned to cover the withdrawal of a squadron of cavalry. We watched their leisurely progress with admiration from the horse-gunners' pulpit, though we could not see the enemy's infantry and guns.

But to return to the infantry. The Turks' flank guard, which had been left behind to hold the 3rd Corps in the Shumran peninsula during the retreat of the main body from Sannaiyat, succeeded in fulfilling its rôle throughout the 24th, though at considerable loss to itself.

All day the 2/4th Gurkhas and Buffs had been heavily engaged with a strong force holding the river bank on our extreme left. During the night the Turks withdrew upstream, and on the morning of the 25th the main enemy force had cleared Shumran. At this point the 18th Division, which had crossed to the left bank on the 24th, took up the pursuit, the 88th Brigade leading. Touch with the enemy was temporarily lost, but at 11.80 on the morning of the 25th, when the Loyal North Lancashires, who formed the rearguard, came under artillery fire at long range, Captain Brooke's battery (66th Brigade R.F.A.) pushed on and came into action three-quarters of a mile ahead of the infantry. This manoeuvre was brilliantly carried out, and diverted the fire from the North Lancashires, who deployed and drove the enemy from his advance posts. For the moment opposition was brushed aside; the King's Own was ordered up in the rear, while the East and North Lancashires formed the main guard. A mile and a half ahead the Herts Yeomanry was in dismounted action with orders to contain the Turks until the infantry arrived. Soon after one o'clock the 88th Brigade were in close touch with the enemy's main rearguard, which had taken up a strong position across the road some four miles downstream of Imam Mahdi. The South Lancashires advanced on the right to the nullah held by the Herts Yeomanry, passed straight through, and occupied a section of the enemy's line in front. Here they spent the day in the same nullah as the Turks, with barricades on either flank, bombing and being bombed, enfilading the enemy and being enfiladed by their machine-gun fire; and they did not relax their grip until the Turks evacuated in the night.

The enemy's right rested on the river. The infantry's business now was to find his left flank and attack it with vigour. The 89th Brigade was called up for this. At 4.80 they reached the battlefield. It was found that the Turkish flank had been hastily extended northwards, and they had fortified two parallel nullahs, the first about 600 yards from the 88th Brigade line, and the second the same distance behind the first. Soon after five the 89th Brigade launched their assault under cover of the fire of the 55th F.A. Brigade, which had come into action within 1,200 yards of the enemy. The Worcesters, Gloucesters and North Staffords were in the front line from right to left, and the Royal Warwicks in reserve. The gallant attack of the infantry was completely successful. The enemy's first line, and then his second, were stormed within fifteen minutes of the launching of the assault. But no sooner were we in than the Turkish guns opened heavily on the captured trenches, and before the position could be consolidated a vigorous counter-attack was launched against our left. The troops on the extreme left of the 89th Brigade were forced back, but the attack was finally checked and driven back. Fighting continued on the left of the captured second line until two in the morning of the 26th, when the enemy began to retire. Several hundred of the prisoners taken in the first attack escaped during the counter-attack and later during the night; but, apart from a large number of wounded, 14 officers and 820 rank and file remained in our hands.

This was the last serious encounter our infantry had with the enemy until the affair at the Diala on March 7th. Our losses were heavy, those of the enemy heavier, especially in killed, but their delaying action was essential to enable them to get the guns of their Sannaiyat force away. During the whole day they put in an unprecedented amount of shell fire, firing rapidly and wildly in all directions. They had no longer any concern for economy of ammunition; they had either to expend it or leave it behind.

So far the enemy had conducted an orderly retirement. It was the action of the gunboats, on February 26th, that introduced panic and converted the retreat into a rout. The Navy had been waiting fifteen months for this chance. It had been a long and tedious period for them, broken only by occasional long-range firing; for the rôle of the Tigris fleet had become that of a heavy battery in trench warfare. In this new phase they were to become cavalry and horse artillery combined; but in their extraordinary rapidity, immunity from exhaustion, independence of transport, and superior striking power, they were given an opportunity which cavalry can never compass, and they turned it to good account.

The day after the crossing the crew of H.M.S. *Mantis* landed and hoisted the Union Jack at Kut; the next morning the gunboats were co-operating with the 38th Brigade in their attack on the main Turkish rearguard; and on the morning of the 26th they received the welcome orders to pursue. The Turks were familiar with our cavalry; they had not reckoned with our fleet. In their garrison-artillery rôle the gunboats take few risks. They must keep their distance and fall back dutifully when the Turkish guns begin ranging on them. For the damage they can inflict by artillery fire on the enemy's trenches is infinitesimal compared with the damage they can receive from one direct hit by a shell. But when the order has gone out for a pursuit it is a different thing. Greater issues are at stake and greater risks are run. It is no longer a question of the pounding of a few Turks in a dug-out. The passing of a certain point by the fleet may mean the precipitation of the enemy's retreat into a rout, the interception of his shipping, the cutting off of his rearguard, and the capture of guns, ammunition, stores and military plant. It is for these supreme moments that the crew of a gunboat live through many uneventful days in a river campaign.

GUNBOAT ON THE TIGRIS.

The Pursuit

On the morning of February 26th H.M.Ss. *Tarantula*, *Mantis* and *Moth* passed our infantry on the bank at full steam; our cavalry watched their disappearing smoke with envy. Soon after passing Baghailah, forty-six miles upstream of Kut, they came in contact with the Turkish infantry who lined the river bund and poured in a heavy fire. But it was higher up, in the Nahr Kellak Bend, that the Turks made their most desperate effort to hold up our fleet. The river here turns back on itself in a complete hairpin bend, so that passing vessels are under fire from three sides. For half a mile before the bend the tongue of land within the loop is nowhere more than a hundred yards in breadth, and the channel, as always, lies on the outside, in this case right against the Turkish position, for which the gunboats steered direct. A Turkish battery and some machine-gun teams had dug themselves in opposite the apex of the peninsula and raked the fleet as they were coming and going, and fired point-blank at them as they passed. Our 12-pounders, pompoms, and machine guns enfiladed the position as they went by, pounding the enemy's trenches and gun pits at 300 yards. It was a hot corner for us both. The quartermaster and pilot in the conning-tower of the *Mantis* were shot dead, and the captain entered just in time to save the vessel running full steam ashore. All the plating was pitted with bullet holes; shells struck masts, ladders and rigging; the *Moth* was badly holed; but by a miracle not one of the three vessels was sunk. The casualties amounted to a fifth of the force engaged; the proportion of killed was slight. Eleven officers were wounded, but not one died.

Swinging round the bend at 16 knots, the fleet reached a point where the road comes in towards the river, and their machine guns played havoc with the Turkish transport and gun teams. More guns were abandoned. Our horse artillery got on to them at the same time. The next morning we found the Turkish dead on the road. There was every sign of panic and rout—bullocks still alive and unyoked entangled in the traces of a trench motor carriage, broken wheels, cast equipment, overturned limbers, hundreds of live shells of various calibres scattered over the country for miles. Either the gunners had cast off freight to lighten the limbers or they had been too rushed to close up the limber boxes. Every bend of the road told its tale of confusion and flight. Here a wrecked field post-office with Turkish money orders circling round in the wind; there a brand new Mercédès motor car held up for want of petrol; cartloads of small-arm ammunition, grenades, a pump, well-drilling apparatus, hats, boots, oil drums, things destroyed or half destroyed, decapitated carcasses of stock which could not keep up with the rout, white columns of smoke ahead telling of further destruction, enough litter by the road to keep the army in fuel for weeks; then a whole battery of 12-centimetre field guns, their breech blocks removed, but buried too hastily near by, and betrayed by an entrenching tool.

The gunboats, while keeping up a brisk fire at the Turks on the bank, were at the same time engaging the enemy's shipping at extreme range; but at four in the afternoon they ceased firing at the army to save their ammunition for the river craft, on which they were rapidly gaining. The hindmost of the enemy's fleet was the first to sink, a ship with a 4.7 gun on her captured from our horse-boat at Kut. Then the *Basra* was hit, and ran herself ashore; she was passed by our fleet and ordered to stand by. Next the *Pioneer*, who had put up a gallant fight, was seen to be on fire and aground. During the whole of the afternoon the *Firefly*, the gunboat lost by us at Umm-el-Tubal in the retreat from Ctesiphon, had kept up a running fire as we pursued. Just as it was getting dark her crew ran her nose ashore, landed, and escaped, leaving her with full steam ahead and a fire in her magazine, but intact save for strained boilers. We salved her, extinguishing the fire just in time. Twelve days afterwards, under her old commander (Commander Eddis), she took part in the entry of the fleet into Baghdad. The loss of the *Firefly* reduced the enemy's fighting fleet to two Thornycroft patrol boats carrying pompoms with a 8-pounder forward. These spent the summer somewhere in the shallows above Tekrit.

The *Basra* was escorted downstream under her own steam. She had two barges in tow, with a cargo of aeroplane plant, engines and bombs; 1,000 Turkish wounded and sick on board and 150 dead. But the most dramatic thing was the restoration of eighteen wounded Indians and eight wounded British, including an officer, all taken in the last fight at Sannaiyat. The moment the *Tarantula* passed in the pursuit and gave the orders to stand by, the wounded British officer took over charge.

Many prisoners fell to the fleet during the pursuit. But the treatment of enemy surrendering on the bank to gunboats in action and under steam is a difficult question. By all the rules and logic of war one is justified in refusing to accept a surrender where there is no guard to leave over prisoners. But this argument translated into action would have meant the mowing down of crowds of Turks who approached the river bank in a trustful spirit holding up their hands. Doubtless they deserved death. Many of them had their arms concealed near by, and would have used them on us again if the chance offered; but we could not fire on men who came in to us unarmed, waving their white flags. As a matter of fact, very few escaped. For another element entered in —the fear of the Arab. The tribesmen, seeing the Turk in a bad way, were stripping and killing him. Prisoners came in at different points all day, many of them naked, and craved protection from their irregular allies. They were afraid to be left without guards. A brigade of cavalry was scouring the country, rounding up prisoners, marking down guns, finding and collecting the enemy wounded. The *Moth*, passing Baghailah after the action, with a crew of fifteen all told, captured 150 prisoners. Four thousand Turks were taken between the crossing of the Tigris on February 23rd and the evening of the fight at Nahr Kellak on the 26th.

The last lap in the running fight on February 26th was a repetition in its main effects of the advance from Qurna to Amara in June, 1915. The gunboats were up against much heavier odds, but their rôle as a kind of super-cavalry was again proved to be essential in a campaign where the main communications are by river. In both cases a large number of the enemy's rearguard were either killed or captured, his shipping was cut off, and vast quantities of munitions fell into our hands. The rapidity of the fleet in pursuit is, of course, beyond anything the cavalry could achieve. In the advance from Qurna (1915) the Navy left Baharan at 1 P.M. on June 1st, and at 1.30 on June 3rd, in spite of mines, obstructions, and forced anchorage owing to the impossibility of navigation in the dark, the *Comet* was in Amara ninety miles upstream; the Turks were completely taken by surprise, and the whole garrison bluffed into surrender. The two actions are examples of how a fleet of gunboats or armed launches can lengthen the arm of a force in a river campaign and double its striking power, paralysing the enemy's communications when he is in retreat. In both cases the manœuvres were of the boldest description; great risks were taken, yet not a vessel was lost, though in the Nahr Kellak fight the fleet ran the gauntlet of the enemy's guns at almost point-blank range.

A great haul was made at Baghailah—bridging

material, ordnance stores, ammunition, carts, tents, telephone wire, trench mortars, maxims, and a number of abandoned guns lying half in the water. We heard from prisoners afterwards that out of ninety-one guns which the Turks had in the Kut area, only twenty-eight were brought away; the others which were not captured were thrown into the river. This is probably not far from the mark. We took thirty-three guns on land and five on ships.

The action on the 26th turned the Turkish retreat into a rout. The enemy now were moving on a broad front, a disorganised rabble, no longer in column of fours. On February 27th the cavalry rode into Aziziyeh in the dark, found the enemy in possession, and engaged them on foot. They did not know that the Turks were in the village until their rifles were blazing in their faces. In the morning the enemy evacuated, falling back on Lajj.

At Aziziyeh a halt was called to reorganise our extended line of communications, and nobody save the private soldier was quite sure whether we were going on. Our policy was not yet clear from home. Government had not anticipated Baghdad, and were afraid of another Ctesiphon. The Force, of course, was not taken into the confidence of the Army Commander as to the future; but so far as it lay with him we had no doubt. His vision was clear enough, his back broad enough for the whole responsibility, and what often seemed optimism in his decisions had its roots in a self-reliance well proved in the past. Also he had the sinews of war that his predecessors lacked. Already he had retrieved the disaster and restored the prestige of 1915. The Turks were beaten, and could not expect reinforcements in time to save Baghdad. The city was ripe fruit ready to fall into his hands. It seemed impossible that political considerations should intervene. We were not kept long in uncertainty. General Maude received, if not an order, a very direct hint, and the military advantage was pressed for all it was worth. It was understood at home that he was acting as an Army Commander in the field would act with a beaten and demoralised enemy in front of him.

At Aziziyeh we were fifty-five miles by direct road from Kut and fifty-one from Baghdad; the river journey, owing to the bends and loops of the Tigris, is more than double the distance. Nothing stood in the way of our going straight on save the important obligation of feeding the army. The mere layman cannot realise the difficulty and complexity of the problems that confronted "Q." Here were two Army Corps and a Cavalry Division on one road, and all the machinery by which they had been fed thrown out of gear during the night. The crossing at Shumran had dislocated the whole system of supply. In twenty-four hours the distance between our firing line and the advance-base depots at Sheikh Saad and Arab Village had been increased, for river transport, by forty miles. The Sheikh Saad-Sinn-Atab railway had served its purpose in breaking the back of the Turk. But it could not help us on; its uses were past; as a means of transport it had become as dead in a single day as an ancient Babylonian canal. Sinn railway station, which had seemed the centre of our universe, was left out of the scheme of things. The S. and T. staffs who were needed for the advance were locked up in the depots as caretakers, or to evacuate supplies down, not up, the line. Three or four thousand tons of ammunition and R.E. stores had to be cleared, and local transport was necessary to collect it and get it away. Thirty train-loads of empty shell-cases and empty boxes alone were removed, and the Arabs were kept off while the gleaning was going on.

But the abandonment of the main artery at Sinn was merely a temporary dislocation; the river was the permanent and compensating gain. Not that it was all plain sailing. Every division had so many ships allotted to it. But some were slower than others; some ran against mudbanks; the channel had changed its course many times since Ctesiphon, and the pilots did not know the way; in some cases coal gave out, and there were knavish units on the bank commandeering other people's food. Often at first we looked anxiously for the smoke of the supply steamers. Once or twice emergency rations were consumed. But soon anxiety was forgotten. "Q" never failed us. When a day's rations went wrong a camel convoy would emerge out of the blue, or a leisurely cortège of Ford vans would traverse the Biblical plain. During the whole of the pursuit only one division was on half-rations, and that only for one day. How it was done Providence alone knows, and Providence was "Q."

By March 4th three days' supplies had been accumulated at Aziziyeh, and we were able to push on.

CHAPTER XXXI

TO BAGHDAD

ON March 6th the pursuit continued. The infantry made an eighteen-mile march to Zeur, preceded by cavalry who moved on to Lajj, seven miles farther on the road to our goal. At this time it seemed that the gunboats would be first in Baghdad, and I became a guest of H.M.Ss. *Mantis* and *Tarantula* in turn. The hospitality of the Navy was doubly welcome in the rapid phases of the advance. On a ship one never had to pack or unpack, or wait in uncertainty for one's kit or rations, or pitch a belated tent, or bivouac without one in the mud or dust. A bed or a bath, or a hot or a cold drink is always handy; one escapes the weariness of a long march, and one is never footsore or tired or depressed at the hard uses to which one has to put the patient, kindly beast that carries one.

The next few days had none of the excitement of Nahr Kellak, but one felt that one was in the van, and that one would not be far away from anything that was going on. All the five arms of the Force—the Navy, Cavalry, Infantry, Artillery, and Flying Corps—were working together in a way that was new in war. We reach a point where the road skirts the bank. A British regiment on the march is so near that one can distinguish the badge on their helmets; the dust of the cavalry floats across our bows; British Hussars and Indian Lancers, watering their horses, exchange facetious comments with the bluejackets on board. At noon an aeroplane comes hovering low over the bank to drop a message, then swings round the ship, circling and banking in an anxious way a few yards above the rigging as if to impress on us that she has borne some urgent communication. When the second boat in the line banks in to pick up the message she sails off contentedly. She has come to tell us of the dispositions of the Turkish troops and to warn us of a battery

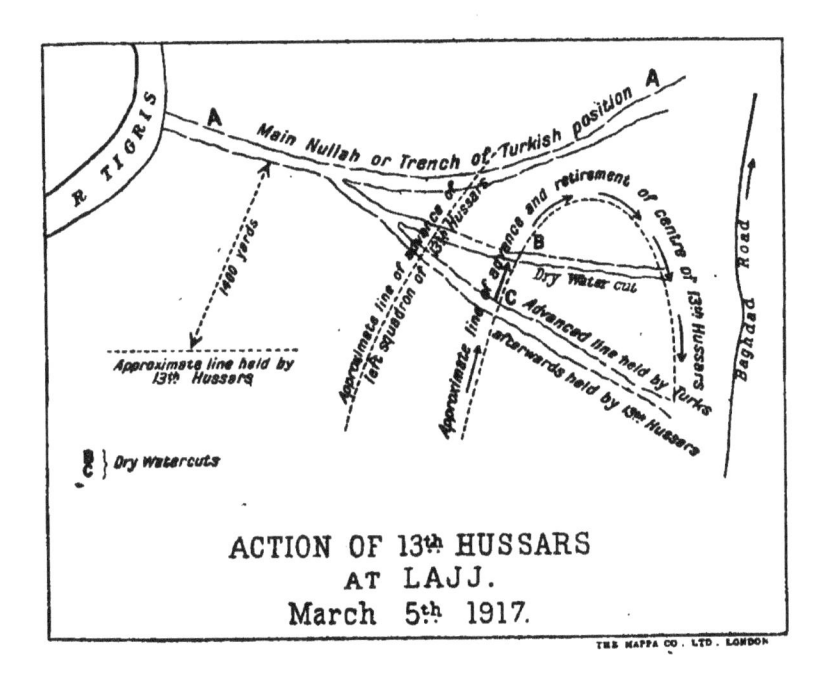

ACTION OF 13th HUSSARS
AT LAJJ.
March 5th 1917.

waiting for us ahead. Later she returned and "spotted" for our ship's guns, but the cloud of dust was too thick for the gunboats to find a target, and they fell back out of range.

The dust isolated us, and left us uncertain of what was happening ashore. At eleven in the morning we heard gun-fire to the north-west and knew the cavalry were engaged not many miles off, though it was impossible to see anything in the thick haze. We learnt afterwards that it was the 18th Hussars. Information had come to them of an enemy convoy some two miles ahead labouring through the heavy dust with an escort of 250 rifles. The chance was too good to lose. The colonel in command had three squadrons. He formed them in echelon and had started the pursuit when a low shrapnel burst disclosed artillery with the convoy, giving a hint of the nature of the resistance they might expect. But their blood was up.

The squadrons, which were now moving at the gallop, extended; they had already drawn swords. They were riding through intermittent rifle fire, when suddenly through the driving dust-screen they saw Turks not a hundred yards ahead. Some were standing holding up their hands; some were running away; and judging by the amount of lead in the air others were holding on to the dry water-cut which formed their position. The order was given to charge. The squadron immediately in front of the position increased their pace and went in. They cleared the nullah. Fifteen or twenty Turks were killed at the point of the sword; thirty were rounded up and sent back to the brigade with a small escort. But the nullah was only an outpost to a stronger position some 800 yards beyond. No sooner had the Hussars charged through than they came into very heavy rifle and machine-gun fire from the second line, and, as some of the regiment believed, from the infantry who had thrown up their hands in the rear. The colonel shouldered his squadron to the right in his endeavour to find a way out towards the convoy; but the Turkish line was extended too far to the north to admit a chance of turning the flank, and he decided to retire his squadrons and advance dismounted.

The Hussars held the first nullah over which they had made the charge, and kept up a fire with their rifles and hotchkiss guns at 800 yards. The enemy were reinforced all day; in the evening they were estimated at a division and twenty guns. A brigade went out to the north and failed to find their flank until late in the afternoon. At 4.30 the shelling became very heavy. The wounded on the field pinned the regiment to the spot. The Hussars lost nine officers (three killed) and eighty-five men (twenty-five killed). All our casualties were cleared or accounted for. There were only two missing, and these were known to be in the hands of the Turks. One does not leave one's wounded on the field in Mesopotamia, as the Arab gives them short shrift. Nor are they always gently treated by the Turk. At Lajj the wounded lay so near the Turkish trenches that the enemy came out and stripped them.

This small action of the 13th Hussars failed in its objective, but it was a very gallant affair. Opportunities are rare in which cavalry have the chance of charging home with the sword. That they were able to go in, come out, and form up again under such heavy fire without loss of control will be remembered to the credit of the arm. In the shouldering movement the left flank of the regiment was brought very close to the Turk. It was a hot corner for mounted troops, yet in spite of loss and the inevitable confusion among wounded and plunging horses, many of them riderless or carrying two men, the three squadrons drew up within 200 yards of the selected position, still in the fire zone, their horses well in hand, returned swords, drew their arms, and advanced on foot as infantry. A test of discipline this which will be a warming memory to the cavalry officers who saw the material they had trained proved in the heat of action.

The next morning examination of the Turkish position showed that the main line (A) ran obliquely backwards from the river to the Hussars' line of advance. This explained the heavy casualties of their left squadron and the squadron next to it; for, as they were endeavouring to keep their left shouldered up, the fusillade poured in on them became enfilade fire. A few men and horses cleared the deep and narrow trench that formed the main line of the Turks' resistance; but none survived. One horse was found dead wedged between the parapet and parados but not touching bottom. The Turks had evidently determined to make a stand at Lajj, but they slipped out of their position in the night and we pushed on. The appearance of the 6th Cavalry Brigade on their left rear towards dusk, coupled with the apparently confident front put up by the 7th Brigade, alarmed them. They thought they were being outflanked and in danger of being cut off. Prisoners taken by us admitted this; and Staff officers who went over the ground are of opinion that the infantry could not have taken or turned the position in less than two or three days' hard fighting. If this were so, the charge of the 18th Hussars, and their dismounted action afterwards, was not merely a gallant effort thwarted; it was a determining action that hastened our advance on Baghdad.

Early the next morning we were in sight of Ctesiphon. The enemy had prepared a strong entrenched position here, but they had abandoned it and fallen back on the Diala. I saw the great arch from the conning-tower of the *Tarantula*; the earliest rays of the sun entering the ruin made it glow like a lighted shrine.

The country as we neared Baghdad was no longer accursed. Even the physical features of the land became less depressing. North of Baghailah the plain becomes undulating. The dead monotonous flat is broken by mounds and the banks of historic canals. There are belts of trees by the river. On the night of the 6th we moored by the throne of the Chosroes and saw the wireless masts of Baghdad. The change in the aspect of the land was perhaps more visible to the inward eye; and a great deal of the ugliness of what we had left behind, and the absence of colour, form, and light, was subjective. The deadness of the country now provoked entertaining ghosts; for mortality was no longer ever present and personal, and a great shadow had been lifted from over our heads.

I had carried Gibbon with me for more than a year, and I often turned to his narrative of Julian's campaign to find parallels with our own. The Roman general had 1,100 ships, fifty armed galleys and fifty flat-bottomed boats which he used for bridging; our original Relieving Force was not so well equipped with pontoons when it left Ali Gharbi. The army marched in three columns on the bank, the brave Nevitta's column always in sight of the fleet, and the cavalry far out protecting the flank. Then, as now, the "Saracens" hung on the skirts of the army and intercepted stragglers on the march; their avarice and cruelty have not changed; nor has the Assyrian habit of opening a dam and opposing a sudden deluge to the progress of invaders. The troops of Julian contended with the same discouraging hardships as ours, the heat, the floods and the flies; inundations poured into their camp; the roads became impracticable; "the unwholesome air was darkened with swarms of innumerable insects."

When Julian found himself on the right bank opposite Ctesiphon his case was ours at Shumran. The Tigris opposed the same barrier to the Roman legions as to the British and Indian force under Maude, a barrier which the troops came to regard as insuperable though the Commander saw a way through. The crossing was the crux; and one feels that the guile and strategy of the one general would have been commended by the other in the different conditions that sixteen centuries impose.

"The stream was broad and rapid, the ascent steep and difficult; and the entrenchments which had been formed on the ridge of the opposite bank were lined with a numerous army of heavy cuirassiers, dexterous archers, and huge elephants; who (according to the extravagant hyperbole of Libanius) could trample with the same ease a field of corn or a legion of Romans. In the presence of such an enemy the construction of a bridge was impracticable; and the intrepid prince, who instantly seized the only possible expedient, concealed his design, till the moment of execution, from the knowledge of the barbarians, of his own troops, and even of his generals themselves. Under the specious pretence of examining the state of the magazines, four-score vessels were gradually unladen and a select detachment, apparently destined for some secret expedition, was ordered to stand to their arms on the first signal. Julian disguised the silent anxiety of his own mind with smiles of confidence and joy; and amused the hostile nations with the spectacle of military games, which he insultingly celebrated under the walls of Coche. The day was consecrated to pleasure; but, as soon as the hour of supper was past, the emperor summoned the generals to his tent, and acquainted them that he had fixed that night for the passage of the Tigris. They stood in silent and respectful astonishment; but when the venerable Sallust assumed the privilege of his age and experience, the rest of the chiefs supported with freedom the weight of his prudent remonstrances. Julian contented himself with observing that conquest and safety depended on the attempt; that, instead of diminishing, the number of their enemies would be increased by successive reinforcements; and that a longer delay would neither contract the breadth of the stream nor level the height of the bank. The signal was instantly given and obeyed: the most impatient of the legionaries leaped into five vessels that lay nearest to the bank; and as they plied their oars with intrepid diligence, they were lost after a few moments in the darkness of the night."

No one who has read this passage will ever forget the scene. It was in my mind as I watched the Norfolks silently load their pontoons and push off in the half-light on the morning of February 23rd. The Roman legionaries pursued the Persians to the walls of Ctesiphon and might have entered the city. But with the army of the West once across the Tigris and a stubborn enemy surprised and routed, the historical parallel changes from Maude to Townshend. History was repeated in

ARCH OF THE CHOSROES AT CTESIPHON.

November, 1915, when another great-hearted leader of men found himself in a pass at Ctesiphon where neither genius nor gallantry could save him. Ctesiphon was a disastrous victory to Townshend as to Julian. The arch of the Chosroes witnessed the setting of their two stars. There was a great deal in common in their character and fate, in their courage and resource, in the persuasion of their tongue and example, in their addresses to their troops, and in their magnetic forcefulness of spirit. And both were disappointed in reinforcements which did not make good. The great difference in the effect of the two campaigns was that in the case of Julian the retirement from Ctesiphon marked the beginning of the end of the Roman Empire in the East; in the case of Townshend the disaster stimulated his race to further conquest. But through the dark months of 1916 the parallel made gloomy reading, and one was glad to be past that fateful and ominous milestone on the road to Baghdad.

On the other side of the river the bare mounds facing Ctesiphon are the ruins of Seleucia, the last remains of the Greek. This thirsty soil has swallowed many empires, but the arch of the Chosroes is the only monument that survives in Mesopotamia to the dignity of man. In the meanwhile the Saracens, "the wretched and unskilful husbandmen" described by Ammianus, till their miserable fields and drive their flocks to pasturage, little concerned with the passage of empires save in so far as they afford opportunity for loot. Whether it be Greek, Roman, or Persian, British or Turk, it is the same thing; it has been their privilege as inheritors of the soil for at least two thousand years to attack, murder and pillage the losing side. The nakedness of the Turks we delivered at Baghailah was their mark. They fell upon the stragglers of Julian's army up at Samarrah in the same way. Townshend's wounded were stripped and mutilated by them. But in the hour of victory they are docile friends.

As we passed Ctesiphon they were lining the banks bowing and gesticulating at the gunboats and waving their white flags. Ten months before these same villagers had paraded for the Turk with great show of jubilation as the ships passed upstream carrying our ill-fated garrison of Kut.[1] There was a dirty white flag on every black horsehair tent, byre or mud hovel within gunshot range. But they are not a timid people. In this running fight they are between two fires, but they go about their work unconcerned, columns of smoke and earth rise on the bank and fountains of spray in the stream, but the "Buddoo" sticks to his yoked bullocks at the Persian wheel where the water-lift feeds the irrigation channel, and his women continue gathering their cow-dung fuel in the fields. They trade with both sides; the only difference is that the Turk pays in paper money depreciated to a third of its face value, we in good coin. Towards evening we pass a village in migration—a procession of men and women and children carrying bundles on their backs and driving or leading sheep, goats and cattle. They are moving a few miles south, to return in a day or two as the edge of the battle recedes in the direction of Baghdad.

The Turks made no stand in their strongly entrenched position at Ctesiphon. We were too close on their heels, and gave them no pause at Aziziyeh. After the action at Lajj their vanguard fell back on Diala, destroying the bridge which crosses the Diala River at its junction with the Tigris. We pushed on in pursuit on the left bank, sending the cavalry with the 7th Division and the 85th

---

[1] "Here and there we passed an Arab village, the denizens of which would come out and gape at us, and cheer and extol the Turks with their haul of prisoners. Linked arm in arm, all the males of the place would run or dance in line, keeping pace with the ship, yelling or chanting a song of triumph, and blazing off any old muskets or pistols they happened to possess. But the Turks only smiled, called them 'canaille,' and shrugged their shoulders."—"Besieged in Kut—and After" (*Blackwood's Magazine*, June, 1917).

Brigade to work round on the right bank, where the Turks had a force covering the city from the south and south-west. Speed in following up was essential, and the column attacking Diala was faced with another crossing from which the element of surprise was eliminated. The village lies on both banks of the stream, which is 120 yards wide. Houses, trees, nullahs and walled gardens made it impossible to build roads and ramps quickly and bring up pontoons without betraying the point of embarkation. Hence the old bridgehead site was chosen. The passage might have been forced with less loss by a wide flanking movement farther inland, but this would have meant delay, and in a pursuit time is essential. One must reckon on the enemy being hustled and weakened in moral, and one must display a boldness which would be foolhardiness in an open fight. The general who does not presume weakness in an opponent in such circumstances, or who hesitates to act on it, would be lacking in initiative. But if the enemy is not hustled, if his moral is good and his dispositions sound, the details who are thrown in on this principle as a feeler have to pay.

The 13th Division were leading on the left bank, and the attack on the night of March 7th-8th was launched by the 6th King's Own of the 38th, or Lancashire, Brigade. It failed completely; but the gallantry of our men has never been surpassed in war. Immediately the first pontoon was lowered over the ramp the whole launching party was shot down in a few seconds. It was bright moonlight, and the Turks had concentrated their machine guns and rifles in houses on the opposite bank. The second pontoon had got into the middle of the stream when a terrific fusillade was opened on it. The crew of five rowers and ten riflemen were killed and the boat floated downstream. The third pontoon got nearly across, was bombed, and sank; all the crew were killed. But there was no holding back. The orders still held to secure the passage. Crew after crew pushed off to an obvious and certain death. The fourth crossing party was exterminated in the same way, and the pontoons drifted out to the Tigris to float past our camp in the daylight with their freight of dead.

Telephone wires were carried over in the boats. In one boat that was drifting downstream the only survivors were a signaller, and a private of the King's Own who appeared to be mortally wounded. The signaller attached his line to the bows of the drifting boat, dived overboard and reached the shore with the other end of the line; by this, with assistance from the bank, he succeeded in hauling in the pontoon with the wounded man. The rowers who went over were volunteers from other battalions in the brigade. They and the Sappers working on the bank share the honours of the night with the attacking battalion. It had become a forlorn hope, but the men laughed and joked, keeping the tragic, sentimental, and heroic at arm's length, as is the manner of their kind. Nothing stopped them save the loss of the pontoons. In the last lap one of the Lancashire men called out: "It's a bit hot here; let's try higher up." But the gallant fellows were reduced to their last pontoon.

The East Lancashire Regiment, which was to have crossed higher up simultaneously with the King's Own, were delayed, as the boats had to be carried nearly a mile across difficult country to the stream.

After the failure of the bridgehead passage this second crossing was abandoned, but the men were still game.

On the second night the attempt was pursued with equal gallantry by the Loyal North Lancashires. This time the attack was preceded by a bombardment. Registering by the artillery had been impossible on the first day owing to the rapidity of the pursuit. It was the barrage that secured us the footing; not the shells, but the dust raised by them. This was so thick that you could not see your hand in front of your face. It formed a curtain behind which the boats were able to cross. Afterwards, in clear moonlight, when the curtain of dust had lifted, the conditions of the night before were established. Succeeding crossing parties were exterminated; pontoons drifted away. But the footing was secure; the dust had served us well. The crew of one boat which lost its way during the barrage was untouched in midstream, but they did not make the bank in time. Directly the air cleared a machine gun was opened on them; the rowers were shot down and the pontoon drifted back to shore. A sergeant called for volunteers to get the wounded out of the boat. A party of twelve men went over the river bund; every man of them, as well as the crew of the pontoon, was killed. Some sixty men had got over. These joined up and started bombing along the bank. They were soon heavily pressed by the Turks on both flanks, and found themselves between two woods. Here they discovered a providential natural position. A break in the river bund had been repaired by a new bund, built in the shape of a half-moon on the landward side. This formed a perfect lunette. The Lancashire men, surrounded on all sides save towards the river, held it through the night and all the next day and the next night against repeated and determined attacks. These assaults were delivered in the dark or at dawn. The Turks only attacked once in daylight, as our machine guns on the other bank swept the ground of the position. Twenty yards west of the lunette there was a thin grove of mulberries and palms. The position was most vulnerable on this side, and it was here the Turkish counter-attacks were most frequent. Our intense intermittent artillery fire day and night on the wood afforded some protection. The whole affair was visible to our troops on the south side, who were able to make themselves heard by shouting. Attempts to get a cable across by rockets, for passage of ammunition, failed. At night volunteers were called for to swim the stream with a line. The strongest swimmer was almost across when Lieutenant Loman, the adjutant of the regiment, who was paying out the wire, fell dead, shot through the heart, and the weight of the line prevented the man in the water from reaching the other bank. At midnight of the 9th-10th, the Turks were on the top of the parapet, but were driven back. One more determined rush would have carried the lunette, but the little garrison, now reduced to forty, kept their heads and maintained a cool control of fire. A corporal was seen searching for loose rounds and emptying the bandoliers of the dead. In the end they were reduced almost to their last clip and one bomb; but we found over a hundred Turkish dead outside the redoubt when they were relieved at daylight on the morning of the 10th.

The crossing on the night of the 9th-10th was entirely successful. With our cavalry and two columns of infantry working round on the right bank the Turks were in danger of being cut off as at Sannaiyat. Before midnight they had withdrawn their machine guns, leaving only riflemen to dispute the passage. The crossing of the Wiltshires upstream was a surprise. They slipped through the Turk's guard. He had pickets at both ends of the river salient where we dropped our pontoons, but he overlooked the essential points in it, which offered us dead ground uncovered by his posts up and down stream. It was so unexpected that the Turks did not realise what was in the air until our footing was established. One man was actually bayoneted as he lay covering the opposite bank of the river with his rifle. The other ferry nearer the bridge also crossed with slight loss owing to the diversion upstream. The Turks, perceiving that their flank was being turned, effected a general retirement; the greater part of their garrison between the two ferries, some 250 in all, finding us bombing down on both flanks, surrendered.

A third ferry had been arranged on the Tigris. Two armed motor launches of the spacious pattern constructed for the landing at Gallipoli were manned overnight by 500 of the Cheshires. These were to be run ashore on to the Turkish trenches facing the Tigris half a mile above its junction with the Diala. The Cheshires were to land, rush the position, skirt the village at the back, and join hands with the small garrison of the North Lancashires, provided it still held out, and with any details that might have effected a passage. It was a gallant venture; but the flats and shallows forbade. One of these ugly, clumsy barges, with its bellyful of armed men like the horse of Troy, grounded on a sandbank, and we on the *Tarantula* had an anxious quarter of an hour the next morning towing her off, before the enemy's guns could register on us. But the Cheshires, had they been in time, could not have added greatly to the success of the action. The passage had been forced before dawn. By half-past nine on the morning of the 10th the whole brigade was across. Soon after eleven the bridge was completed and the pursuit continued. The splendid gallantry of the 38th Brigade will never be forgotten, and if there is any perspective in history, the Diala will be remembered—not as the stream in which Cyrus lost his horse, but as a kind of Lancashire Thermopylæ.

At Bawi, four miles above Ctesiphon, we bridged the Tigris again, and threw a force of all arms on to the right bank. The 35th Brigade had crossed by ferry on the night of the 7th and 8th, and were working up the river bank. The Cavalry Division crossed by the bridge on the night of the 8th; the 7th Division on the early morning of the 9th. The Turks were holding a position at Shawa Khan, some five miles south-west of Baghdad, with their left resting on the river. They had no natural defences on this bank comparable to the Diala. By this time they had abandoned all hope of saving the city and were fighting a delaying action. The dust storm which blew hard on the 9th and 10th helped them, screening them from our guns in their retirement.

On the 9th there was a scattered fight on a very wide front, and we advanced, driving the enemy's patrols and pickets before us. By two in the afternoon the 7th Division were in touch with the 35th Brigade on the right.

As the line of our advance drew in towards the bend of the river our flank was exposed all day to an enfilade fire from the enemy's guns on the other bank. Behind his huts and walls and in his hastily improved watercuts the Turk had a strong rearguard position, and it was immensely improved by the support he received from his artillery across the Tigris, where his guns lay concealed in palm groves and safe from attack so long as the Diala defences held. Inland our troops on the extreme left were seven and a half miles from water. A force consisting of the 51st Sikhs, 56th Rifles, 92nd and 28th Punjabis, who were sent out to find the enemy's right flank, failed. And the cavalry lent no aid, as, through want of water and the exhaustion of their horses, they were for all practical purposes immobilised. When darkness fell the Turks were still holding the position, but before dawn our patrols pushed forward and found that they had evacuated. The morning of the 10th discovered the enemy in a new line of trenches covering the iron bridge. The day was spent in a gradual advance under a heavy fire. All the time the Turk must have been slipping away, but in the blinding dust our guns had no target. The wind served him in good stead; a clear sky would have doubled his losses. Our own casualties in the two days' fighting and marching, though there was no bayonet work or rushing of trenches, were not small. For the Turk, having little transport to fall back upon, was reckless in his expenditure of shells, and he had the advantage of us in the dust as he knew the ground and had registered the positions. The losses of the 7th Division exceeded a thousand. But the Turks were not for staying. They could hear the sound of battle on the left bank which told them that we had crossed the Diala. Towards evening they were firing salvoes from all their guns—no uncertain sign of impending departure; and their uneasiness was betrayed in the wild, rapid and continuous fire opened by their infantry on our patrols. Then, soon after midnight, the glare of the flaming city indicated the organised destruction of a retreat. At 1 A.M. a patrol under a Gurkha officer of the 2/4th Gurkha Rifles reported that the enemy's gun pits were empty, and that there were no Turks in the Iron Bridge nullah. The order for the attack in the early hours of the night had not been cancelled, and no further move was made till 2 A.M. on the 11th. The 21st Brigade then passed through the 19th Brigade; patrols were pushed forward, and it was found that the Turk had only left a few riflemen to cover his retirement. At 5.45 A.M. a half company of the Black Watch under Lieutenant Houston seized the Baghdad railway station with the loss of two men. Two hours afterwards the 35th Brigade had occupied the suburb opposite the site of the bridge of boats, and before noon the cavalry were in Kadhimain.

On the left bank, after the crossing of the Diala, there was fighting in the palm groves of Saida and Dibaiyi. The Warwicks went in and the Turks were cleared with the bayonet after our artillery had combed the wood. The enemy's main body was holding the Tel Mahomed position a mile and a half farther north, a trench line running nearly four miles inland from the Tigris. The 38th and 39th Brigades attacked this in front while the 40th Brigade made a wide turning movement on the flank. The enemy evacuated the position in the night; and early on the morning of the 11th the corps cavalry, two squadrons made up of the Herts Yeomanry, the 10th Lancers, and the 32nd Cavalry, rode into Baghdad. The column on the right bank had the start of us on the left, and if Baghdad railway station is Baghdad, the Black Watch had the honour of being first in. It fell to them to seize the terminus which the Hun had designed for the triumphal progress from Berlin, the pledge he had advanced of his spiritual, kultural and material conquest of the East.

CHAPTER XXXII

THE FIRST DAYS IN BAGHDAD

A YEAR or two of war in Mesopotamia dulls one's sensitiveness to impressions. As we entered Baghdad our thoughts should have been sweeping back through the cycle of history to Nebuchadnezzar, Alexander, Cyrus, Julian, the Chosroes, Haroun-al-Raschid. And now it was Maude. Our General of the quiet smile had become one of the immortals. Method, vision, and decision had earned him his niche in the temple of Fame. The most fabled city in the world had opened its gates to embodied precision. The Afrits fled before practicality to the nth; ghosts abdicated, legends were dissolved in fact. In vain on the day before our entry did the Osmanli destroy the Bab-el-Kilissim, through which the conquering Murad rode, and which he blocked behind him lest others should follow to victory in his steps. It seemed that no spiritual or superstitious aid or favour of the goddess of chance was ever invoked in this campaign by Turk or Briton with success. All through, from the day we landed at Fao, Science had been inexorable. Very merciless were the laws of cause and effect. Every mistake was paid for, and interest exacted. For months the smallest dint that we made in the iron wall of the Turkish defence was the result of countless hammer strokes, untiring vigilance and zeal, and a resolution that the most depressing circumstances could not relax.

We were fixing a memorable link in the continuity of history when we rode into Baghdad, but it is the most difficult thing in the world to associate what is familiar with what is great. Romance flies before revelation.

And Armageddon has destroyed the poetry of adventure; it has flattened out everything, leaving nothing salient anywhere, no perspective or beauty of light or shade, only barren and confused undulations like a field of battle pitted with shells.

Nothing could have been more casual, easy and unofficial than our entry into Baghdad. Four of us, the colonel and adjutant of the King's Own, a gunner officer and myself—for I had left the gunboat, seeing that the Army would be in first—were riding ahead of the column through the palm groves talking of some action of a week ago.

It was the ordinary day's march in column of fours, ready to deploy against a new position and with guards thrown out, until, as we drew near the city, the high-walled gardens confined us to the road. We were not quite sure whether we were going to bump up against the Turk. He had slipped out of the Tel Mahomed position the night before, and after the way he had fought for every nameless ditch between Sheikh Saad and Shumran it was difficult to believe that he would leave the city of the Caliphs behind without a last ambush. As a matter of fact two squadrons made up of the Herts Yeomanry and 10th and 32nd Cavalry had already entered, and the 7th Division and 35th Brigade had reached the right bank soon after dawn and were waiting for boats to cross.

We were talking about something far away—I think it was the Western Front—when the colonel in command of the vanguard pointed to some figures emerging through the haze of dust.

"By Jove!" he said, "I believe these fellows are bringing us the keys of the Citadel."

We saw three men in black approaching along the unmetalled road between the walled gardens, probably the three men in Baghdad who were most confident that the Turk was "beat." For it requires some courage under

Ottoman rule to greet the enemy at one gate a few hours after the dominant race has ridden out at the other. Needless to say the welcome was unofficial. As they drew near they waved their red fezes and called out to us, "Good morning, how are you?" This bold and confident and familiar greeting was amusingly unexpected. As we rode on other groups joined them and they all repeated the same greeting. Then they began to cheer. Among them were girls and matrons of fair complexion and unveiled, whose forwardness was almost embarrassing to men who had seen nothing in the shape of a woman for years beyond black bundles filling their pitchers on the Tigris bank.

We had been bivouacking out in a blowing dust. We were dirty, unwashed, unshaven, unfed. My mare, who a few days before had broken tether and dispossessed herself of the best part of her bridle, had on a makeshift headstall of rope. On the whole we did not make up a very imposing cortège for an historic state entry.

We came along a nameless road to a dilapidated bund. Here stood the ruins of the Southern Gate. We swung round to the left and found ourselves by the river where the first of the great houses on the Tigris bank forms the abrupt beginning of the city. A great crowd had collected to cheer the British. They clapped and hurrahed, and the soldier man, who is apt to regard anyone who wears a red fez as a Turk, was a little contemptuous. But it was no fickle demonstration. I rode on ahead into the American Consulate. The Consul was out, but an Armenian dragoman invited me to the luxury of a white cloth and a steaming cup of tea—very refreshing after the Tigris water and bully beef seasoned by the wind-driven dust of the last few days. He had been told to have it ready "for the English," he said, and in two minutes he told me enough to explain the attitude of the Baghdadi to the invading army.

The hand of the Turkish Government had lain heavy on the people of the city. The struggle in Iraq was for the survival of an antagonistic governing race, and the Christian, Jew and Arab population had had to pay. Each of these communities far outnumbered the Turk. The huzzaing on the river bank was genuine enough. Our arrival was a deliverance. In the last ten days the oppression of two years had degenerated into brigandage. For nearly three weeks, ever since our crossing the Tigris at Shumran sealed the fate of the city, the Ottoman Government had been requisitioning private merchandise and sending it off by rail to Samarrah. The bazaars were nearly emptied when the last Turkish train left Baghdad early on the morning of the 11th. Then the Kurds and Arabs came in. There were still hidden stores, and the Jewish merchants say that they lost two million francs' worth of goods between 2 A.M. and our entry at 9. The cost of an hour's delay was reckoned in so many thousand liras.

When we entered, Arabs and Kurds, the riff-raff of the city, were carrying off shutters and benches, heavy bedsteads, wood and iron mantling, the seats and balustrades of the public gardens. Everything easily movable had been removed. British and Indian troops were soon patrolling the bazaar, firing good-naturedly over the heads of the rabble, striking with the blunt edge of the sword the villain who would not disgorge. In some quarters where there had been resistance the shops had been gutted; the woodwork was smouldering. Under the Northern Gate a man lay huddled in the dust giving up the ghost; a massive iron safe which had defeated violence and ingenuity was lying in the road. I believe there was little spoil left by daybreak, and the tardy brigand must have been disappointed in the sacking of Baghdad.

A group of our officers had soon collected in the

First Days in Baghdad

American Consulate. Then the Consul arrived. He had been looking for us. The merchants were asking for a guard. They had been hiding all night waiting for the British to come and disperse the mob and police the bazaar. Soon we were cantering along Khalil Pasha Street to the scene I have described. The roofs and balconies were packed with women in bright dresses. Children danced in front of us uttering shrill Arab cries and clapping their hands. There was none of this gala display when the British and Indian prisoners marched through after Kut.

Khalil Pasha Street, through which we rode, the only broad thoroughfare in the city, received the name of the local Hindenburg in commemoration of the fall of Kut. It is not a beautiful or imposing thoroughfare, and, like most Turkish reforms, its growth had been intermittent and subject to caprice. Demolition and construction had not kept pace. The dismantled walls and pillars of crumbling brick still bulge out in the street. The landlords, we were told, received no compensation. Loss of property was to be paid for in the gratification of patriotic sentiment. But by a stroke of irony the road that was built to memorise our reverse at Kut was completed just in time to afford us a passage through Baghdad.

Nineteen years earlier, when I passed through Baghdad, there was no carriageway on the left bank. There was barely room for a camel in some of the streets, and the small white ass of the city was a convenience which the wealthiest did not disdain. I remember being driven in a cumbrous kind of ark drawn by four mules across the desert to Babylon, Hilleh, and Birs Nimrud; but the vehicle had to be stabled on the other side of the bridge of boats. On both sides of Khalil Pasha Street, which has been cut right through the city parallel with the river, the Moslem, Jewish and Christian quarters have not changed. It must be a dull and unimaginative spirit that does not find romance or suggestion here. The narrow streets will just admit a horse. The spacious bow windows, often covering the whole frontage of a wall, almost meet above. There are women peeping from every one of them, veiled or unveiled, according to the quarter of the city, Moslem, Christian or Jew. The woodwork is fretted. The doors have curious antique brass knockers and are studded with nails. From alleys where one can span the two walls with one's hands a gate will open into a wide courtyard planted with orange trees and pomegranates in the centre. As in all old cities of the East, the cramped approaches contrast with the spaciousness of the dwellings on either side. The roofs, which offer the adventurer, lover or thief a thoroughfare for miles, and the windows through which Romeo and Juliet might converse in whispers, give one the impression of a city architecturally designed for a Lothario.

In the cafés the Arabs squat on their pew-like benches gravely gossiping, or absorbed in meditation, or in a game of dominoes or dice. There is very little coffee to drink, very little tobacco to go round. It is a sombre, unimpressionable crowd. When we had been in the city an hour they ceased to take any interest in the army of occupation.

The bazaars which I remembered as the life of the place were a depressing scene. The shops were all empty and shuttered, some of them gutted. It was a long time before they could be restocked. The human interest was now the contact of strange races, the realisation or rejection of ideas formed by one about the other, the quickness with which remote things become familiar. The Indian *drabi* and British transport driver soon learnt the commonest Arab cry, " Ba-lak, Ba-lak "—Get out of the way.

In these arched and vaulted thoroughfares, congested with our transport, troops, and guns, one witnessed strange encounters. The wheel of a 60-pounder gun limber breaks through the roof of a cellar and discloses the head of a terrified Jew. A battery mule thrusts his nose into a dish of sweetmeats carelessly carried by an Arab girl. A Sikh duffadar in a signalling section is talking the French of Festubert fluently and with appropriate gestures to a French Carmelite priest of Lyons lately delivered from internment at Mosul. A fat Persian beggar howling on a doorstep uses the word for "hunger" which the sepoys understand, and a grinning Dogra points at the fellow's paunch, which betrays him if it does not lie. A Chaldean astronomer receives a nickel piece from a black Ethiopian slave; one wondered if it were the price of a prophecy which we were fulfilling.

Hard by a soldier of France is explaining himself to a young British officer. The man is an Algerian, and had been a prisoner of the Turks. He was gassed and captured at Verdun early in 1915, and taken to Berlin, and thence sent East that he might see the Khalifa in Stamboul, as they told him, and strike a blow for Islam. The Khalifa did not materialise, and the blow was never struck, but now at last he has crept out of some prison hole into the sun, and he is explaining with lively gestures that he is a Spahi, a brother in arms, and no dirty Turk or Hun, that it is the hour of his deliverance, and that his immediate need is a cigarette. "Pas de cigarettes!" he lamented. "Jamais, jamais de cigarettes—those unclean beasts would never part with one."

As the King's Own marched through the city the weariness of the long pursuit was forgotten. The dust of Baghdad was a lenitive for bruised feet. But it was not the golden dust of romance they were treading; it was not in the architecture or personages of the Arabian nights that the enchantment lay; it was not the city of Haroun-al-Rothschild, as I heard a soldier call it, or even of Nebuchadnezzar that our troops wanted to see; but "the old Turkey cock's" stronghold, the enemy's capital, their visible goal, the prize in substance of as stubborn a fight as has ever been fought. For they had sweated and fought for months without end in a continuous offensive with little in the way of physical or mental recreation. No billets between trench work; often not a tree or a house to break the monotonous horizon. And here they were in Baghdad, the goal of their desires, with a certain sense of achievement, yet illogically expecting a little rest. But there was to be no rest; and all the djinns of Baghdad could not raise a single glass of beer. The Turk was not yet beaten; he was being reinforced. There were nearly a hundred miles of road ahead, and two and a half months' hard marching and fighting, before we had secured the railroad at Samarrah and broken up the enemy's forces that threatened Baghdad.

The King's Own and three battalions of the 85th Brigade (the Buffs, 87th Dogras, 102nd Grenadiers), who were ferried across the river to garrison the city, were the only battalions of infantry to see the inside of Baghdad on March 11th on the left bank. The 40th Brigade, which had made its long enveloping movement round the flank of the Tel Mahomed position, struck the road beyond the cavalry barracks to the north and camped in the palm groves outside of the city. The 14th Division halted at Hinaidie; and the remaining battalions on the left bank, the 39th Brigade and the 88th Brigade, less the King's Own, received orders to march round, and not through the city. The colonel of one of these regiments told me that the order to keep outside Baghdad took all the heart out of his men. After a year or more in the trenches the troops were not in a condition for long marches. Whole companies were limping, and the physical stimulus that kept them on their feet sprang from a moral source. In the long, tedious, and circuitous route by the bund, the distant houses and the minarets of Baghdad became as the houses and minarets of any ordinary Eastern city; the clouds of glory that should have invested them melted into the light of common day. Many of the men who passed Baghdad without entering it never saw the city at all; and for this reason we who stayed and rested there a time, enjoying the fruits of their achievement, were sadder when we read the roll of honour. The soldier of the old school will find this point of view vicious, illogical, unduly sentimental; his contempt does him honour; the sentiment is none the less natural and true.

The 7th Division were first in on the right bank, and the patrols of the Black Watch were ransacking the railway station at 5.45 A.M. The last train had gone out at two in the morning, and somebody found the waybill. There was a rush for the deserted booking-office, and a vain search for tickets to Constantinople and Berlin. Officers of the Black Watch will always regret that they omitted to carry off the station bell,[1] an historic bit of loot which is now a trophy in the mess of the ———s. But of all the things we saw in and near the city, I think the inscription " BAGHDAD " written large on the walls of the terminus pleased us most. It was like a phrase that slips out in an enemy's boastful communiqué betraying defeat. We all smiled at it, though we could not have explained exactly why. It was partly the Huns' inadvertent admission of the futility of his deep-laid schemes. But it was more than that. There was something subtle and ironic in it which we could not interpret. It shouted to us that we had arrived. And it bridged in a humorous and unexpected way the past and the present, romance and the familiar things of life, dismantling proportion, making the impossible of the day before yesterday the commonplace of to-day. It was an odd thing to strike coming out of the desert over mud and sand five hundred miles from the sea. A kind of mirage trick. And I thought of the easy

[1] The Black Watch made good with the station bell at Samarrah.

assurance in the old nursery rhyme now dispossessed of its haunting irony :

> "How many miles to Babylon ?
> Three score and ten.
> Can you get there by candlelight ?
> Yes, and back again."

If the Hun had been gifted with a sensitive imagination he would have destroyed the nameboard of the Baghdad railway station. He destroyed nearly everything else, venting his brutish sentimentality on a wire-haired terrier which we found shot in a house near by, and his gross humour on the walls of the power house. Pursuit was on the heels of retreat, but he had had time to smear ironic texts in red paint on the wall. A singularly inapt one was, " It is a long way to Baghdad." Another, " 100 Tommies = 1 Askeri." And there was the inevitable caricature of the Englishman with big teeth and a pipe, and a picture labelled " London," with a Zeppelin as big as St. Paul's dropping bombs as big as St. Martin's-le-Grand.

All this modern Babylon of the Huns on the right bank had been destroyed as cleanly as doomed cities one reads of in Holy Writ. The wireless station had just been completed at enormous cost; it was one of the most powerful installations of the German system, and in direct communication with Berlin. It had been receiving messages for six months, but the transmitting plant was not working until we had crossed the Tigris at Shumran. In its short life of two or three days at the most, it was a messenger of disaster. It was blown up early on the morning of the 11th. We found the roof carried away and a deep crater in the centre of the floor. The giant mast had fallen away, crashing through the outer wall. One of the great boilers was blown up, the other half filled with titanite, but the charge not fired. The money

GUFARS AT BAGHDAD

locked up in the wireless, railway station, sidings, workshops, water towers, cranes, engineering plant, must have run into millions. And on the railway, as in the wireless, it was a case of wreckage before completion. The pointing of the mortar in the power house was half finished; the numerals in fresh paint on the new rails and couplings told of work barely a month old.

It was a relief to leave this scene of scientific havoc and to cross the river again in the spinning *gufar* familiar to Herodotus, Trajan, and Nebuchadnezzar. The right bank is not Baghdad proper. The quarters on this side of the river are merely a suburb, and the railway and power house and workshops lying in the desert beyond belong still less to the city of the Caliphs.

At 9.80 on the morning of the 11th three battalions of the 35th Brigade were crossing the Tigris in *gufars* from the right bank to the left. The bridge of boats had been broken up and destroyed. Soon after 10 A.M. the 1/5th Hants hoisted the Union Jack on the Citadel. They and the 37th Dogras, and the 102nd Grenadiers garrisoned the city on the left bank, the 2/4th Gurkhas the right. A cavalry brigade occupied Khadhimain. The remainder of the Force camped outside Baghdad, but they were soon pressing hard on the heels of the retreating Turks. General Cobbe's column on the right bank and General Marshall's on the left pushed on in pursuit, while a third column was dispatched to the Euphrates, and a fourth to join up with the Russians in the direction of Khanikin in the hope of cutting off the Turkish 18th Army Corps, which was falling back from Hamadan.

Very few of us were left behind to explore the city. Half my kit had gone on in a gunboat, the other half was with the 40th Brigade; but for the moment Baghdad was evidently the place to stay in. As I only had the clothes I stood up in, the opening of the Hotel Tigris, the one Europeanised hostelry in the city, was a piece of good fortune. I dined there alone on the night of the 11th, and the proprietor, an Arab Christian, asked me the name of the general commanding the British forces. The next morning "Hotel Tigris" had become "Hotel Maude." It was soon the centre of attraction for officers from neighbouring camps. By the horses in the street outside you would think a regiment of cavalry was billeted there; and as units were always changing, one met men at every table whom one had not seen for months. There were no stores; drinks were soon exhausted, and meals were of a very simple kind. But we had been cut off from civilisation so long that there was something very homely in walking into an hotel, ordering lunch, and drinking one's coffee and smoking one's cigarette in peace on the terrace overlooking the river. Force D was not exacting in its standard of comfort. For afternoon tea, the *khobez* or Arab *chapatti*, a flat cake of coarse wheaten flour spread with the cream of buffalo milk, made a pleasant change. And it was good to be among English flowers again. I was told of a Red Cross nurse who, landing in Baghdad after two years' hot weather in Mesopotamia, burst into tears when she saw the roses, stocks, wallflowers and poppies in this garden by the Tigris.

There is no path along the river front. The chief houses and consulates are built on immensely solid revetments, and have their foundations in the water, mostly in the form of bastions. Many of them have small gardens and steps running down to the river. At intervals between these there are approaches, in some cases through archways under houses, where the women of the city draw their water in tapering copper vessels with fluted necks, and the boatmen ply for hire, and the water carriers fill their skins, which they load on their white asses.

At the northern end of the city the civil and military *serais* cover a quarter of a mile of the river front. They comprised the infantry barracks, Judicial Court, Council

Chamber and all the administration offices of the wilayat. There was ample room here for all the troops needed to garrison the city. The quadrangles are very spacious and solidly built. In the *serdabs* or underground chambers, ventilated by shafts from the roof, the temperature is 8 or 10 degrees cooler than on the ground floor. I found a company of the 87th Dogras here. The jamadar shook me by the hand and said with a smile, "Sahib, we have arrived. It is a very good place."

There was plenty of human interest in Baghdad, but those of us who looked for lions in this ancient, dirty and dilapidated city were frankly disillusioned. What they expected to see and did not find it is difficult to imagine. Here we were helping to turn the wheel in the most rapid revolution of fortune that the city had witnessed since it grew out of Babylon; and the writing was fresh on the wall for us to read. The cryptic nature of the script with regard to its bearing on the future of the people whose new destiny was bound up with ours lent it the greater fascination. Everywhere there was evidence of what the Turks had done yesterday and what we were doing to-day. The people of the city were waiting and looking for a sign. One could wander in the Christian quarters, where the Armenian, Syrian, Chaldean, and Latin churches were approached by doors in a dead wall in the same secretive way as the houses. One had to knock hard and many times on March 11th and 12th before the latch was tentatively lifted. The habit of suspicion had become ingrained. Some of the churches had been used by the Turks as hospitals. The Latin church had been burnt. "Out of vengeance," the priest told me, though the Baghdadi Moslem has not the reputation of being fanatical. In the Armenian church we found a haggard crowd of refugees from Mosul, and among them the deserters from the Tigris army who had extricated themselves on the night of the rout and who were eloquent of the miseries of the retreat from Shumran. In the Jewish quarter, too, one heard tales that helped one to understand the huzzaing in the streets.

One might have spent days exploring the *serais* and the Citadel. There is a great deal to be learned from the litter left behind in a capital abandoned by a government who have not had too much time to get away; and we were ransacking these offices twelve hours after the Turks had left. Anyone who has changed houses knows the difficulties of sudden transport. These were complicated in Baghdad by a single-line railway, a great shortage of ships, and a congested bridge of boats. In nearly every room were things the Turks must have been reluctant to leave behind. In one of the offices we found the survey maps; another contained the trade returns of the notorious Wonkhaus; a third the portfolios and membership tickets of the Committee of National Defence. A courtyard enclosing an orange garden contained papers of the Irrigation Department. Hanging on the walls and littering the floor were the maps and plans drawn up by Sir William Willcocks which might have made Iraq as fruitful as Egypt. In the Citadel the stack of arms grew higher as the house-to-house search continued. Besides the rifles, swords, and revolvers we found a great deal of curious ordnance, valueless from a military point of view, from the antique brass cannons of the time of Sultan Murad to the guns we left in Kut last year. The inscriptions in Arabic and Persian engraved on the muzzles between figures of warriors and beasts carried one back to scenes of ravage in the past. "Victory is of God and is at hand," one of these stern old pieces has proclaimed since the year 1546. "The Lord of Victory, the Safavi Shah, to destroy all trace of the Turks, decreed the casting of this gun. It belches fire like a dragon and flings flame among them." And a grim companion the other side of the gate, once the " gun of Captain Ali Akbar, of the gunner Mehdi Khan,

OLD ORDNANCE IN THE CITADEL, BAGHDAD.

of the driver Bagir," whose inmate is a "world-devouring dragon who roars with awful thunder like a lion," demands of all the friends of Ali, "Didst see the tortures of the seventh hell?"

How often in history, one wondered, has the cellarage in Baghdad been stuffed with merchandise which the people dared not display in their shops. For a few days after we entered the city nothing could have been more gloomy than the empty, shuttered bazaars. One heard that there was stock still concealed, but, what with official and unofficial looting and the blockade of the Tigris from the south for nearly two and a half years, it was difficult to believe there was anything left. Yet before a week had passed the bazaars began to fill, trade was brisk, and a deal of stuff was disinterred from hidden places. The din of the copper market resounded as of old where the six smiths, stripped to the waist, hammer the white-hot metal at the forge. These groups were the most admired sights in the city. One stopped and watched the straining muscles of the men's backs as they stood in a circle by the bellows and swung their enormous hammers so quickly that you would think they were striking one concerted stroke, if it were not for the sound of the rapid chime. The din pursues one down the steps into the silversmiths' quarters in the next bazaar, where the women sit all day haggling with the Jews for an extra piastre or so for a bangle or ring, and into the grain market, now the quietest corner of the bazaar, where the huge, half-empty granaries, like elephant stables, with their cage-like grille, are open to the streets.

The only colour in Baghdad and its environs is the peacock blue and old gold of the mosques and minarets. This bright mosaic is a relief in a land which is dun-coloured from the dust at one's feet to the walls and roofs of the houses and the hot haze floating over everything. As in the outskirts of all ancient Moslem cities, death is the one obvious thing. On the inside of the bund that rings the city the crowded graveyards meet, the low tombs all lying east and west with the feet of the faithful pointing Meccawards ready to spring up at the first note of the trump of doom. There is a smell everywhere of dry decay, and the road beyond the bund leading out into Persia through the desert is marked only by skeletons and calcined bones. Every landmark is a mosque or tomb. Under the tall tapering crenellated minaret, like an inverted fir cone, on the right bank rests the wife of Haroun-al-Raschid. All along the ridge from the mausoleum to the mosque the graves are so thick that there is not room to bury a month-old child. But as we rode by they were bringing in another corpse wrapped in linen on a bedstead, not for interment under the same heap of earth as covered the Queen's bones, but as near as might be, in the dusty palm grove opposite, where the professional mourner is howling his lamentations to the little dust devil which comes swirling towards us, dancing and pirouetting on its base, the only live thing in this dead plain. Very dead is Zobeide in her tomb, dead her legends and romance, and dry and withered the sap of all romantic inspiration in these iron days.

My impressions of Baghdad, in spite of all detraction, are of a kind of mournful beauty. Those who deny the city's charm should see the broad sweep of the river front from the north at sunset, when the mosques and blue-tiled minarets are echeloned, as it were, and catch the slant rays of the sun. The colour on the left bank in the reflected light of the east melts from orange to the dull glow of the siris pod, while in the west the palms silhouetted against a clear iron-grey sky give one the impression of being soft and metallic at the same time. I have described Baghdad as it appeared to us in the first two or three days of occupation, and I will leave it to another chapter to tell what we made of the city.

how under our régime the smells became centrifugal and the roads and drains and water supply were improved. For the moment it was our business to increase the bills of mortality. Only a few officers of the troops garrisoning the place had time for leisurely exploration. The greater part of the Force was engaged in hunting down the Turk east, west and north; for we had not yet carried the points on the Tigris, Euphrates and Diala which made our hold on the city secure. After a peaceful interlude of a few days I caught up the column which was moving north-east towards Khanikin, Persia and the Russians.

CHAPTER XXXIII

THE TURK IN BAGHDAD

TO THE PEOPLE OF BAGHDAD WILAYAT

In the name of my King, and in the name of the peoples over whom he rules, I address you as follows:

Our military operations have as their object the defeat of the enemy, and the driving of him from these territories. In order to complete this task, I am charged with absolute and supreme control of all regions in which British troops operate; but our armies do not come into your cities and lands as conquerors or enemies, but as liberators.

Since the days of Hulagu your city and your lands have been subject to the tyranny of strangers, your palaces have fallen into ruins, your gardens have sunk in desolation, and your forefathers and yourselves have groaned in bondage. Your sons have been carried off to wars not of your seeking, your wealth has been stripped from you by unjust men and squandered in distant places.

Since the days of Midhat, the Turks have talked of reforms, yet do not the ruins and wastes of to-day testify the vanity of those promises?

It is the wish not only of my King and his peoples, but it is also the wish of the great Nations with whom he is in alliance, that you should prosper even as in the past, when your lands were fertile, when your ancestors gave to the world literature, science and art, and when Baghdad city was one of the wonders of the world.

Between your people and the dominions of my King

there has been a close bond of interest. For two hundred years have the merchants of Baghdad and Great Britain traded together in mutual profit and friendship. On the other hand, the Germans and Turks, who have despoiled you and yours, have for twenty years made Baghdad a centre of power from which to assail the power of the British and the Allies of the British in Persia and Arabia. Therefore the British Government cannot remain indifferent as to what takes place in your country now or in the future, for in duty to the interests of the British people and their Allies the British Government cannot risk that being done in Baghdad again which has been done by the Turks and Germans during the War.

But you, people of Baghdad, whose commercial prosperity and whose safety from oppression and invasion must ever be a matter of the closest concern to the British Government, are not to understand that it is the wish of the British Government to impose upon you alien institutions. It is the hope of the British Government that the aspiration of your philosophers and writers shall be realised, and that once again the people of Baghdad shall flourish, enjoying their wealth and substance under institutions which are in consonance with their sacred laws and their racial ideals. In Hejaz the Arabs have expelled the Turks and Germans who oppressed them, and proclaimed the Sherif Hussain as their King, and his Lordship rules in independence and freedom, and is the Ally of the Nations who are fighting against the power of Turkey and Germany; so, indeed, are the noble Arabs, the Lords of Koweit, Nejd and Asir.

Many noble Arabs have perished in the cause of Arab freedom at the hands of those alien rulers, the Turks, who oppressed them. It is the determination of the Government of Great Britain and the Great Powers allied to Great Britain, that these noble Arabs shall not have suffered in vain. It is the hope and desire of the British people and the Nations in alliance with them that the Arab race may rise once more to greatness and renown among the peoples of the Earth, and that it shall bind itself together to this end in unity and concord.

O people of Baghdad, remember that for twenty-six generations you have suffered under strange tyrants who have ever endeavoured to set one Arab House against another in order that they might profit by your dissensions. This policy is abhorrent to Great Britain and her Allies, for there can be neither peace nor prosperity where there is enmity and misgovernment. Therefore I am commanded to invite you, through your nobles and elders and representatives, to participate in the management of your own civil affairs in collaboration with the political representatives of Great Britain who accompany the British Army, so that you may be united with your kinsmen in North, East, South and West in realising the aspirations of your Race.

The flowery periods of the proclamation amused the soldier. He had no love for the Arab, and he rather liked the Turk. And his estimate, though it ran counter to received opinion, was the outcome of two years' acquaintance, which, if not intimate, or subtle, or scholarly, at least touched the ultimate decencies of life and was related to the behaviour of the two races when brought face to face with first and last things. All that the ancestors of the " Buddoo " had contributed to literature, science, and art left him indifferent; and he smiled sadly as the moral side of the campaign was presented to him. It is pleasant to learn that one is a liberator. And when one has been fighting with one's back to the wall for one's very life, it is gratifying to discover that the knock-down blow one has given the tyrant has freed a number of other people besides oneself. But in listening to the story after the fight the soldier is a little uneasy when this incidental salvage is made too much of, as if it were the motive that brought him into the lists. He smells cant. In this case no doubt his values had all been upside down. He had not sufficiently recognised the nobility of the Arab, the iniquity of the Turk. And as he read the proclamation he was conscious of appearing a little ridiculous, as if he had been seen going into the trenches spurred and plumed for a Crusade.

No one for an instant believed that the manifesto was the conception of a soldier, much less of the Army Commander. Its diplomacy, persuasiveness and fine literary quality were generally approved by the Press. And one could not but admire the happy Oriental vein in which it was written, and the almost Biblical denunciation of the Turk, by which it was hoped to impress upon the Arabs the beneficent change that had come over their fortunes. But one missed the directness of Maude. The inspiration was from Whitehall, but whatever the source of the pronouncement, ambiguity as to the future of Mesopotamia was inevitable; for it had been agreed among the Allies that until the last shot had been fired in the War there should be no settlement.

As to the Turk's unfitness to rule, everyone except the Turk is agreed; and the consequence has been a combination by which he has been reduced to a strip of land in Europe about two-thirds of the size of Belgium. There is no question that he deserves eviction. The only regret is that he was not frankly declared an outlaw instead of having his possessions juggled out of him one by one by ostensibly friendly powers. The fight he put up for them at the Tchataldja lines compels admiration. It is his fine military qualities, combined with his *bon camaraderie*, which is genuine in spite of all cynical denials, that have won him the esteem of fighting men. We had heard a great deal about his inhumanity, yet he continued to be a gentleman when we met him. We ought to have shrunk from him with horror, but after fighting him in Gallipoli and Mesopotamia the British soldier had a sneaking affection for the man, and was unwilling to damn him on hearsay. In the newspaper tirades we recognised official inspiration. Even in Baghdad, with his iniquity proven, our sympathies were not entirely estranged. A Tartar and savage under the skin, unscrupulous where his interests are concerned, a bandit and a humbug, driven into the arms of the hated Hun by the irony of circumstance, with all the rest of the world against him, yet possessing qualities which in these iron days are irresistible to the man of action—so we saw him and yet liked him; and it should be remembered in our defence that we never came in contact with the wirepullers and politicians and the scum of officialdom, and we had not then learnt of the brutish neglect of our prisoners in the desert march to Aleppo.

There was abundant evidence of the Turk's misrule in Baghdad. At last we were brought face to face with his atrocities. Until our entry we had taken him as we found him. The Armenian business had been so remote, so incredibly barbarous, that it had never seriously entered our thoughts. We could not associate the assassins with the men we were fighting. When we met the unfortunate Jew or Armenian in Baghdad we only believed half his story, or discredited it *in toto* on account of too much colouring and palpable additions. But evidence, from unbiased as well as from prejudiced sources, was cumulative. There were cases of stark realism beside which fictitious barbarity paled.

Baghdad has never had the reputation of being fanatical. This did not mean that the Turk of the city was different from the Turk elsewhere. There were local causes. Apart from the garrison the Turks made up a very inconsiderable part of the population, and this was largely official. The bulk of the inhabitants are Arabs,

Jews and Christians, of which latter the Armenian community is but a small fraction, not large enough to constitute an economical menace or even a pretext for political uneasiness. In consequence the Armenians have probably suffered less from the Turk in Baghdad than their co-religionists in any other part of the Ottoman Empire.

The campaign in Mesopotamia and the gradual approach of the British Force up the Tigris naturally altered the situation. The subject races no longer felt secure. A number of Armenians were deported, and no reasons given; these were afterwards restored. The Baghdadi Armenians escaped the general massacre, but the exactions of the Government fell heavily on them. And they were not the only sufferers. All subject races, other Christian communities as well as the Arabs and Jews, had been bled white during the last two years; and if all this gold had gone into the Treasury instead of into the pockets of officials the harvest would have provided the Turk with very considerable sinews of war. Requisitioning was excused as war contribution, and the excuse would have been valid if the tax had been levied with any consistency or under any system other than that of the Turk.

Those who are familiar with Ottoman ways will know the kind of thing that went on. When, for instance, wool was commandeered for the Army Clothing Department, the rich Armenian would be told that his stuff was dirty and not worth four piastres the kilo. At the same time it would be discovered that the stock of the influential Moslem was no good at all. "I very much regret, Effendi," the purchasing officer would exclaim, "that your material is worthless for our purpose. We cannot take wool in a condition like this." And as a makeweight this subtle functionary would confiscate the entire stock of a small Arab merchant on the pretext of incorrect declaration, or failure to declare. Later, when things went ill for the Turk, all pretexts were forgotten. The bazaars were officially looted.

A much simpler method of extortion was the compulsory exchange of gold for notes. By this system nearly all the available cash of the Arabs, Jews and Christians in the city passed into the hands of the Turks. When debts were paid in paper currency a profit of from 60 to 75 per cent. accrued. And when there was no opportunity for a transaction, the officials summoned the Jews to their houses at night; they came with gold and went away with paper. The most dreadful penalties were held out against those who would not accept Government paper on its face value. In the meanwhile notes fell to a third, and even a quarter, of their accredited value; and orders kept coming through from Constantinople that, as the depreciation of Government paper in Baghdad was greater than elsewhere in the Empire, immediate steps must be taken to revive credit. The officials were frightened and vexed, and the weight of their displeasure fell chiefly on the Jews. There had been actual trafficking in notes. Merchants had been selling them at a discount for a third of their value. This was viewed officially in the light of a studied conspiracy to depreciate Turkish credit. The higher officials, of course, understood; but the slow-witted Turk genuinely believed that the motives of the Jews were political and mischievous. When Government ordains that paper is the same value as gold, he argued, then paper becomes gold by law; or "if not gold for you or me, gold for Mirza, Abdul, Ezra, and Johannes." A proclamation was issued that all trade transactions and purchases must be made in paper money. The result was a financial panic. Shops were shut; there was no market; you could not buy meat or bread in the bazaar. To keep his household alive the Baghdadi had to slink about and make surreptitious purchases in cash after dark. Another proclamation was issued. Merchants were to open their shops. Those who did business secretly, or hid, or refused to sell, their goods, would be deported, and their property confiscated.

The Jews who had been guilty of trafficking with notes were summoned secretly to the Court of the Prefect of the Police at night. They were confined by day and taken out after dark and tortured. Finally they were murdered and thrown into the Tigris. When their families brought round breakfast in the morning they were told that they had gone down river to see Khalil Pasha in Kut. Or that is the story in Baghdad, and everybody believes it. The nineteen Jews have never been seen alive since, though the bodies of five of them were restored by the Tigris. Haron Mealem, Abdullah Isaac Mesafy and Ibrahim Dabool were identified on March 7th, Shelemo Siom and Isaac Messim Mina a few weeks afterwards. The two legs of Haron Mealem had been cauterised, apparently by a hot iron, just above the ankle.

When the police came round, a cousin of one of the men who was wanted and who had fled was sleeping in the house of his relative, the accused, and he was taken as a hostage, in the hope that he might betray the fugitive's whereabouts. As he was not actually implicated his case was left to the last, and he managed to slip away in the confusion caused by our approach to the city. He and other prisoners in the house at the time bear witness to the groans and cries for mercy uttered by the Jews at night. These torturings and assassinations were by way of a deterrent. The Turks argued that by no milder methods could they give discredited paper the value of gold. The idea was that if they killed one or two, the others would soon come to their senses and the mischievous trafficking would cease.

This story puts the Baghdad officials on the same plane

as those responsible for the Armenian massacres. If the city had had a reputation for tolerance in the past it must have been because there was nothing countering Turkish interests to call for repression. No sooner had the paper exchange difficulty supplied the irritant than the mediæval torture chamber came into being.

Yet Baghdad was a relatively safe asylum for Armenian refugees. On the afternoon of March 11th I found them huddled in the Christian churches, still uncertain as to their fate, half afraid that the Turks might come back. But there had been no killing. In a few days we were engaged in the salvage of Armenian women and children who had survived the massacre in the north, and were now living in Mussulman families. They were gathered into homes financed by Government. Ladies of their own community were put in charge. One learned a great deal in a visit to these institutions. The inmates of one I visited were all young, many of marriageable age. A great number of the children were under six, and had already forgotten their language and their faith. The bald statement of what they had suffered and seen is a damning and unanswerable arraignment against the Turkish Government. It is quite possible that many of the details that I gathered may be inaccurate; but collectively they are convincing as to the methods employed by the Turk. It is hard to sweep aside the vivid story of a child of twelve; and the evidence is supported by Americans in other parts of Turkey in Asia, by escaped Indian prisoners from Ras-el-Ain, and by such documents as private diaries found on the dead.

The first girl I saw was a child of ten from a village near Erzeroum. She and her family had started on donkeys with a few of their belongings, but in three days the Kurds had left them nothing, and they had to walk. The Turks had issued a proclamation in all the villages that the Armenians were to be sent away to a colony that was being prepared for them, and that their property was to be kept under the care of Government during the War and then restored. This was more than a year before. The gendarmes were very pleasant to them in their homes, and told them that they were to be given new land to cultivate and that their journey would not be long. The first assurance as they guessed, was visionary; in the second the gendarmes did not lie. For many of them it was all over on the third day. Two or three hundred of the men were separated from the women and killed at a distance, shot or cut down with the sword. After that the same sort of thing happened nearly every day. The guards were very haphazard; there was no system. Some of the women were pushed into the river; others thrust over precipices. Twelve hundred left the two villages near Erzeroum; 400 only reached Ras-el-Ain. The survivors were all women and children; there was not a man among them, nor a male child over the age of nine. The girl thought that it was the gendarmes' policy to tire them out, to make them walk over stones, and to keep them at a distance from water. This may have been imagination. It was very distressing, she said, to be at the end of the procession; for then one had to pass the corpses of one's friends and drink water from canals where their dead bodies were floating. She saw a hole in the earth in which a number had been burned. In Ras-el-Ain a Syrian family took in the girl and her sister—the mother had died. And so they reached Baghdad.

There were small children of four or five in the home—hardly two from the same village. They had been with their adoptive families a year or more and forgotten their own language. Kindly Turks had picked them up, as one might a small puppy or a small kitten, and taken them in. This is the Ottoman nature all over. The massacres are a very unpleasant business. The less civilised elements of a heterogeneous army are turned on to the dirty work, and the Turk shuts his eyes to it as much as possible. His social and domestic relations are always pleasant. An Armenian mistress enjoys the privileges of the home; a servant is well cared for; children, when adopted, are treated kindly. It is good work for Allah to take an infant and make a true Moslem of her.

Some of the women and girls are given to Arabs, who also treat them well. I met a refugee from the Kala Hissar district, who with six companions had been saved by some Armenian women he found established in a Bedouin camp. Eight hundred families in all left Kala Hissar. Half of these were capsized and drowned in *shakturs* (Arab boats) on the Euphrates. The survivors, when they reached Deir-el-Zor, were placed in an internment camp. They had been allowed to take money with them, and those who could pay the sanitary inspector got a clean bill of health from him, and were permitted to live in billets in the town. They were kept at Deir-el-Zor some weeks in suspense. While here they approached the Mutesarrif, hoping to purchase their release. They offered him 8,000 liras. It was not enough. They made a second collection; every piastre they could raise was thrown into the pool. This time the sum was nearly 5,000 liras and the Mutesarrif accepted the bribe on condition that they should sign a paper: "We the Armenians of . . . . . . give this sum willingly to the Turkish Army." But it did not save them. The hated gendarmes accompanied them on the march, and nine miles from the city the massacre began. Sticks and stones, and knives and daggers, were employed, and a few merciful bullets. But, as always happened, the assassins tired of their work; even the physical part of it was exhausting; and the last act was postponed from day to day. In the end a tired gendarme gave them the hint to go. The night was dark and the guard more careless than usual, and the last remnants of the party, fifty-five in all, made their escape. They fell in with a caravan of tribesmen the next day, who stripped, but fed them. On the third day they crossed the river and struck an encampment of the Anizeh Bedouin, a tribe always hostile to the Turks. It was here that they found the Armenian women, who had been with the Anizeh for a full year, relics of an earlier persecution. From this hour they were safe. The women were now part of the tribe, and when they cried out: "These men are of our own people," the Anizeh took them in. They worked for the Bedouin, feeding the camels, gathering fuel, loading and unloading packs. The tribe were moving south, and after a month they reached Hilleh, where the name of the Turk is hated.

In the rising of the spring of 1916, after the Kerbela trouble, the inhabitants were shot down in the streets, and Arab women carried off. The Armenian found himself among friendly people and stayed in the town until the British came to Baghdad. He is now engaged as a mechanic and is one of the ever growing colony of refugees in the city.

I met other Armenians who had had strange escapes. One was taken from a raft at Mosul, and offered his life if he would become a Mussulman. The man temporised and asked to be instructed in the faith. In the inquiry that followed he revealed a scholarship and a knowledge of Arabic that none of the local Mullahs possessed. He was taken into the family of the Sheikh as a reader of the Koran. As regards conversion nothing more was said.

Another man I heard of was the sole survivor of a group of refugees who disappeared between Ras-el-Ain and Nisibin. They were taken into the desert and formed up in line, as in a Chinese execution, to be dispatched with the sword. There was no shortage of ammunition, I was told, but the sword was employed for reasons of economy (*pour économiser*). While waiting for his turn it occurred to the Armenian that a bullet would be an easier death. So he broke from the line. In the confusion the gendarmes missed him. It was almost dusk; he hid in the brushwood; by a miracle he escaped and found his way to Baghdad. The main features of the massacres are much the same. The immigrants, if they are not killed on the road, are taken to some depot where they are kept a few days. Here they form a large camp of two or three thousand or more and the rationing becomes a difficult question. Soon notice comes from Constantinople that the refugees of a certain district have been allotted land for cultivation, and they are told they must start on their journey again. This, they know, is probably the death sentence, but they nourish a thin hope. Others, they argue, have survived. There have been instances of humane governors. There was one at Deir-el-Zor, though he was afterwards removed, not being, as an Armenian explained to me, "a specialist for massacre."

For the first half-day they were generally safe, as murder on a large scale is deprecated near a town. Nobody, for instance, saw anyone killed in Trebizond; but a few days after the Armenians had left the city their bodies came floating down the river. The desert is a non-conductor. What is done there leaves only vague rumour, nothing definite enough to shock politicians in the West. The tribesmen, Kurds and Arabs, are called in, if possible, as that gives the Turk the pretext of "a regrettable affair." The Kurd and the Arab, he explains, are a very uncivilised people, and have not yet been educated up to the "progress" part of his programme engraven on the heart of the Young Turk. Meanwhile the unhappy Armenians never know when their turn will come. The gendarmes have no system in elimination; one never hears of a case of clean dispatch; and the miserable affair may drag on for days. Generally the first act is the separation of the men and women. If the women cling to the men it is their own affair. The brutality of the scene may be left to the imagination. The "kindly old Turk" himself weeps tears when he hears of it, and says that the killing of women and children is not in the Koran, and that it will bring down the displeasure of Allah upon the Ottoman race.

The refugees, though unarmed, sometimes turn on their guard. More than once the assassins have paid dearly. There is a woman in Baghdad who was one of a band of two or three hundred Armenian women from the hills who held a pass near Urfa. Their men had been treacherously killed off earlier, and they knew that obedience to the proclamation of exile was as fatal as resistance. They held the pass with their rifles nearly a week, and the Turks had to bring up artillery. Some fifty of them escaped. The woman now in Baghdad was rescued by a Turk of the better school, who respected her honour, and on the journey treated her as his own daughter, though he failed to convert her to Islam.

Few Armenian women were so fortunate. Many were killed with as little scruple as the men. Plainness and good looks were disastrous in different ways. The old and ugly died by violence or starved; the young were taken into the families of the Turks. A traveller I met in Baghdad was given a letter by an official at Ras-el-Ain to deliver to the gendarme in charge on the road. "Choose a pretty one for me," he wrote, "and leave her in the village outside the town." Some smeared their faces with mud and coal to hide their attractions. In many cases they arrived naked out of the desert, save for a sack or a bit of matting.

Ras-el-Ain, the railway terminus, is too near the centre of things for massacres in the old style. The women and children are permitted to starve. I heard of two women who could not feed their babies holding them under water until they died; and of another who lulled her child to sleep and eased its pain by lighting a cow-dung fire. There was nothing to cook, but the fumes carried the smell and suggestion of cooking and a momentary peace. Djemal, the modern Nero, kept up the pretence of feeding the refugees, and even sent a copper dole to the internment camps in the desert for the purchase of supplies where the only commodity was sand, laying the charge upon Allah that his miserable captives died. At Aleppo and Ras-el-Ain the German officers stalked side by side with these spectres of famine and murder and death, and not a finger was raised or a word said. " It is impolitic to interfere " is the Hun watchword. And it was by the same politic forbearance that Kaiser Wilhelm won the love of Abdul, when the other Great Powers waxed indignant and threatened to sweep the Turk from Europe and tumble the Sultan from his throne. But Abdul's massacres of 1895-6, when the killing began with the blowing of a horn and ceased three days afterwards with the same sign, were a clumsy business compared with the fine art to which murder has been brought by the Young Turk.

The Hun apathy or sympathy we can understand. The difficult thing is to reconcile the atrocities with what we have seen of the Turk. There are very few officers in the Force who will not bear witness that, winning or losing, he has fought cleanly on the whole. This Jekyll-and-Hyde-like nature of the man is a perpetual riddle. One has often heard the two sides of him explained away, but never convincingly. He is half Tartar, half European, one is told, and when he meets an Englishman or a Frenchman it flatters his self-esteem to exhibit the polished side; but when he meets an Arab, Armenian, or Kurd the barbarian will emerge. I have heard it argued that his individual courtesy and chivalry, all that has distinguished him from the Hun in war, is a form of guile, a nicely calculated investment from which he expects a usurer's interest on demand, as if his social and personal relations were dictated from Stambul in an official Irade. But few who have mixed with the Turks will accept this is an unprejudiced estimate. The virtues of the man are too normal, too much a part of his daily routine, not to be instinctive. Still, the whole case against him is damning. The Turcophile may argue that the Ottoman Empire is not a homogeneous whole, that the officials are a race apart, that the governing classes have nothing in common with the people, and that the good Turk views these crimes with dismay. The Osmanli is none the less collectively responsible. And he is chargeable individually. The officials implicated, of course, deserve the fate of assassins. As for the better class of Turk, who is a gentleman in all the simple bearings of life, he may proclaim his horror. But so long as his kindliness has not got its roots deep enough in humanity for sacrifice he, too, by his acquiescence, has forfeited his right to belong to a governing race.

CHAPTER XXXIV

AFTER BAGHDAD—THE MEETING WITH THE RUSSIANS

LOGICALLY a history of the Expedition up to the fall of Baghdad should include the operations by which we secured and consolidated our hold on the city. The end of this stage of the campaign was the capture of the Turkish railhead at Samarrah.

We could not, of course, stop at Baghdad. The city is without natural or artificial defences, and it is open to attack by columns advancing down the Tigris, Euphrates and Diala. To hold the city one must occupy advanced posts on these rivers. These had to be secured, and the enemy in front of us, who was now well shaken, had to be completely crushed and demoralised before we could call a halt. Some of the stiffest fighting in the campaign was ahead of our troops; and with the hot weather imminent we had little more than six weeks left to us during which a vigorous offensive was practicable.

Thus, when the Force entered Baghdad on March 11th they had still four main objectives to realise. The first was to continue the pursuit up the Tigris and to complete the rout of the 18th Turkish Army Corps retreating in front of them; the second, to seize the enemy's railhead at Samarrah; the third, to intercept the 13th Turkish Army Corps which was falling back before the Russians from Hamadan and to prevent its junction with other enemy troops; the fourth, to control the inundation of the Tigris and Euphrates north of Baghdad. All these immediate objectives served the ultimate one of throwing out posts to stop the three channels by which troops could be poured down upon the city.

The control of the inundation was really the most vital of the four main objectives I have enumerated, for on it depended the issue of the other three. The river was rising, and in a normal flood season an enemy who held command of the banks of the Tigris and Euphrates at

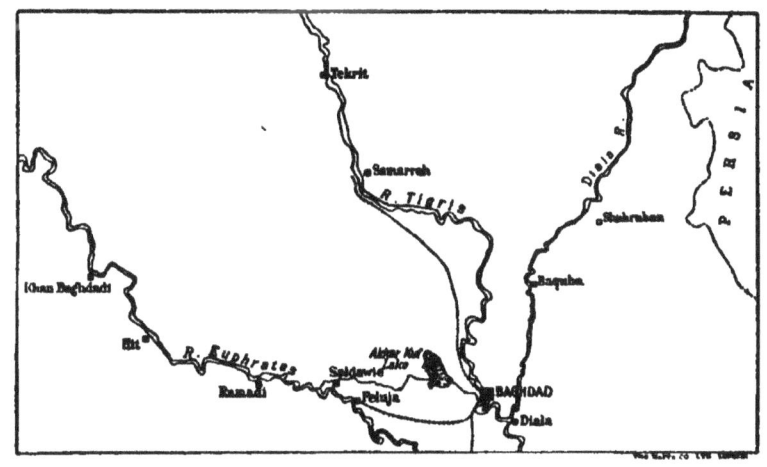

CONVERGENCE OF RIVER ROUTES ON BAGHDAD

certain points north of Baghdad would be in a position to flood out an invading army and bring all further operations to a standstill. The Euphrates was the greatest danger-point, for its flood level is 14 ft. higher than that of the Tigris; and the bursting of a dam five miles upstream of Bustan, where the Saklawie channel leaves the river, would inundate the whole country between this point and Baghdad, submerging the suburbs on the right bank of the Tigris. In the same way, when the Tigris is at high flood the left bank is open to inundation from several points north of Baghdad. Thus the ground on which the city stands might be converted into an island surrounded by a vast lake, beyond which, some six miles inland from the river, the Turks would be able to move freely while the British force was waterlogged.

Thus the control of the floods, should the river continue rising, depended on the advance of the army; the military necessity of pressing hard on the heels of the enemy was doubled by considerations affecting the security of our hold on Baghdad; and the Turk was given no rest. Our columns on both banks of the Tigris pushed on in pursuit, while a third column was dispatched to the Euphrates, and a fourth prepared to advance on Khanikin with the object of cutting off the force which was retiring before the Cossacks over the Persian border. In spite of the enormous difficulties involved in the rapid and complete change of dispositions called for by the new situation, our supply and transport never broke down, and the four columns were effectively fed, munitioned and equipped from the start.

The stiffest fighting after Baghdad was on the Tigris and the Shatt-el-Adhaim. On the Tigris the Turkish 18th Army Corps, now reinforced, fought desperately to save Samarrah; on the Shatt-el-Adhaim the 13th Army Corps, with the same object in view, drove in repeated attacks on our flank in their efforts to divert our main thrust at their railhead. But before dealing with these operations we must follow the columns dispatched to the Euphrates and Diala.

The Euphrates Column (7th Brigade) had two objects in view, to save the dam above Bustan and to cut off the small Turkish force which had begun its retirement upstream from Samawa as soon as the defeat of the Tigris army became known. The 7th Brigade occupied Feluja on March 19th, but the Turks had the start of us. We captured a few prisoners, a launch, and many rifles; and the cavalry, pushing on towards Saklawie, engaged two gunboats towing coracles filled with Turks, and inflicted some loss on them. The Turks fell back on

Ramadi, 25 miles upstream. The 7th Brigade remained to garrison Feluja, cutting off the enemy from communication with the Lower Euphrates. We were not in time to save the dam at Saklawie. The Turks burst it soon after they heard that our troops had entered Baghdad, and the water flooded through into the Akarkuf lake, which overflowed and swamped the intervening ground right up to the bund protecting the railway and suburbs of Baghdad on the right bank of the Tigris. In a normal season the embankment must have been swept away; but the river in 1917 was exceptionally low, and the bund held back the flood. Flood and weather were as favourable in the advance on Baghdad as they were perverse and malignant during the attempt to relieve Kut.

On the Tigris the flood danger zone was passed when our troops reached a point forty miles upstream of Baghdad. Our advance on both banks of the river served three of the main objectives in view—the breaking up of the remnants of the Turkish 18th Army Corps, the seizure of the enemy's railhead, and the securing of the country behind us from inundation. The 7th Division advanced on the right bank, the 18th and 14th on the left.

On March 14th, after a long march from Baghdad, the 21st and 28th Brigades engaged the enemy at Mushaidie. The Turks had evidently expected our attack on the river, where they were strongly entrenched with guns. The railway lies some six miles inland, and the position lay east of this, centred in two dominant heights, linked to each other and to the river by a series of trenches, nullahs and irrigation cuts. The Turk, in preparing for our attack on the east of the railway nearer the Tigris, was no doubt counting on the water shortage, which he thought must render an advance impracticable so far inland as his left flank. But here he miscalculated. General Cobbe, by switching the 21st Brigade to the left and crossing the line, was able to find the enemy's extreme left flank, and thus to turn his whole position. The 28th Brigade advanced on the right of the railway, the 21st on the left, the Black Watch (right) and the 1/8th Gurkhas (left), with the 9th Bhopals in the rear. It was a very simple action and very gallant. But for the dropping casualties it was the kind of thing that everybody had done or tried to do a hundred times on field-days, except that no mistakes were made and everything went off "pat" according to the text-book, the two brigades deploying and advancing in short rushes under better cover than the division had seen for many a long day, but not without heavy loss.

The first line of Turks in advance of the main position was dispersed soon after four in the afternoon and fell back on the second line. As we advanced a heavy enfilade fire was poured in from a big mound on our left. This sandhill, which came to be known as Sugar Loaf Hill, appeared to be the Turk's extreme flank, and the fire from it was so intense that a platoon of the Black Watch changed commanders six times in as many minutes. But the remnants pressed on unchecked, led by a lance-corporal with the same gallantry and coolness as the fallen officers had shown. The two companies of the Black Watch on the left lost half their strength in this advance over 500 yards, but they forced the Turks back and occupied the low sandhills 200 yards in advance of their main position. At the same time the two companies on the right, working in conjunction with the left company of the 56th Rifles on the east of the railway, charged in and rushed the advanced trenches with the bayonet. The capture of this position changed the whole face of the battle. The Lewis gun teams of the Black Watch and the 56th crept forward among the sand dunes and under the railway embankment, and a hot enfilade fire was brought to bear on the enemy's main position. Their fire grew less intense, even from Sugar Loaf Hill it slackened; and it soon became clear that the Turks had evacuated the crest of the ridge nearest the railway. A halt was called for the guns to come up. The final rush was made, after a brief bombardment, by the Highlanders and Gurkhas on the left of the railway. The Turks cleared as our men closed in, and the position was ours. Soon afterwards the 9th Bhopals, who were echeloned out far away on the left, assaulted and captured Sugar Loaf Hill.

It was during the advance after the attack had been launched at 4.30 that we had most of our casualties. The Black Watch lost ten officers in the action (five killed or died of wounds) and 227 men. The 8th Gurkhas lost every officer who went into action but one. But in the final assault on the second line at 6.30, which was covered by a good barrage, we lost very few. Small batches of the Turks stood, but the bulk of them made off, and a little before midnight the Black Watch and 8th Gurkhas had pushed the enemy back another three miles and captured Mushaidie station. The men were tired out. It had been a twenty-one miles' march with a stiff fight at seventeen miles, a position that was taken cheaply at the cost of over a third of the effectives in officers and men of the regiments attacking, and no water save what they started with at midnight on the 13th—altogether a lap of thirty hours' marching and fighting. The Turkish retreat was precipitate. During the night and the next day they fell back rapidly along the line. On the morning of the 16th our airmen reported them spread over a depth of twenty miles, their rearmost stragglers still pressing on in flight fully twenty-five miles north of Mushaidie.

Mushaidie was a hard-fought and determined action, and the fame of it should have been far-spread. A victory of the kind in any other phase of the campaign would have thrilled England; it might even have stirred

Simla in her sleep, but at the moment the eyes of the world were not to be diverted from Baghdad.

After the action at Mushaidie our further advance along the railway was dependent upon operations on the left bank, where the Turks were soon concentrating in order to create a diversion and to draw off our force which was threatening their railhead. To understand this new concentration it is necessary to follow the movements of the Turkish 13th Army Corps, which at the time we were threatening Baghdad was retiring before the Cossacks by the Kermanshah-Khanikin road over the Persian border.

On March 3rd, a day or two after the news of our occupation of Kut, the Turks fell back from the Asarabad Pass fifteen miles north-west of Hamadan, fighting a succession of rearguard actions until the 10th, when they held up the Russians at the Kara Su River, where they had destroyed the bridge. The Russians captured Kermanshah on March 11th, the same day that we entered Baghdad. From Kermanshah the pursuit continued, with two short checks, to the Tâq-i-Garra Pass, a natural corridor in the mountains, where the Turks occupied a strong, previously prepared position across the gorge. A rearguard action was fought here for ten days. The enemy retired on March 30th. The Russians, pursuing in close contact, arrived at Qasr-i-Shirin on March 31st.

In the meanwhile our "Khanikin Column," consisting of the 8th and 9th Brigades commanded by General Keary, had pushed out to the Diala from Baghdad on March 15th in the full hope of intercepting the Turk and crushing him between the British and Cossack nutcrackers. We had heard little or nothing of the political conditions in Russia which were paralysing the sinews of her army. We did not realise that our allies were starved of ammunition, transport and supplies, and in no position to take up a vigorous offensive. We expected to meet a force half-routed and broken in moral. But the Turkish 18th Army Corps showed no signs of being hustled; they were greatly superior in numbers to the small column we could oppose to them, and they were able to hold the Jebel Hamrin range until their whole force had crossed the Diala. It is true they were in retreat, but it was an orderly retirement, rapid on account of the danger of our cutting off their communications, not through the pressure of the Russians behind them. The withdrawal was, in fact, in the nature of an offensive, for it was part of a converging movement by which the 18th and 18th Army Corps were to join hands and drive in an attack on our flank.

General Keary's column met with little opposition at first. On March 18th his advanced troops crossed the Diala five miles downstream of Baquba, and, by threatening the enemy's rear and flank, manœuvred him out of a position he was preparing to hold with machine guns and artillery. On the 20th the column concentrated at Baquba, and the cavalry occupied Abu Jisra, fifteen miles farther on the Khanikin road, without opposition. On the 23rd the enemy was shelled out of his position at Shahraban. These were merely delaying actions, and the Turk made no resolute stand until we ran up against him on Jebel Hamrin, the first low range of hills through which the Khanikin road rises and dips towards the Persian frontier. He had a strong natural position here, and he was holding it in strength with his right flank on the Diala and his left two and a half miles east of the road, while his front was covered by the Ruz Canal, a high-banked stream 80 ft. wide, which formed a natural moat to the glacis. Facing the road there were three tiers of traversed fire trenches with a line of picket posts thrown forward. The whole ridge commanding the plain formed an ideal vantage post for observation. On the right bank the enemy held a line of trenches west of

Mansuriyeh-el-Jebel, while a regiment and two batteries occupied Deli Abbas.

We with our two brigades were hardly in sufficient strength to attack. On the other hand, inactivity would have been unpardonable. Had the Turks got away without our engaging them it would have been a blot on the

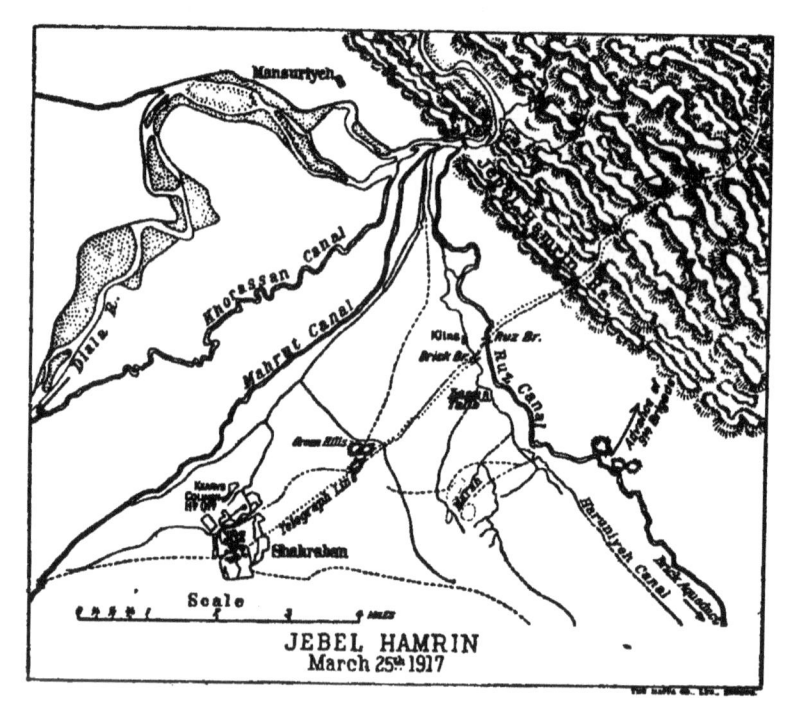

JEBEL HAMRIN
March 25th 1917

conduct of the campaign. Theoretically they were a force in retreat jammed in between two hostile converging armies. Judging by every precedent in war their moral ought to have been badly shaken. Yet, knowing the Turk, we doubted it. These were not beaten troops. To them the Tigris disaster was merely hearsay, and it is not in the Ottoman nature to suffer vicarious discouragement. Physically they had the best of the situation, but the psychological test had to be applied.

After Baghdad

But it was not quite easy at this stage to read the Turk's mind. Why was he holding the Jebel Hamrin position at all? He stood to lose everything between the Bear's arm and the Lion's paw. At first we thought he was making a stand through necessity with his back to the wall. He had no pontoons, we were told, and was collecting material for a bridge. A deserter brought some foolish tale about a faint-hearted engineer who had left them in the lurch and slipped off to Baghdad.

Then we heard the Turk was collecting supplies to carry him over the desolate tract between Kifri and Mosul, and incidentally exhausting the land for us. The Turk apparently had no Q. Branch, and was living on the country, getting in supplies from as far east as Mendali; it was part of his business to sterilise the district before our occupation. But he was in no hurry to move, and he exhibited a coolness which is generally associated with strength. We came to learn afterwards that the Jebel Hamrin garrison was not merely a covering force to an army in retreat. It was, or soon became, the bulk of the army itself.

On the night of the 28rd General Keary's plan of operations was to work round to the east with the 9th Brigade, capture the Jebel Hamrin heights and roll the enemy back on the Diala, leaving the 8th Brigade to press in frontally as soon as this movement had become effective. To effect a surprise it was necessary that we should be on the hills at dawn, but the nature of the country defeated us. The water-cuts between Baghdad and Shahraban had swallowed up the greater part of our bridging material, and the Ruz, the third stream we had to cross at night, would have entirely exhausted it. There was nothing to be done but to send back for more pontoons. These arrived on the 24th, and the bridge was built that night. But concealment, of course, was no longer possible. Early in the morning the Turks were observed by our airmen moving their guns along the ridge to meet the 9th Brigade; they registered the point where we were building the ramp to a nicety; from the hidden folds in the hills they could mark all our movements. Nothing was to be gained by changing the site of the bridge; it would be only time and labour wasted.

As the vicious little shrapnel burst low over the bank I felt the senselessness of war more than I had done for a whole year. In these iris fields I had almost forgotten we were fighting. The great objective had been grasped and left behind. None of us could have felt very warlike. A blue sky, willows, a running stream, an English spring, banks bright with charlock; buttercups, clover, veronica, pimpernel; scarlet anemones glowing through the grass; beyond the stream a plain rolling up to a scalloped ridge of rock; beyond this again, forty miles or more, the snows, and every promise of a flowering, undulating country in between. It seemed hard on our men to have to go on attacking entrenched positions after a lull like this. War carried out of the accursed dead plain, where it had become a normal kind of hell, into this green spot, seemed less a phase, more an eternal fact, than ever.

In the early morning, after a ride in the dark, I followed the telephone wires from the Ruz bridge to the battlefield in the hills. Not a head was visible of the British, Indian or Turk from the plain, but the wire led me over a sudden rise to a wing of the 93rd Burmans and on to the headquarters of the 9th Brigade. The force had bivouacked 500 yards from the ridge at 1.30. At 5.30 they advanced, the 1st Gurkhas on the left, the Dorsets in the centre, the 105th Mahrattas on the right. The 93rd Burma Light Infantry, who were in reserve, were called up afterwards to fill a gap between the Gurkhas and the Dorsets, and one company of the

84th Pioneers, who had come up for roadwork, were thrown in with the Gurkhas on the left. At eleven the Divisional Reserve, Manchesters and the 124th Baluchis, came up from the bridgehead in support.

As the Dorsets and Gurkhas appeared over the crest of the first mounds the Turks were seen slipping away, but only to concentrate and return. They were in greatly superior force. When I reached the scene soon after seven they had already established superiority of fire. The enemy had the advantage of knowing the ground; they had had time for reconnaissance; and the position was well registered by their artillery. We had no artillery support, owing to the difficulties of observation. Our gunners on the plain had good targets, but it was impossible to distinguish in this irregular interlaced system of mounds and depressions whether they were our men or the enemy; and signalling flags to mark our position had to be abandoned, as they drew a storm of shrapnel from the Turk. For once the enemy had the bombardment all their own way. The burst of their shrapnel was perfect, and we discovered that shell fire was much more formidable among rocks, where every splinter ricochetted from the natural parapet, than in the yielding clay of the Tigris valley. Also the Turkish gunners had the best of the ground. The guns on the second, and higher, range of hills could clear the crest of the first range, and so give their infantry effective artillery support, whereas our own shells, if they cleared the first range, passed over the heads of the enemy engaged with our infantry.

The scene of the battle was a welcome change after the Mesopotamian plain. It was the North-West Frontier again. We had to adapt ourselves to new tactics, or rather to the tactics of hill fighting familiar to the Indian Army before the War. Not that we had profited by it. Force D by this time had had more than one incarnation, and it is doubtful if there were a single sepoy on Jebel Hamrin who had seen a frontier campaign. The Turks had no regular line, and we could not see where their flanks lay. Small parties of skirmishers conformed to the irregularities of the ground. There were no trenches. The country was broken like the Sewaliks, a series of low scallop-shaped hills with rounded crests and flanks falling away—a bumpy wave-like panorama with few continuous lines. And here lay the danger. It was not the skirmishers coming over the ridge we had to fear, it was the parties working round the flank. You could not tell until the bullets came cracking over whether you were on dead ground or exposed to fire from some projecting salient in the opposite ridge. Our advance at dawn established us on the first line of crests; there was a second line some 2,500 yards away flanking the Khanikin road; the enemy appeared to be concentrating on a line half way between, but there were skirmishers in front of us anywhere between 150 and 1,500 yards.

I struck a knoll held by a mixed platoon of Mahrattas and Dorsets, once more together as in 1914, and commanded by an officer who had been wounded at Ctesiphon. He had got another bullet through his arm a few minutes before. A young havildar was tapping away with his Lewis gun at some black figures which kept crossing a ridge at long range. He was a mere boy, not yet 20, and as absorbed in his gun as in a new toy. What the depression concealed between us and them nobody knew. The Turks had come in with a machine gun between us and a company on higher ground to the right and enfiladed them, forcing them back; they were bringing it to bear on another ridge nearer us, and we saw the garrison retire. Far away on the right the other half battalion of the 105th held a hill on the extreme flank. On the left the Gurkhas held higher

After Baghdad

ground. A party of Turks had worked round under cover to within bombing distance. This was no doubt a diversion to persuade us to withdraw troops from the point against which their main stroke was being prepared on our right. But General Campbell kept up an even line as far as possible, weakening no point. We were now palpably on the defensive. It looked like an impasse, a sticky day's fighting, and probably a retirement at night.

In the heat of the day I left the burning rock for the river and the shade of willows two miles to the west, where my orderly was waiting for me with my horse and lunch. It was not till after three that we heard of the retirement, and the first intimation of it was the enemy's artillery barrage sweeping slowly towards us over the plain. Under it were our infantry. They had been within an ace of being enveloped.

At one o'clock the enemy were observed to be working round our right flank. At two heavy attacks were delivered on the centre and right. Another enveloping movement on the right compelled a local retirement. Our left was exposed to renewed attacks, lost ground, but 'recovered it. At 2.15 large reinforcements were seen moving up for the counter-attack, line upon line of fixed bayonets; the enemy had apparently drawn from the Khanikin reserves. A general retirement was ordered. The Manchesters on the right, the 98rd in the centre, and the 124th Baluchis on the left, fought a steady rearguard action. The enemy made one attempt to follow up the withdrawal of the infantry, whose retirement they covered, but it was easily repulsed. At 8.80 the Turkish cavalry on our right had formed up and were preparing to charge, but were dispersed by the rifle and machine-gun fire of the 18th Lancers and the battery protecting their flank. Our infantry had three miles of plain to cover swept by the enemy's shell fire. The artillery barrage of twenty-two guns was well directed; the fire was mostly shrapnel in bursts of three. Had the attack in the morning succeeded and the enemy been driven back along the ridge we should have had the support of the whole of our artillery, which, with the exception of one 18-pounder battery and a section of R.H.A., was in action close to the Khanikin road countering the enemy's guns; but it was held too great a risk to push our batteries across the Ruz until the second bridge had been completed, an indication, this, that the attack was launched tentatively and with no great hope of success.

The enemy's shell fire was particularly heavy on the two bridges over the Haruniyeh and Ruz canals, and on the road between. The 9th Brigade lost nearly a third of their first line transport. The casualties of the whole force, the 9th Brigade and the two supporting battalions of the 8th, were 1,177, more than a third of the troops engaged. And for the first time for nearly a year the Roll of Honour contained a large proportion of "missing," many of them wounded men whom we had to leave behind in the retirement.

Jebel Hamrin was a reverse. But there was no help for it. We had to take the chance. The Turks were in too great force, too well disciplined, and too well handled to be pushed out of one strong position after another and rolled back on the river. Reserves had been called up from Khanikin. They had 6,000 rifles—picked men, their prisoners told us—250 sabres and twenty-four guns. Their moral was good, and they were not to be hustled. But it was essential that the attempt should be made. Against other troops of less stubborn fibre the thrust might well have succeeded. The discouragement of a retreat is infectious, and it is a commonplace in military history that the fear of envelopment weakens the hold of an army on the strongest positions. The general who did not presume weakness in an opponent in such circumstances, or who hesitated to act on it, would be lacking in initiative.

In any case an assault was called for. If the attack were only partially successful, we hoped to be able to entrench on the heights and to pin the enemy to his ground so closely that an attempt at withdrawal would imperil his whole rearguard. But the Khanikin reinforcements made even this alternative impracticable, and we had to take up the line of the Ruz again.

For the next few days we were in continual uncertainty both as regards the movements and intentions of the Turks and the advance of the Russians.

The bulk of the Turkish 18th Army Corps were already across the Diala, and had swung south-west with the intention of joining hands with the Turkish force on the Tigris in the neighbourhood of Deltawa. But this move was thwarted. We engaged the two forces in detail. The Tigris force was met and defeated and driven back to the Shatt-el-Adhaim at Dogameh on March 29th, while our cavalry, which had moved up rapidly on the right bank of the Diala, contained a hostile division at Deli Abbas, our artillery, horse and field, co-operating effectively from the right bank.

The Dogameh action has been called the Battle of the Marl Plain. The ground where the advance was made to the east of the dry bed of the Narwan Canal was hotter, figuratively if not literally, than "the burning marl" which received Lucifer and his fallen host. Its surface was as smooth as a liquid which has congealed on a still night; there were stretches where you could not find an inequality that would have given bias to a marble. It was over this ground that the 89th and 40th Brigades attacked frontally. The 40th Brigade was to make a holding attack, to be pushed home if circumstances warranted, while the 89th made an enveloping movement on the Turks' left. They found the enemy's flank, however, too extended to turn, and had to go in on the front. Both brigades attacked over this marl plain with the surface of a cement floor. The 5th Wilts made a memorable advance over the last thousand yards of flat. They started a bare 500 strong, though they were the strongest battalion in the brigade; 195 dropped going over, including seven officers, but they got in and drove the Turks from their line of rifle-pits in front of the position. The lie of the main Turkish line was still uncertain, and the 40th Brigade were ordered to advance no farther until the action of the 89th Brigade made itself felt. The 89th Brigade, after a ten miles' night march, found themselves still some distance from the ruins. The advance was checked by enemy skirmishers pushed out well to the east, and it was not until 2.80 P.M. that the assault on the main line was delivered. The three battalions present with the brigade, the 9th Royal Warwicks, the 7th Glosters and the 7th North Staffords, were all put in. The advance was carried out without a pause, and the three battalions gained their objectives, capturing 180 prisoners. During the night the Turks fell back on the Shatt-el-Adhaim, and the desired result of the battle, the prevention of the junction of the 13th Army Corps with the 18th, was attained.

Upon the defeat of their Tigris force the division at Deli Abbas fell back on to the hills and joined the rest of the Turkish forces from Persia. We occupied the village at dawn on March 81st. The same morning the enemy evacuated Jebel Hamrin, on the left bank of the Diala. The Diala crossing had been completed, and it was believed the enemy were retiring on Mosul along the Kifri road. This movement had evidently been contemplated until the bolder strategy of an offensive against our column on the left bank of the Tigris commended itself to the Turkish Commander, Ihsan Bey.

After Baghdad

On April 1st the 8th Brigade advanced after a reconnaissance to join hands with the Russians. Reports as to the whereabouts of the Cossacks were still conflicting, as their advanced troops had no wireless with them, and relays of riders had to carry dispatches through to Headquarters many stages back on the road before a message could be transmitted to Baghdad.

The dramatic encounter of the Allied armies which we had been anticipating so long took place at Kizil Robat on April 2nd. A small body of cavalry was sighted on the horizon riding towards us. General Edwardes, in command of the column, seeing their squadron standard, a blue and white pennant, called up a squadron of the 18th Lancers, who pushed forward, wheeled into line, saluted, and turned back, bringing the Russians into camp. It was a sotnia of Cossacks who had been sent forward to establish communications far in advance of the main body. They had crossed the Persian frontier at Qasr-i-Shirin the day before, and bivouacked in the night ten miles north-east of Kizil Robat. They came in at a walk, riding with short stirrups, toes down, heels up, leaning forward, their weight thrown upon their stirrups. They wore jackboots and sheepskin caps. Besides their rifles they carried knives and curved Caucasian scimitars without handguards. Their small horses, mostly under fourteen hands, looked thin and spent, and were heavily laden. They had been fed on the dry leaves of scrub oak. There was no grain, no transport. The troopers had been reduced to two *chapatties* a day. They had had a hard trek from Hamadan through an inhospitable country, over snow passes trodden into the consistency of ice, down into the burning heat of the ravines of the foothills. The country between Kermanshah and Khanikin was an uninhabited waste. Seven armies had passed through in ten months. Villages were abandoned. Supplies did not exist. Even in the districts which were least exhausted the two armies were dependent on a country that could barely support a brigade.

The retreat of the Turkish army from Hamadan was well ordered. The Russian army of the Caucasus was beginning to feel the paralysis that must devitalise the fighting machine when the interior economy of a country begins to crumble. At the end of February they knew that the British advance was pressing on towards Baghdad, and that the Turks in front of them, with their communications threatened in the flank, would have to fall back. Yet they had no scheme, and they were not prepared to follow the enemy up and seriously harass his retreat. An organised transport system no longer existed, so the Turks were able to fall back with few casualties inflicted by arms, though hunger, disease, and exhaustion took their toll. Fighting was confined to artillery action and to rifle and machine-gun fire at very long range. There was no bayonet fighting, save in the case of one regiment when the Turks held up the pursuit three days on the line of the Kara Su in front of Kermanshah. The Cossacks forded the stream at night near Tâq-i-Bustan and attacked the Turks in their lines; a second crossing turned the enemy's flank. But the Turk had time to evacuate his wounded, and before he quitted he destroyed the British and Russian consulates, which were burning as our allies entered the town. The pursuit was held up again at the Nal Sikhan Pass, and again in the Tâq-i-Garra, where the Turks held the gorge for ten days where the spur runs down on the right of the road two and a half miles above Sakhadisa Khan. We were to pass that way ourselves less than a year afterwards on the way to the Caspian. It is the strongest point on the old Babylon-Ecbatana road, and no doubt armies used to hold it before the days of Darius and Hystaspes.

The Turks suffered heavy losses through sickness and exhaustion. All the way the road was littered with dead mules, horses, camels, asses, buffaloes. Their ranks were thinned with typhus. The infantry were footsore; their light Hamadan boots only lasted a few days, and most of them went barefooted. Many of them fell from exhaustion; the cemeteries of every village showed signs of new graves; nearly a thousand were counted in Kermanshah alone. The country was full of deserters. Many of the Turkish rank and file slipped away from the retreat. The people at Khanikin described a scene in which batches of them were driven over the bridge by officers pointing their revolvers. At Kermanshah the last remnants of the French Algerian and Moroccan prisoners, who had been impressed for pioneer work, made their escape and joined the Russian troops. The Turks destroyed everything as they retired. They demolished the European telegraph station at Qasr-i-Shirin, the Russian and British consulates, the Imperial Bank of Persia, and most of the bridges on the road, indulging a Hunnish instinct of havoc which seemed to indicate that they had little hope of return. The three Russian officers lunched with us and we drank the health of the Russian Army in our last bottle of rum. In the afternoon a small motor convoy brought in bully beef, ration biscuits, jam, and dates for the sotnia, and they enjoyed the best meal they had had for a month. The Cossacks were a hard-bitten, weathered, cheery crowd, and they were soon fraternising with our troops. Their fair eyelashes and moustaches looked almost white against their tanned skin, giving them a homely northern appearance welcome to our eyes after Mesopotamia. In the evening they rode back to Qasr-i-Shirin, their thin, game little horses stumbling under their loads, and we saw them no more. We, too, had come to the end of our tether in transport, and marched back the same night to Jebel Hamrin, and the next day to Shahraban and on to Baquba, where we had established a strong post.

Our immediate objective had been gained. Persia was clear of the Turk, and there were no enemy left east of the Diala River. But we were a disappointed column. The nutcrackers had closed on emptiness. The 18th Army Corps had extricated themselves and had not even been badly mauled. We had expected great things of the Russians and our joint offensive, and we drew no comfort from any abstract promise of a liberated humanity that the revolution in Petrograd might portend. All we wanted just then was the power to deal hammer-blows at the Turk. If the Russians had come down in their might on Mosul, Diabekir, and Khanikin, while we were thrusting north from Gaza and Baghdad—if they had had half the vitality of eighteen months before, we might have so crippled and broken the Turk that his usefulness to the Hun would have become negligible. Or so we believed. And the chance might never come again. Questions of autocracy or democracy left us cold. We only saw these long-enduring gallant troops starved and neglected in a crisis which might have decided the struggle for which we and they had paid so dearly in sacrifice and blood.

CHAPTER XXXV

THE SHATT-EL-ADHAIM

ONCE across the Diala River the 18th Army Corps was able to adopt an offensive rôle. The Corps Commander, Ihsan Bey, was one of the ablest of the Turkish generals, a man of great initiative, and quick to seize an opportunity. His objective now was to threaten General Maude's right flank in order to thwart or delay the advance of our Tigris column on Samarrah. The 7th Division could not advance along the railway on the right bank until the left bank was cleared of the enemy. Thus, after the battle of Mushaidie on March 14th a halt was called on this side until we had swept clean the left bank of the Diala, and fought the action of Dogameh (p. 145) in which we drove the left wing of the enemy's Tigris corps back on the Shatt-el-Adhaim while our cavalry contained the Turkish division at Deli Abbas, preventing a junction of the two forces.

With the left bank clear up to the Shatt-el-Adhaim progress along the right bank could be continued. On April 6th the 7th Division advanced along the line to Sumaikcha, the enemy retiring before them, and on the 8th, Easter Sunday, the 28th Brigade occupied Beled station and village after a brisk action with the Turkish rearguard. The Turks had machine guns mounted on the station buildings, but the 53rd Sikhs and Leicesters rushed the place with the loss of only 80 men, and took 200 prisoners in the low hillocks beyond.

On the 9th the advance was continued to Harbe. Here the resources of the supply train were very nearly exhausted. The column consumed 120 tons a day, and transport was wanting. Riverhead was at Fort Kermea, whence supplies were sent through to Sumaikcha on carts. But at Harbe the Turks left behind thirty broad-gauge trucks on a side line running off to some gravel pits. To these were harnessed the mules of the ammunition column, and "Catty's Express," as the new link in the communications was called, after the transport officer who originated it, gave us just the extra mobility we needed. Had it not been for this providential windfall we could not have pressed on to Samarrah that April.

At Harbe, however, the advance was held up for a week while another hostile concentration was dispersed on the left bank. Ihsan Bey and the 18th Army Corps were active again, preparing a descent on our Tigris column from their new base in the Jebel Hamrin range. The movement was anticipated, and the Turks driven back into the hills. These repulses of the enemy east of the Tigris synchronised with our advance along the railway. From this point I shall deal with the operations separately, concluding the present chapter with the fighting on the Shatt-el-Adhaim and reserving for a separate chapter the story of the advance by the 7th Division on Samarrah.

The 3rd Corps, General Marshall, was on the left bank, the 18th Division commanded by General Cayley, and the 14th by General Egerton. The forces opposed to it were the left bank column of the Turkish 18th Corps on the Tigris and the 18th Corps, which had its base in Jebel Hamrin. It was General Maude's object to prevent the Turks from Jebel Hamrin joining hands with the left flank of their Tigris column. We have seen in the last chapter how the first sortie from Jebel Hamrin, part of the enemy's thwarted converging movement on Deltawa, was held up by the Cavalry Division, while the force it intended to join on the Tigris was engaged at

The Shatt-el-Adhaim

Dogameh and driven back on the Shatt-el-Adhaim. The Turks were now entrenched on the north bank of the Shatt-el-Adhaim near its junction with the Tigris, with the intention of opposing our crossing. It was necessary to disperse this force in order to open up our river communications, and also to protect the 7th Division in its advance along the right bank from enfilade fire from across the river. But first we had to force the passage of the Adhaim.[1]

It was intended to cross the Adhaim on the night of April 11th, but on the 10th the Cavalry Division reported that the Turks were advancing in strength from Jebel Hamrin. This entailed a postponement of the operations on the Adhaim, while two brigades, the 89th and 40th, were sent across the desert to assist the Cavalry Division, which, while holding Ihsan Bey's column, was withdrawing slowly, taking up line after line west of the Diala. As the cavalry fell back before this force of infantry, Ihsan Bey diverted the whole of the Turkish 2nd Division to turn their flank and take them in the rear. This column was nearing the pivoting point from which it was to close in the net behind the cavalry when it met the 89th and 40th Brigades, which had made a night march of twenty miles across the desert from the Adhaim. The result was an encounter battle in the open, a rare experience in modern fighting, and one not likely to occur unless one party is unaware of the other's advance. The two forces met at a point near Shialah, at least twenty miles from their last entrenched positions, and there was a race for the nearest rise, a gentle enough gradient, but the one dominant bit of ground in the plain. The wave of steel and khaki, as the Cheshires and Royal Welsh Fusiliers advanced at a double to the crest of the slope, was the first hint the Turks had of the

[1] I am indebted to Mr. J. A. Sandbrook for his description of the fighting on the Shatt-el-Adhaim, part of which I quote verbatim. My thanks are also due to numerous regimental and Staff officers.

presence of an enemy force within twenty miles other than that against which they were marching. The arrival of our two brigades on the spot at the moment is only one instance of the good work of our Intelligence, which was becoming almost uncanny in the certainty with which it forestalled every movement of the enemy.

The cavalry withdrew through our advancing infantry. As the two battalions reached the ridge they met a staggering fire. The Turks had still 600 yards to cover and were coming on in waves looking enormous in the mirage. Our infantry lay down with bayonets fixed. Their steady fire and the guns supporting them checked the enemy's advance. Colonel Peck, commanding the 55th Brigade R.F.A., realising the supreme importance of the ridge, galloped his batteries to within 800 yards of the infantry and came into action at 1,500 yards. This action was decisive. Gradually we gained superiority of fire. The Turks fell back two or three hundred yards, but held on to this line, a shallow nullah, all day. Before daybreak on the 12th they withdrew, leaving 815 dead on the field, and took up a new entrenched position at Bint-el-Hassan, six miles to the north-east. They were forced out of this on the 13th, which was a gunner's day. The action of the 11th decided the issue. On the 12th, 13th and 14th the fight developed into a runnng battle, the Turks retiring before us. The infantry were seldom in touch, though there were dropping casualties from long-range fire and enemy's guns. The 40th Brigade advanced on the left, while the 35th Brigade on the right, the Buffs leading, carried Bint-el-Hassan by assault. The Turks' withdrawal was well ordered. They maintained their old rearguard tactics, holding a series of rifle pits, echeloned in great depth, firing through each other, offering no definite objective, but a certain heavy loss, to the attack, while their machine guns, skilfully concealed, poured in a cross enfilade fire. On the evening of the 18th the

The Shatt-el-Adhaim

Royal Welsh Fusiliers had advanced to within 600 yards of their position. The Turks fell back at night, and on the morning of the 14th were holding a new line at Serajik, 1,500 yards in front of our infantry. Early in the morning our guns registered on their position, while our cavalry worked round their flank. In the evening our artillery threw an intense barrage on their trenches, and our machine guns got a good target as they retired. Before sunset they marked a further development on their right. It was the 40th Brigade making a feigned enveloping movement with much noise and dust and clatter of empty carts. Before daybreak on the 15th they had melted away into the shelter of the hills.

Our flank was now clear on the Adhaim, and the 88th Brigade prepared to force the passage of the river a few miles from its junction with the Tigris. The Turkish position facing east and north was strong, and there was little chance of decisive results by an enveloping movement to the north. Away to the north, however, there was an old ford (A), the only way then known of crossing the stream without boats. A little downstream of this a reconnaissance had discovered another ford (B). The actual crossing took place here while a demonstration was made at the old ford, against which the enemy's fire was directed, while we forced the passage downstream without a casualty. In the meanwhile the uncertainty and bewilderment of the Turk was increased by a manœuvre on the part of the cavalry. Supported by a battery of field artillery, Cassels' Cavalry Brigade worked up the river and threatened the enemy's left. The Turk had learned to expect, and prepare for, envelopment, but this time General Marshall's plan was to break through his centre. The Corps Commander alternated his tactics, to the confusion of the enemy, and always did the unexpected thing. While the North Lancashires were crossing with some ostentation and occupying a spur of high ground which enabled them to contain the enemy, a far more important passage (C) had been effected by the East Lancashires and South Lancashires in the dead of the

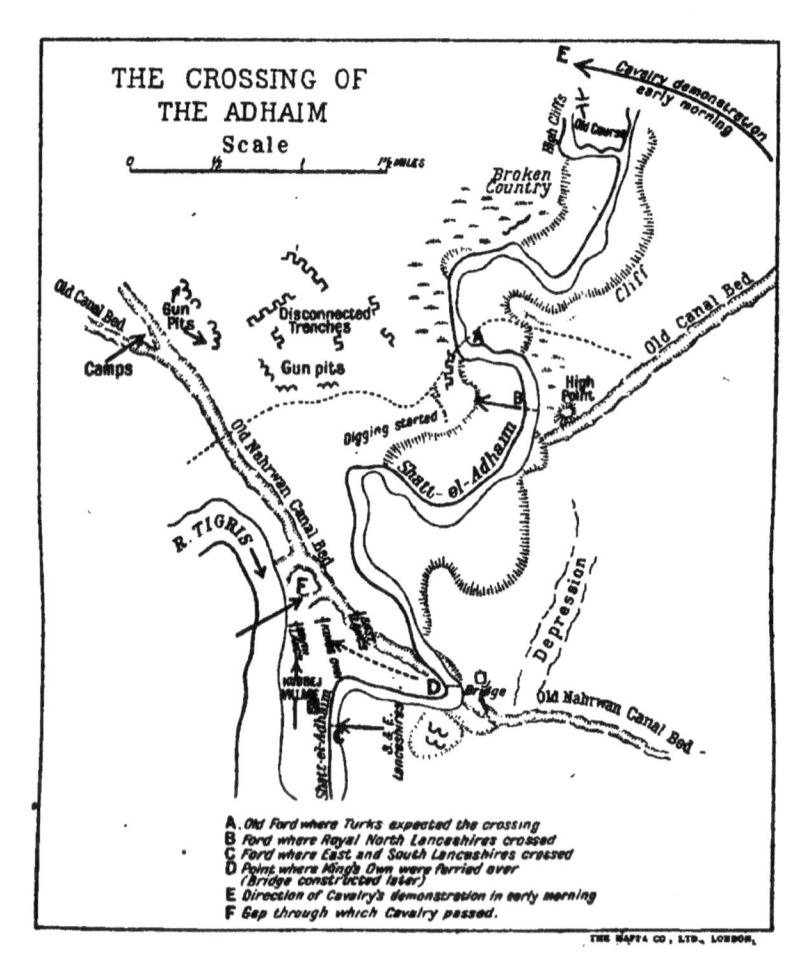

THE CROSSING OF THE ADHAIM

A. Old Ford where Turks expected the crossing
B. Ford where Royal North Lancashires crossed
C. Ford where East and South Lancashires crossed
D. Point where King's Own were ferried over (Bridge constructed later)
E. Direction of Cavalry's demonstration in early morning
F. Gap through which Cavalry passed.

night lower down the Adhaim. It was pitch dark when the two battalions marched at 10 P.M. from the rendezvous in the dry bed of the old Nahrwan Canal and crept stealthily across the low-lying, scrub-covered ground. The darkness concealed the clouds of dust; the soft ground deadened the sound of movement as the two battalions marched in close order to preserve touch. When the leading companies reached the bank, less than a mile from the enemy's position, there was nothing to show that the Turks were alert or had even suspected General Marshall's plan. Each company carried a pontoon, and in these the men were silently ferried across the stream. Forming up on the other side, the Lancashire battalions pushed on past the Kubbej village, and at 4.50 A.M. they were at the foot of the cliffs of crumbling earth that marked the bed of the erratic river. The march had been so silent that not a casualty was sustained. The occasional maxim fire of the Turks was directed blindly. They were unsuspicious of any menace from this side. Just before dawn our men scaled the cliffs and rushed the pickets, breaking the silence with a cheer that could be heard a mile off. For a few seconds the Turks replied with a wild fire, then threw down their rifles and surrendered.

As soon as the South and East Lancashires were established on the high ground the King's Own were ferried over (D), while the Sappers threw a bridge over the Adhaim. The King's Own, with the two Lancashire battalions, then formed for the attack with their left on the Tigris and their right slightly overlapping the Nahrwan Canal. The plan of action was to drive in a wedge between the enemy's right and the Tigris. Through this gap the cavalry were to pour in and round up the Turk in the rear when the infantry had driven him out of his position. Everything fell out according to plan. At 12.15 the artillery and the gunboats on the river opened a hurricane bombardment on the position. At 12.80 the three battalions advanced under this barrage to the assault. The Turks were completely routed. Over 500 prisoners were taken. Then the cavalry came in. They were well handled on the

Shatt-el-Adhaim. After this feint of a flanking movement in the early morning, which had kept the Turk uncertain and cramped his dispositions, they had been withdrawn and brought into reserve near the spot where they were to start in pursuit when the infantry's work was done. They had been resting unsaddled; the horses were watered; the men fresh and keen; the enemy tired and dispirited. Galloping over the soft sandy country, Cassels' Brigade bored a way between the Turks and the Tigris, cutting them off from the river and water. Only a small remnant of the force that opposed the crossing managed to get away. Over 1,200 prisoners were taken; 700 surrendered to the cavalry alone; and as the original force was reckoned at 2,000 men, after allowing for killed and wounded, it is no exaggeration to say that it practically ceased to exist. The few stragglers retreated in a northerly direction; our cavalry pursued until 8 P.M.; nothing but darkness and the exhaustion of their horses prevented them from rounding up the enemy's guns.

News now came to hand from aeroplane reconnaissance of the advance of the Turkish 18th Corps down the Shatt-el-Adhaim. They were attempting a fresh offensive in the last desperate hope of saving Samarrah. By some extraordinary marching viâ Kara Tappah they emerged from the Demir Kapu defile, where the Shatt-el-Adhaim issues from the hills, and moved southwards against our right flank. They were too late to prevent our crossing the Adhaim; but their leading division, the 14th, was not far distant from the Tigris, and on the night of April 23rd they took up a strong position at Dahuba to oppose our northward advance. The Turks' 14th Division was estimated at 2,000 rifles, and their 2nd Division was some six or seven miles to its rear. It was our object to engage the 14th Division before it could be reinforced by the 2nd. The 88th Brigade, as they neared the end of their night march, saw the enemy's lights ahead, and naturally took this casual illumination for the fires of an Arab encampment. But in the false dawn they saw the Turks silhouetted against the sky still digging their position. The surprise was mutual, and the battle broke out with startling suddenness. The North Lancashires swung round and attacked due east, advancing to within 600 yards of the enemy's position, supported by the 66th Brigade R.F.A., which came into action 1,200 yards behind them and kept down the Turks' machine-gun fire. Here a halt was called for the 85th Brigade, which was making a wide outflanking movement on the enemy's right. When the two brigades advanced the Turk; no longer able to count on the support of the 2nd Division, and seeing his flank threatened, broke and fled across the Adhaim. This was on April 24th. The action only lasted a few hours, and the Turks suffered heavily from our guns as they crossed the river.

The Turks withdrew to a strong position under Jebel Hamrin, some thirty-six miles from the mouth of the Adhaim. Here, with the 14th Division on the left bank and the 2nd on the right bank, they awaited our attack.

On April 26th General Marshall's column, which included the 6th Cavalry Brigade, got into touch with the enemy, and on the 27th seized a large island in the river bed. The stream itself here is of insignificant proportions, but it has wandered far and wide between the high banks that rise like cliffs, and the bed of the river varies in width from 2,000 to 8,500 yards. About 2,000 yards beyond the island the cliffs of the right bank jut out into the bed, forming the shape of a boot, and on this lofty irregular mound the Turks had established their centre. On their right a line of trenches ran back some 4,000 yards till they rested on a hill. Their left extended across the river bed, climbed the banks in a series of formidable machine-gun emplacements and redoubts, and, circling in front of the Band-i-Adhaim village, was carried round to the north, an effective guard for the left flank. Altogether the position covered some seven or eight miles of front and commanded a wide field of fire over an almost level plain.

The 27th, 28th, and 29th of April were spent in reconnoitring the position and preparing for the attack. At nightfall on the 29th, the 88th Brigade marched out

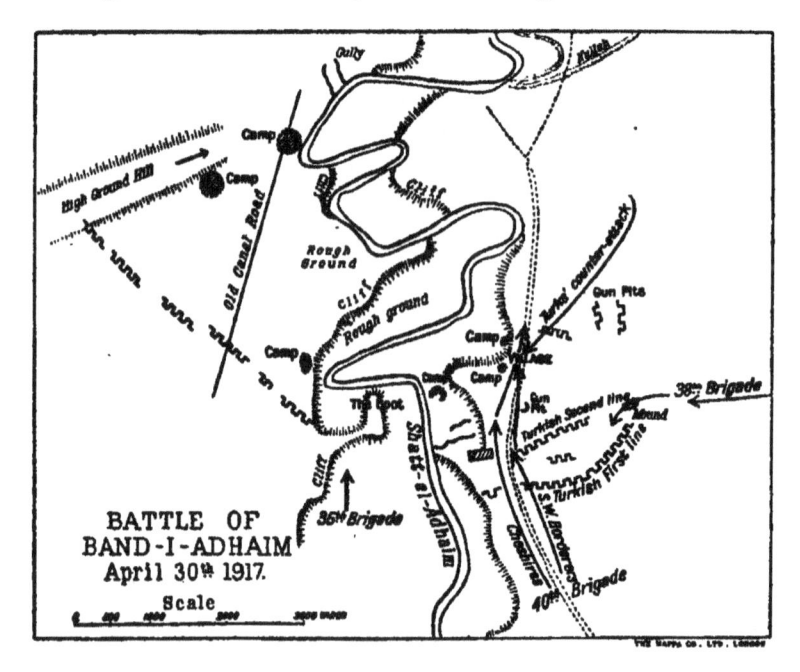

BATTLE OF BAND-I-ADHAIM April 30th 1917.

from our right front and threatened the enemy's left. They were held up by strong and active enemy patrols, as anticipated, creating the impression that General Marshall intended to envelop the Turkish left. The 40th Brigade in the centre, which was to deliver the decisive attack, was on the left bank of the Adhaim; and our left, the 85th Brigade, extended from the island in the river bed to the right or western bank of the stream. At 5 A.M. on April 30th, when the day was beginning to break, the two battalions of the 40th Brigade, the Cheshires and

The Shatt-el-Adhaim

South Wales Borderers, advanced across the bare plain supported by a heavy artillery barrage. They gained their objective and drove the Turks out of their line of trenches. The 85th Brigade, on the left, advanced to within 600 yards of the main position, "The Boot," which bristled with machine guns and rifles. Here at six in the morning they dug in, as ordered, and awaited developments.

In the centre our objective was an empty village of mud huts that stood on the high banks of the river and the second line of the Turkish trenches to the east of it. General Lewin, commanding the 40th Brigade, sent out the Cheshires and South Wales Borderers on the left and right. The Cheshires on the left drove the Turks out with bomb and bayonet. On the Borderers' front the defence had been more or less paralysed by the barrage; and the enemy surrendered in masses. Two-thirds of the Cheshire officers had fallen in the advance. Colonel Crocker,[1] their Commanding Officer, fell wounded. Lieutenant Welsby, the Adjutant, was killed. The men pushed on and overshot their objective. Their blood was up. There was no holding them. The Borderers, on the right, swept on in line, missing in the confusion the Turkish second line trenches and strong points they were ordered to hold. Right in front were the enemy's guns, two batteries of four guns each. They seized them, and took 800 prisoners. At 7.80 in the morning the guns were ours. The Cheshires had advanced beyond the village with the Borderers on their right, when a sudden dust storm swept over the battlefield, obscuring everything. It shut out the whole scene. No one could see what was happening where the two battalions stood round the guns, tired and winded by the long charge, but keen and confident, though a good 8,000 yards ahead of their supports.

[1] Colonel Crocker had been wounded in the action at Shialah on April 11th, and his second in command, Major Mitchell, Royal Sussex Regiment, killed.

Ali Ihsan, as we have seen, was a man quick to seize his opportunities. He realised that our men were disorganised after a successful assault; he heard that his guns were captured, and decided without hesitation to take advantage of the screen of the dust storm to counter-attack in mass. He must have counter-attacked in any case, but the dust storm was his opportunity and it delivered the two battalions into his hands. Only those who have seen these typhoons blotting out all the landscape hour after hour can realise their blinding intensity. Behind the clouds of dust Ali Ihsan delivered his counter-attack. He thrust what was probably his main reserve of a couple of thousand men across the river. Hidden from the view of the 88th Brigade on our right, these reinforcements passed right across their front, their daring march not even suspected. Our artillery would have pulverised the assault had the screen lifted, but it was impossible to get our guns on to them as they came up, for the telephone communications were broken in the storm. Ali Ihsan took the risk, and fortune favoured him. His counter-attack passed in front of the 88th Brigade, fell on the two front battalions, drove the right into the village and through it, cutting off our left. The Turks came on in a solid continuous line, "like a horn" as one of the Borderers put it, a complete semicircle bent into the cliff on our left and far outflanking our right. And behind the impenetrable veil of dust there raged a bloody hand-to-hand struggle. Two or three thousand Turks were massed on a front of 400 yards. They swept into the village in overwhelming numbers, recaptured it, and enveloped our troops beyond. Cut off from support by the murk of the storm, the odds were too heavy against our men, and seven of the captured guns were lost to us, and 450 of the Turkish prisoners. But the Turks never regained their lost trenches; nor did they hold the village long. The counter-attack was held up by the steady fire of the machine-gun section, and by the Wilts and Royal Welsh Fusiliers who had been moved up rapidly when it was found that the Borderers and Cheshires had overshot their mark. The quick decision of General Lewin saved the brigade from complete disaster. By four in the afternoon the dust storm had spent its force. As soon as it was realised that the Turks were again in the village an intense artillery fire was opened on the group of mud huts, and the enemy were once more driven out.

Towards dusk the 85th Brigade on our left, who had been lying low in the river bed, pushed forward officer patrols to the edge of "The Boot," upon which was concentrated from time to time the fire of all the British batteries. At 9 P.M., under cover of the officers' patrols, we started a bombing attack on the position. But the Turks had been shaken by our artillery; after the punishment of our guns they did not wait for our grenadiers. By midnight the field was ours and the Turks were in full flight towards the Jebel Hamrin hills. The punishment they had received had entirely broken the moral of the 18th Army Corps, and only a few remnants of what was once a considerable force watched from a respectful distance our column packing up its traps and departing down the valley of the Adhaim. Two days afterwards our aeroplanes flying low dropped half a ton of bombs on the retreating army.

"The Battle of Band-i-Adhaim," or "The Boot," as it was called, was the bloodiest action in Mesopotamia, if one counts loss in proportion to the force engaged. Our battalions were far below strength at this stage of the campaign. In spite of new drafts the Cheshires had dwindled to 880 after four and a half months' almost continual fighting, and of this small remnant they lost 126 in the last action on the Adhaim; and the South Wales Borderers lost 208 out of 840. We found over 100 dead Turks where the struggle had been hottest, round the pits where the guns had been taken and lost, and over the ground where they had counter-attacked; and most of the dead, Turks and British alike, had bayonet wounds, for both sides were running short of ammunition. It is to the eternal credit of those thinned battalions that they drove a numerically superior force out of a formidable position, and retained a field gun and 800 odd prisoners, including the Brigadier—all sent back before the counter-attack was driven in.

The last day in April marked the end of the operations during the hot weather in 1917. The heat already was barely endurable, and the men were still marching and fighting in their winter clothes. The enemies of Force D once more became the sun and the dust and the flies. Folk who have never left a temperate clime cannot imagine a summer under canvas in Mesopotamia. The sun rises somewhere about 4.55. At five the flies begin; they will be a torment through a day of fourteen hours. The earlier they are astir the more cumulative is one's depression. The only parallel I can think of in the way of imaginative anticipation is the horror one had in childhood of hell-fire when one was told that it must be endured without end. At eight in the morning one's glare glasses singe one's eyelashes; one's lips hate one's teeth and gums; one's throat becomes a ladder of hard and sore protuberances leading down to an internal slake heap which no water can appease.

I confess that I did not think it possible that troops who had been through the hot weather of 1916 on the top of four months' reverses in the winter and spring would be fit for a big offensive in the cold weather. But Force D will live in history as the most perfect example of the British habit of " slogging on."

CHAPTER XXXVI

SAMARRAH

IN bringing the story of the Shatt-el-Adhaim fighting to an end, I have anticipated by a day or two the capture of Samarrah. As soon as their right flank was cleared by the dispersal of the enemy on the opposite bank, the 7th Division continued their advance along the railway. On April 19th they occupied the ridge at Al Khubn, within a mile and a half of the enemy's trenches at Istabulat station. The Turkish position here was one of great strength, and had the advice given by their late commander been acted upon it might have been very much stronger. Shortly before the capture of Baghdad the Turkish 18th Army Corps had been commanded by Kazim Karabekir Bey, a general with a long and distinguished service record. When the fall of Baghdad seemed imminent—and with the Turkish army flying and broken it was bound to fall—he ordered a retirement direct to Istabulat, there to strengthen the position already prepared. He did not believe in frittering away his diminished forces in fighting for small positions. He was, however, overruled, and, as the Turkish prisoners told us, resigned his command to Shefket Pasha. The series of battles between Baghdad and Istabulat was the result. They availed the flying Turks nothing. As events proved, it would have been more profitable to them if they had fallen back on Istabulat and made the position still more formidable.

Even as it was, the Istabulat position was extraordinarily strong. Its left, guarded by well-placed redoubts, rested on the Tigris. The main line of trenches ran along a ridge to a point about a mile southward of the railway; thence they ran parallel with it in a north-westerly direction for several miles. These trenches commanded a flat, open plain across which the British had to advance to the assault. The Dujail Canal, a narrow

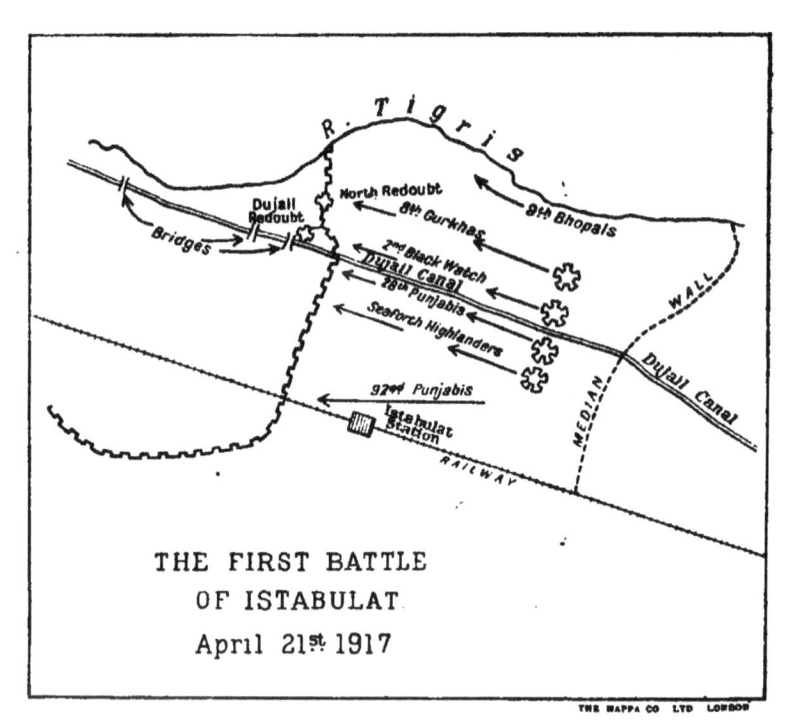

THE FIRST BATTLE OF ISTABULAT
April 21st 1917

watercourse, 20 ft. below the level of its banks and spanned by three small bridges, passed through the centre of the position; but this was a disadvantage, if anything, to the defence, as it increased the difficulties of bringing up reinforcements.

On the 19th strong fighting patrols were sent out, both on the north and south of the canal, from the British outpost line which ran along the Median wall. During the night we consolidated the ground we had gained, building four strong points, some 400 yards from the enemy's advanced posts, and 2,200 yards from his main position at Istabulat. On the morning of the 20th the assaulting troops were massed for the attack in and in the rear of these redoubts, and it was from this line that the attack was launched.

Standing on the ancient Median wall, the Staff could see the battlefield spread out before them, with the ruins of old Istabulat, now nothing more than a series of mounds on the sky line. The 92nd Punjabis attacked in the early morning of April 21st, advancing on Istabulat station, taking it by assault and digging themselves in in front of the main position, half a mile beyond. The key to the Turkish position, the two redoubts to the north of the canal, stood some 40 ft. above the level of the plain. The 21st Brigade operated to the north of the canal, the Black Watch (left) advancing on the Dujail Redoubt, the 1/8th Gurkhas (right) on the north redoubt; the 9th Bhopals were sent round to attack on the flank, while the Black Watch and Gurkhas went in frontally. On the south of the canal one company of the 28th Punjabis co-operated with the 21st Brigade, advancing in line with them and attacking the enemy's trenches on the high ground near the Dujail.

The infantry moved steadily on to the assault, line upon line, in open order, through machine-gun and rifle fire that swept the bare plain. On the north of the canal the ground afforded sparse cover to within 500 yards of the enemy's position; from this point onwards the ground was flat; on the south of the canal the whole stretch of over 2,000 yards from the Median wall to the Istabulat lines was absolutely flat. At 6.80 A.M. the Black Watch and Gurkhas reached the foot of the high ridge, where the enemy lay waiting for the assault. The artillery barrage lifted, and nothing now remained between the successive lines of our infantry and the grim line of trenches with their hidden machine guns and battalions of rifles. Highlanders and Gurkhas stood face to face with the Turk separated only by a few yards, but the Turk was raised above the plain, and from his maze of trenches he poured in a deadly fire on the assaulting battalions. The line went on unchecked, and when the first wave reached the foot of the redoubts the men gave a wild cheer as they swept up the slope and came to grips with the Turk. It was a desperate struggle, but there are no troops in the world so resistless with the bayonet as the British; and though the assault was delivered at the key-point of the battle by a force numerically weaker than that of the defenders, our men gained the Turkish trenches, an exhausted but cheering crowd.

The Gurkhas and Black Watch reached their objectives almost at the same moment. The Gurkhas took nearly 200 prisoners in the north redoubt, where the enemy's resistance was not so stubborn. But in the Dujail Redoubt the Turks gave and asked no quarter. The Black Watch had cleared this strong point at 6.45 A.M.; a quarter of an hour afterwards the Turks threw in a heavy counter-attack and reoccupied the greater part of the position. Once more they were evicted by the Highlanders, and at 7.15 A.M. the redoubt was in British hands. But the Turk was not yet beaten. He launched counter-attack after counter-attack along the banks of the Dujail, and it was not until after an hour and three-quarters' hand-to-hand fighting, bombing and bayoneting, that we held the north bank of the canal unchallenged. The 9th Bhopals in their flanking movement overshot their objective and came under a staggering fire from the banks of the Dujail. Two hundred fell in ten minutes; they lost all their officers but one.

South of the canal one company of the 28th Punjabis advanced in line with the 21st Brigade. The Seaforths on their left launched their attack some three hours later, and, advancing splendidly over the level plain, drove the enemy from his first-line trench. The intention in pressing in first on the right with the 21st Brigade was to give the enemy's line of retreat a bias to the left, driving him on to our cavalry and away from the water, and also to distract his attention as much as possible from the troops who had to advance over more open ground. But the Turk continued to hold on all day, and it was not until early on the morning of the 22nd that our patrols reported he had evacuated the position.

The first battle of Istabulat was a stubbornly fought action. The fighting was stiff all along the line, but the Turks hung on to the Dujail Redoubt as though their continued existence in Asia depended on it. The railhead was at stake; and this, strategically, was more important than Baghdad. The Black Watch lost ten officers (five killed or died of wounds) in their assault on the position. They had lost the same number of officers, and almost as heavily in men, at Mushaidie a month before. After sixteen months of Mesopotamia and over a year of France the spirit of the battalion was as unquenchable as ever. It shone forth memorably at Istabulat in Private Charles Melvin. When the leading company of the regiment were waiting for reinforcements within thirty or forty yards of the main position of the enemy, this gallant Scot rushed forward with a shout that stirred his comrades and terrified the Turk. The gods favoured his pluck, for he was not hit as he fired six rounds into the trenches, dropping his man with nearly every bullet. Away back in the early stages of the advance, when his company came under shrapnel in the open plain, his bayonet had been hit. It would not fix on his rifle. But with his rifle in one hand and his bayonet in the other he leapt into the Turkish trench. Most of the Turks fled in terror at the sight of this cheering, yelling, slaughtering Scotsman, but eight or nine remained, cowering. These he bustled into surrender with his bayonet flourished in his hand. He bundled nine unwounded Turks out of the trench and three wounded. One of the wounded, his own victim, he bandaged and lifted over the parapet, giving him a shoulder back to the British lines as he drove the other eleven in front of him. Then he returned with ammunition to the trenches and reported himself to the platoon commander. I have quoted the adventures of Private Melvin, for of such are the traditions of a regiment made. It is not merely the contagion of the moment that tells. The inspiration is communicated and renewed. There will be something of Melvin in the collective spirit of the battalion long after his great-grandsons' day.

Many tales of chivalry will be found in the regimental records of Istabulat. There is a story of a Jharwa in the 8th Gurkhas, an aboriginal of Assam, who became detached and achieved great things on his own, though wounded in the head, proving the small black man of the woods to be the equal of seven Turks. This disproportion is on the face of it absurd in the light of permanent values. If victory gave us moments of superhumanity, it was the reward of the long, close grip in which the spirit of the opponent was gradually crushed. The Turks we were fighting were not an inferior breed; only we had shaken their moral. Istabulat was won by the same troops on earlier fields. An advance of the kind against a strong position over 2,000 yards of flat could not have been driven home in the Sannaiyat or El Hannah phase, when the Turk was confident and contemptuous. And this should be borne in mind by those who underestimate the quality of the troops opposed to Townshend. The Turks were made to feel the irresistibility of the 6th Division in the early stages of the advance; the ascendancy of Townshend and his men was moral; and moral, as we are constantly reminded, counts as three to one against mere physical resource in the essentials of victory. Happily the ratio is not so certain in its application to British troops; or rather it would be a mistake in an enemy to presume any weakening of fibre in defeat. These Highland regiments were as magnificent in the third attack on Sannaiyat as at Mushaidie and Istabulat. Jock does not go in much for degrees of moral; he is, if anything, more dangerous when he is down than when he is up on top, and this is true of most British ranks, as it was of the Turk—up to a point. It is in reverse, discouragement and disaster that the spirit of the British army most shines forth. If one looks for the top and crest of heroism, one will find it in the men who made the forlorn and doomed attack on Sannaiyat on April 22nd (1916), or in the men who walked into the mouth of hell at Dujaila, on March 8th (1916), with no hope, or incentive other than stark discipline.

The Turk, as we have seen, stood a deal of hammering, and he was not beaten yet. In the night the 18th Corps retired to another position in front of the Samarrah railway station, which they had evidently prepared to hold. The position ran along a ridge of pebbly ground which commanded the open plain, and more severe fighting was necessary to capture it. After the fighting on April 21st, when the first Istabulat position was captured, the 28th Brigade marched through the advanced troops and kept in touch with the enemy, who were preparing to make a stand the following day. It was mid-day on the 22nd when the Brigade headquarters reached the ruins of old Istabulat, and here, as from the Median wall behind them on the previous day, they could see the whole battlefield spread out before them, the flat roof of the railway station several miles distant, the golden dome of the mosque of Samarrah flashing in the noonday sun, and the curious spiral tower that rises high above the surrounding landscape. The terrain slopes gradually up towards these distant landmarks, none of which was within the battle zone, until it reaches a series of undulating mounds and sharply defined ridges which run from the river to the railway station. On these ridges the Turks had elected to make their last fight for Samarrah.

Soon after mid-day our infantry were in touch with the main body of the Turks in an entrenched position between the river and the railway. The position was too extended to be bombarded and assaulted on the whole front with the guns and infantry at our disposal. It was therefore decided to force back the Turkish left from the river while the cavalry worked round on the right flank preceded by a battery of light armoured cars.

It was afternoon when the 28th Brigade began their advance. The Leicesters led the attack. They had not gone far when they came in for heavy enfilade fire from the left. Here the 51st Sikhs, who were in support, came up and swung half left to cover their flank. The 51st lost heavily, but their steady advance enabled the Leicesters to proceed, though the cross-fire was still troublesome. By 1.80 they had advanced 1,200 yards, and were near the ridge held by the Turks. At four o'clock our guns opened a tremendous fire on the trenches, and the weight of metal poured in on the Turk was augmented by the artillery of General Thomson's column, which had moved up on the left bank and enfiladed the enemy's trenches from across the river with deadly effect, and shelled him in the rear almost as far back as Samarrah.

As soon as the guns lifted, the Leicesters swept forward up the slope. An officer on the spot told me it was the most inspiring, whole-hearted charge he had ever seen. And apparently the Turk thought so, too, for he did not wait for the bayonet. The leading company reached the first summit tired and winded, but still game. The Turkish trenches were crossed without a check. The sight of the enemy bolting and holding up his hands was too much for Thomas Atkins; he threw caution to the winds and pressed on in pursuit. Soon the flash of artillery was seen through the dust, and they knew they were right on the guns. The heat was intense, but such a moment was not to be lost. Exhausted, breathless, scorched by the sun and thirsty to the point of desperation, the first wave of pursuing infantry raced on and did not halt till they burst over a battery of astonished gunners in a depression a full fifteen hundred yards beyond the trench. The captain of the leading company was too hoarse even to call on the commander of the battery to surrender. His revolver was empty. His men were close at hand, but few in number. The battery commander came forward, shook the British officer by the hand, and surrendered with fifty or sixty men and seven guns. Other guns were seen hurriedly retreating on the plain, and it looked as if the enemy were in full flight. This was about five o'clock. The three advanced companies of the Leicesters began to consolidate their position, but they had been carried on beyond the immediate reach of their supports, who had, in fact, been diverted to deal with the enfilading fire from the left.

When Shefket Pasha heard of the loss of his seven guns he began to reconsider his position, and a halt was called in what appeared to be a precipitate retreat. The Turkish Commander took careful stock of the situation. The Leicesters had been carried beyond the original objective, lured by the flash of the guns that invited capture. The ground to their rear was swept by gun and rifle fire, shrapnel and high explosive. Their weakness must have been apparent. A bare three companies—and it was sheer gallant bluff that had given them the guns. Shefket Pasha was taking no risks. He had brought up his reserve of two or three thousand men, and went straight for the nullah where the guns had been lost. The small handful of Leicesters could not hope to hold up such a counter-attack. The supports were still far behind, and there was no means of getting the guns away. There was nothing to do but to damage them as much as they could, retire on their supports and dig themselves in. Later in the night they had the chagrin of hearing their trophies being hauled back to the Turkish lines.

The Turks counter-attacked in very great force, and at one time threatened to roll up the flank of the brigade. The wave was held up by the 56th Rifles and a machine-gun company. The 56th advanced against the counter-attack with a steadiness and coolness which even in these days of hard fighting was memorable. Two companies of the 53rd Sikhs who had been in reserve with them lost their C.O. (Grafton), second in command (Adams), Adjutant (Blewitt), and Quartermaster (Scarth). The 56th and 53rd lost heavily, but they and the machine-gun company saved what might have been a very critical situation.

The V.C. of Istabulat was Lieutenant Graham, of the 186th Machine-Gun Company. Lieutenant-Colonel Pessick, of the 56th Rifles, who was a hundred yards behind and saw him dragging his guns over the traverses, has given me an account of Graham's action which ought to be preserved :

"Graham volunteered to go with us with two guns. The Turks left their trench when our leading line was 500 yards away, and it was occupied with little loss. Our first line pressed on, but while in the open the Turkish main counter-attack reached the railway embankment and shot down practically the whole of our first line. Fortunately Graham's machine guns and our second and third lines had reached the trench, and they opened a hot fire on the Turks. Their officers could not induce the men to come over the embankment. I consider that the presence of the machine-gun detachment contributed greatly to this. The position, however, was very critical. The embankment was some 200 yards away from the left of our line, and to make matters worse, a party got through a culvert, 200 yards in rear of our position, and fired into the backs of our men. The Indian officer in command on the left faced his men about and sent word to Graham asking for help. One machine gun was already out of action, but Graham brought over the other to the threatened point. I was just behind the trench, and saw him bringing the gun over to the left. The trench was traversed and very narrow, and he had to carry the gun over each traverse in the open, as the trench was blocked with men. He was wounded twice. Finally he got his gun over to the left, but all his detachment except his orderly had been hit. I believe he fired the gun himself, but was wounded again. He then removed the lock of the gun and made his way back to where I was, wounded for the fourth time. He handed me the lock and explained the situation as far as he knew it. Just before I left him he collapsed from loss of blood.

"His hand was bound up, his cheek had been laid open by a bullet, we found another wound high up in his thigh, and he had stuffed a handkerchief under his puttee to staunch a wound in his calf. I thought he had two other wounds, but I cannot remember now. There was too much to think of at the time."

To turn to our left flank on the west side of the railway, Colonel Cassels had moved from bivouac early in the morning south of Al Khubn with the object of turning the enemy's right flank near the junction of the Aj Jali and Izhaki canals. The brigade was reinforced by some extra guns and by armoured cars which went ahead reconnoitring as far as Samarrah station.

Moving north-west from Main Ridge on the Aj Jali canal over an open plain, slightly undulating, but offering little or no cover from view, the brigade was intermittently, and at times heavily, shelled, but with little effect. A wrecked hostile aeroplane was passed on the way, destroyed in a duel by one of our airmen, with the German pilot lying dead beside it. The enemy's advanced infantry scouts and pickets between the railway and Aj Jali canal, in reality a low, shingly, waterless ridge, were gradually driven in, and, as they retired over the open ground, offered good targets to our guns, which played on them with effect.

Near the junction of the two canals the enemy stood in a prepared position running astride the ridge and with rifle pits thrown out at intervals to join up with the railway. He had been reinforced to meet our enveloping movement, and, with machine guns in position, and supported by artillery, he barred our way up the canal, the only covered approach; the complete lack of cover and the exhaustion of the gun teams precluded a wider turning movement on our part.

In the afternoon, under cover of gun and machine-gun fire, and supported by the armoured motor cars, renewed efforts were made to gain ground on the flank. The Turk, however, stood firm. Finally a most gallant attempt by the 32nd Lancers to capture the position by a *coup de main* was all but successful. The Lancers charged over and beyond the enemy's trench, and the Turks occupying it threw down their rifles and surrendered, or doubled back in confusion. The enemy was apparently on the move, and had the armoured motor cars been in close support, as the Lancers believed, their flank must have been turned. But, once beyond the trench, our cavalry came under heavy machine-gun fire, the Turks rallied, and the assault was driven back. Colonel Griffiths, in command of the 32nd, and Captain Hunter, the Adjutant, fell leading the charge; the losses of the regiment were heavy. Yet the assault was not without its value in the action. Apart from the splendid spirit it showed, it was of material assistance to the infantry brigade at the very moment when the Turkish counter-attack was threatening to develop into serious proportions. The activity of the cavalry on his right acted as a caution to Shefket, and he was content with recovering his guns and retiring.

But the thing which frightened the Turk more than

anything else, and determined his retirement, was the artillery of our column on the left bank. Our batteries across the river wrought bloody execution on their flank and rear all day. In the evening they were recalled to the Shatt-el-Adhaim fight, but Shefket had every reason to believe that, if he dallied, they would be in Samarrah before him.

The ground we had gained in the main attack on the riverside was made good. The guns we had taken had been recaptured, but we had put them out of action, and soon after the Turks' counter-attack the 19th Brigade arrived to support the garrison. Before darkness fell the position was consolidated. The Turks retreated in the night. We continued the pursuit at dawn and occupied Samarrah station, the enemy falling back on Tekrit. Their outposts faced us across fifteen miles of desert throughout the long Mesopotamian summer.

The railway station, goods sheds, and workshops were gutted. We expected to find the locomotives and rolling stock destroyed, but the Turks had evidently determined to defend Samarrah at all costs, and their reluctance to quit did not give them time to complete their work of demolition. Among the spoils of war were a number of broad-gauge engines and trucks, all more or less damaged, but some were repaired, and in a few days trains were running between Baghdad and railhead made up entirely of the plant they had left us.

Samarrah became our advance summer quarters. The temperature rose to 119 degrees in the shade, but Force D, with all its objectives gained, had earned such rest as the sun and flies and sandstorms permitted—and the preparations that had to be made against a great enemy offensive in the autumn. During the fighting in April they had defeated the 18th Turkish Army Corps three times, and the 18th Corps five times, driving it back over sixty miles. Within the month our columns on both banks of the Tigris had captured 8,000 prisoners and sixteen guns. The same troops which had been engaged almost continuously since our first advance on December 18th achieved these results, exposed all the while to the hardships of a desert campaign, and fighting in their winter clothing under the fierce heat of a Mesopotamian sun.

Samarrah has seen the making of much history, and we felt that it would see more. Julian lies buried there. He fell near by, in the retreat from Ctesiphon, and the tomb of the Emperor is visible from the walls of the city, a mound of earth encircled by a ditch, a crumbling memorial of the death of Rome's Empire in the East. The place is historic, too, in that it has witnessed the end of a spiritual sway on earth. The twelfth Imam disappeared here in some obscure cellar of the town, and will rise again—the Shiahs say—and many look for his advent on the spot. And then the Hun came and laid his defiling hand on Samarrah, branding it as an outpost of Kultur. So here the two forces faced one another, and the struggle at hand was pregnant with issues deciding the system, philosophy, or religion of the life to be lived after the war.

CHAPTER XXXVII

THE BLOSSOMING OF THE DESERT

ANOTHER hot weather lay before us, for most of us the second summer in Mesopotamia, and for a few hardy veterans the third. The sun was more malignant in 1917 than it had been in either of the two previous years, and the dog-days began a month earlier. According to the Baghdadis it was the hottest season in the memory of man. Most things were too hot to touch. The rim of a tumbler burnt one's hand in a tent. The dust and sand burnt the soles of one's feet through one's boots. Even the hardy Arab and Kurd made such an outcry that one had to water the ground where they worked.

In July the temperature rose to 122.8 degrees in Baghdad and 122 degrees in Basra. In tents and dug-outs it was often ten degrees higher than the standardised official reading. And I gathered a great deal of collective evidence, from persons otherwise normally truthful, of even higher readings. But these I will not record, for it is hard to believe that anything save a salamander could live through such heat.

The health of nearly everyone in Mesopotamia broke down at one time or another. In my own case, after sundry spells of hospital, I was definitely immobilised a few days after the meeting with the Russians at Kizil Robat. I missed the advance on Samarrah as well as the Shatt-el-Adhaim fighting.

The moment of waking on a still, hot-weather morning in Mesopotamia is one of the least pleasant of the day. The air is charged with apprehension, just as the waiting room at a dentist's is sometimes more depressing than the actual chair in which one submits to his severities. Happily, the nights are generally cool and the mornings fresh, however burning the days; but when the north wind drops or, worse, when there is a south wind bringing up the moisture from the Gulf, it is hateful when one is awakened by the sun to think of the day in front of one.

At the end of May, 1917, when I left Baghdad, the mornings were still tolerable, but the sun was taking hold. We were all, according to the custom of the country, sleeping on the roof. Early in April the housetops were deserted, but in May every Baghdadi, man, woman, or child, ascended to the roof to sleep. When one woke in the morning one overlooked a sea of beds. The well-to-do lay in four-posters with mosquito curtains; the poor on hard benches with a mattress thrown over them. The three families who lived in the small house next door to our mess had twenty-eight children. These were disposed with the dozen odd grown-ups in ten large square beds like wooden platforms fenced with rails to prevent the smaller fry from falling out. The searching for insects that went on in the morning suggested disturbed nights.

On one roof was a lamb; on another a promenading turkey. And there was generally a stork on the neighbouring minaret standing above the head of the muezzin as he uttered his call to prayers and flapping his wings in accompaniment to the man's beating of the breast. One bird had a nest on a Christian church in view, and she defended it fiercely against invaders. Then, having asserted her dignity and modesty, she would throw back her offended neck, clack her beak, and emit her machine-gun rattle.

That was in April and May. When I returned early

in September the lamb and the turkey had gone; even the storks had taken themselves off; but the men and matrons and the teeming children remained—they had apparently increased. I was immensely thankful that for the two hottest months of the year, July and August, I had escaped, and that instead of the panorama of Baghdad *en déshabillé* the first thing that greeted my eyes in the morning had been a Himalayan forest. Even the September heat was oppressive. The first twelve days of the month were eight degrees above normal, and the atmosphere was moist and sticky—114 degrees by the official reading, and 118 degrees in some of the offices and billets.

Most of the houses in the city are provided with a *serdab*, or cellar, sunk some six feet under the ground level. The temperature in these *serdabs* is generally ten degrees lower than in the rooms of the first floor, and one is glad to escape to them, though the air is close and oppressive. The ventilating shafts which run up from the cellar to the roof end in hoodlike cowls, and all point the same way to catch the shamal, or prevailing north wind, which alone conveys any alleviation that the gods may provide.

Up in Baghdad and Samarrah the nights generally bring relief, but in Basra one often fidgets restlessly through them with little sleep, fighting the sandflies. The official reading when I passed through was 115 degrees; six weeks earlier it had been 122 degrees. That was a dry heat. Basra suffers most when a lazy south wind, the date wind of September, under which the crops ripen, rolls up the moisture from the Gulf and then drops, leaving a humid film in the air which suffocates one like a blanket until the wind changes. A clamminess pervades everything. Even inanimate material things seem to sweat in this air. To imagine it one must wrap one's head in hot pudding cloths and one's chest in mustard plasters.

The period from May to the end of September was recognised in the force as "the close season for the Turks." We and they bowed to a common enemy and dug deeper into the earth. We æstivated, in fact, just as the old Romans used to hibernate. Yet, though serious military operations were out of the question, we put in a deal of spade-work. The spirit of the troops was high. They had accomplished great things and achieved victory out of defeat. The gallant and enduring 7th Division were holding the ground they had won, and it was their dearest wish that the Turks would be emboldened in the hot weather to descend and attack them. "The more the merrier" was the verdict of Sergeant Macnabb. "It would be a welcome change for the boys to see the old Turkey-cock hopping the parapet."

On the Diala side there was movement in June and again in August, but happily no fighting. It will be remembered that after the meeting with the Cossacks in the first week of April we fell back on Baquba to shorten our line. Early in June, on account of the increasing heat and the difficulty of supplies, the Russians found it necessary to evacuate the line of the Diala River, and they withdrew beyond Kerind towards Kermanshah. This withdrawal necessitated a forward move on our part, and on June 23rd we occupied Beled Ruz without encountering any opposition. Then early in August our airmen reported that the Turks were entrenching a position south-west of Shahraban. In order to dislodge them and to occupy the town, which we could not afford to leave in the hands of the enemy, two converging columns were dispatched from Beled Ruz and Baquba on the night of the 18th-19th. On the 19th Misdad was seized at dawn, and on the 20th Shahraban. The Turk decamped hastily on to Jebel Hamrin and left us in possession.

The attack on Ramadi in July was the only movement in the hot weather of 1917 which involved both marching and fighting. On July 8th we advanced our line on the Euphrates from Feluja, a few miles upstream, to the high ground on the right bank at Dhibban, which dominates the left bank of the river at its junction with the Saklawie Canal. This move was necessary for the control of irrigation and inundation. The enemy at the time were holding Ramadi lightly with a force estimated at 1,000 rifles and some Arab irregulars, and as the advance to Dhibban brought us within striking distance, General Maude thought the opportunity favourable for attacking him with a view to covering our forward movement. But the elements defeated us. Our column was in touch with the Turk early on the morning of the 11th, and had made some progress in the assault, when, on account of a duststorm which interrupted communications, both wireless and land line, the order for the attack was cancelled. The day marked the beginning of an abnormal heat wave, abnormal even in a land where the sun is an habitual scourge. Men in camps and officers leading sedentary lives were struck down with sunstroke or heat exhaustion; to march or fight under these conditions was to invite disaster.

On the night of the 11th-12th the force withdrew to the river bank at Mushaid, and as the Turks showed no signs of evacuating their position, they fell back on Dhibban on July 14th. The casualties from the heat were almost as heavy as in the bloodless, but costly, occupation of the Sinn position in May, 1916. The moral drawn from the frustrated advance on Ramadi in July was that nothing save the very gravest military urgency justifies an offensive in a Mesopotamian midsummer.

Peace was yet a long way off, but it was comforting to think that the war which had let loose destruction in Europe was bringing new life to Mesopotamia. The settlement and development of the country kept pace, as we advanced, with the occupation. The Political

Officer, in most cases a soldier, arrived on the scene with the troops—sometimes, as in the Euphrates area between Samawa and Feluja, before them; and an hour or two after the Turk had decamped, while the white flags still fluttered on the walls, he would be holding court and the Arabs would be bringing him their petitions and complaints, as if it were the most natural thing in the world.

In Baghdad a year of occupation had brought many changes. The city was dead to all appearances, or moribund, when we entered it on the 11th of March, 1917. Now it is a bustling hive of humanity. Thousands of workmen pass through the streets early and late. The main thoroughfare, metalled and lighted, is a constant stream of traffic; the sleepiest old women who haunt the bazaars have become adepts at dodging the Ford van. A police force has been organised, and a fire brigade. The street lamps have given place to electric lights. The water supply has been extended. Electric lighting and electric fans have been introduced into offices and billets. Mosques have been repaired, roads metalled, schools opened, including a survey school, and a training school for teachers. Water-carts ply in the streets; sanitary squads have penetrated the most hidden purlieus of the city; smells have been exorcised. Galled, injured, sick and starved animals are received into a home until they are fit for shaft or pack again. The markets are controlled; the grain supply has been taken in hand; the prices are moderate; the municipality pays its way, and the Tigris is crossed by two bridges.

These are only some of the outward changes, and though most of them affect the Baghdadi and the British and Indian soldier alike, they are probably little noticed by the army of occupation. The soldier in the street, if asked if he marked much change in the city, would probably say that it looked cleaner, smelt less, and seemed more alive. He might remark upon the good behaviour and contented appearance of the citizens, but it is doubtful if he would associate these conditions with the work of the Administration—with the Police, the Revenue or Judicial Department, the Municipality, the reorganisation of the Courts, the provision for agricultural and garden developments, and the control of grain and markets in those lean months when we had to feed the civil population. Least of all is the soldier in the street likely to grasp the complicated nature of the machinery we have been getting into gear, the complex relations of labourer, tenant, landowner and State, the difficulty of adjusting their rights, and of assessing property and taxes with no revenue registers or land records to go upon. Yet all this is being done, and a system is being evolved, based on what is sound in existing organisations. We have adopted and modified these to meet the new needs, preserving as far as possible local traditions and employing native agency.

To realise the difficulties of the civil administration one needs at least a superficial acquaintance with the system of our predecessors. One has always known that the territories subject to the Osmanli lie dead under his hands; that the Turk has not yet repaired the ravages of his ancestor, Hulagu; and that the blight where he governs is as certain as famine after drought. In Mesopotamia a comparison of the present with the past proves him the greatest sterilising agent the world has known. Every ancient embankment where ran some fertilising canal, every relic of the civilised generations that preceded him, every barren, treeless acre on the Tigris bank is an indictment of him and a reproach.

The Turk is a Providence for himself only, and that only for the hour. An Ottoman Governor of a province that nature intended to be fruitful is like a greedy, hungry, and irresponsible child left in charge of the jam cupboard and pantry—mere appetite without provision. There is an authentic tale of a Turkish administrator who boasted that his budget showed no expenditure at all, but consisted entirely of receipts. All the officials from the Mutasarrif down drew no pay, but lived on questionable perquisites, while repairs, maintenance, public works, were neglected. The Turk is a conservative without the art of conservation. In his character of a destroyer he is fond of felling trees, but he never plants them. He is pleased with expensive, civilised toys, but as quick to forget and neglect them as a child. Thus for mechanics and aviators he was largely dependent on the Hun. He will order the most up-to-date medical appliances, and leave them to rust in his hospitals, where the patients are lying in the most filthy and insanitary surroundings with their wounds septic and undressed. You would think that sterilisation was a cult with him. In Mesopotamia the Ottoman Government had evolved an excellent and elaborate agricultural system on paper, but in practice it did not work. It was the same with education. It was found upon investigation that many of the schools referred to in the files of the Department existed only on the map. Baghdad, a city with a population of over 200,000, boasted only four Government school buildings. As for instruction, the attempt to suppress the indigenous Arabic with its traditions of culture and learning and to introduce Turkish in its place was in keeping with the general policy of blight. Turkish, too, was the language of the Law Courts, though it was a tongue not understood by the mass of the population. The Judicial system, like the Revenue and Educational, was excellent on paper, but in fact the salaries paid to the judges and the subordinate staff were so inadequate that it was impossible for a decent standard of honesty and efficiency to be maintained.

But the Revenue Department more than any other

branch of the Administration was responsible for the general blight. The Turkish system was to farm out districts to the Sheikhs. A Sheikh would offer such and such a sum for the land watered by a certain canal and its affluents. The purchaser was given no security of tenure, and so was not encouraged to effect improvements. The high rates forced him to grind down the cultivator. The system was as vicious politically as it was economically, for the Turkish Government ruled by dividing, rousing the hostility of one Sheikh against another by making them bid for one another's districts.

Patronage was one of the most valuable sources of a Wali's income. The revenue officials received a nominal salary. Their aim was to enrich themselves, to remit as much money as possible to Constantinople, and to invest as little as possible in public works and agricultural development. In Mesopotamia, owing to the effects of continual misgovernment and the lack of control of irrigation, the area cultivated and the yield harvested varied from year to year. Thus there crept in the evil of the fluctuating assessment. The assessor took just as much as he thought he could exact, and was indifferent whether the fellah was left a living wage. The natural consequence of the system was to discourage outlay and initiative. It amounted to a tax on improvements, as the cultivator experimented at his own risk; he was out of pocket if he failed, whereas the greater part of his profits was absorbed in revenue if he succeeded.

The stock-in-trade of the successful assessor was optimism—a high appreciation of the value of crops. It was a fluent and not a stable optimism, and the assessor was open to disillusionment at a price. Mahmoud Effendi, visiting the fields of the cultivator, Ali Ibn Hussein, would hold up his hands in wonder. "Marvellous!" he would exclaim. "I have never seen better crops in my life—a yield of 400 to the hectare at least." The cultivator would receive this compliment with a wry face. "Alas! not 40!" he would protest. After a little discussion profitable to the assessor the difference between 400 and 40 might be reduced in favour of the cultivator. The assessor might even be induced to write down 40 in his book if the cultivator were prepared to pay; but the price of depreciation would not leave much in hand for the payment of the modest tax. Nor could Ali Ibn Hussein evade the revenue collector. If he were slow in paying his dues a body of mounted gendarmerie would be sent to stay with him, and he would have to feed these guests and their horses until it was borne in on him that it was cheaper to pay.

It will be gathered that the Arab has benefited by our presence in Mesopotamia; even allowing a large margin for mistakes, we must have done more for him in a couple of years than Turkish reformers have accomplished in a century. But it must not be supposed that he welcomed us with open arms. The Asiatic as a rule dislikes an alien tutelage, no matter what gifts it may bring; and the reality as well as the name of independence is becoming more important to his peace of soul. To the Christian population in Mesopotamia the British occupation was undoubtedly a godsend, but we must discount a great deal of the smug nonsense that has been written about the Arab eagerly waiting for the British to deliver him from the yoke of the Turk. He cares for neither of us; both are intruders. It is true that the Turk as a member of the dominant race was an unpleasant person to deal with, but the Arab often got even with him. We on the other hand are admittedly efficient and men of good faith. But the Arab does not appreciate these gifts so much as he would if he were a European; in all the simple contracts of life the Asiatic will feel more at home with the Asiatic.

Yet there is one thing that will bind the settled Arab

The Blossoming of the Desert

cultivator, or fellah, to the alien official with hoops of steel. Bring the water to his land; make his crops grow, and leave him to enjoy them in peace, and he will go far out of his way to requite you. He will drag you into his mud tower or into his black goat-hair tent as you pass. He will make coffee for you and entreat you to stay and partake of his *pillau;* and his hospitality will be the measure of his love.

The first time I came on a large area in which the Arabs were demonstrative in their friendliness was in the district between Roumethwa and Diwaniyeh, where before the war the white man was seldom seen. It was early in February, 1918, but the great Euphrates irrigation scheme had already changed the face of the desert, and green corn was sprouting everywhere.

The peaceful penetration of the Euphrates from Feluja to Hilleh began in April, 1917, a month after we entered Baghdad. Before the Turk was finally routed on the Tigris we had begun to tap the resources of the Euphrates. For months during the hot weather the roads from Hilleh and Museyib to Baghdad were obscured by the dust of camel and donkey convoys bringing in corn. Arab levies were raised to police the roads, villages, and towns; and the country was cleared of bands of marauders. During the summer we were at work on the irrigation scheme connected with the Hindieh barrage. The barrage, which was designed by Sir William Willcocks and constructed by Sir John Jackson's firm, was finished before the war; but the Turk by his supineness neglected to profit by it. The canalisation work connected with it was left incomplete, and the area to be cultivated was never brought under irrigation.

The Euphrates divides at Hindieh into two branches, the Shatt-el-Hilleh to the east and the Shatt-el-Hindieh to the west, and the two channels of the river meet again a few miles above Samawa. Until the nineteenth century the Hilleh branch carried the main channel, but during the last century the bulk of the river has been diverted to the Shatt-el-Hindieh, which was the main channel more than a thousand years ago. The function of the barrage was to provide water for the Hilleh branch, which was silting up, while the bed of the Hindieh branch was scouring out and its water was being wasted. A month or two after we got to work on it nearly a hundred canals on the Hilleh branch which had fallen into disuse were dug out; three hundred thousand acres were brought under cultivation; and the summer of 1918 saw the greatest harvest in the memory of man, possibly the greatest since the days of Nebuchadnezzar.

But the Shatt-el-Hilleh developments were only part of the scheme. For several years the land on both banks of the Hindieh branch below the barrage down to Kifl had been out of cultivation, as the canals provided in the Willcocks scheme to irrigate that area were neglected. We were not long in getting to work at them. In May, 1917, as soon as the Tigris operations were completed, we began to open posts on the Euphrates. The work on the canals was started early in June; they were finished by the end of October, and the ground they irrigate is now under cultivation. There was a gap in our communications between Nasiriyeh and Hilleh in the hot weather, but we bridged it in the autumn, establishing posts south of Hilleh and north of Nasiriyeh, so that we administered the whole country from Basra as far as our arms extended. It was a singularly peaceful penetration.

Needless to say, the Arab cultivators welcome the new regime. Their property, which had lain fallow for years, has become rich and profitable. All the summer and autumn they were busy getting their water channels clear. Below the barrage some 14,000 Arabs were engaged in making the new canals and clearing the old ones. Nearly every able-bodied man in the district was working

The Blossoming of the Desert

for us. The irrigation works at Hindieh affect the land from Feluja upstream above the barrage as well as downstream as far as Kifl on the Hindieh branch, and Diwaniyeh on the Hilleh branch. The whole scheme puts many thousands of acres under irrigation for wheat and barley. A great part of this is Government land (*sanniyah*), from which the Government share is a third of the harvest.

Thus nearly two-thirds of the grain collected for the army is in the form of revenue. The first charge on all land brought under cultivation is a return in kind for the expenditure in seed provided for the sowing and the necessary advance to the cultivators.

The effect of the work on which we were engaged on the Euphrates was far-reaching. The irrigation scheme brought in enough grain to feed the whole of the forward army, it reduced the tonnage required for foodstuffs on the lines of communication by thousands of tons, and freed rolling stock and river transport for ordnance and other supplies—not to speak of the economy that the development of local produce effected in overseas shipping. At the same time our blockade posts on the two rivers were preventing stuff getting through to the enemy while collecting and sending in supplies to our troops. Then there is the political side to the Euphrates development, which will be ultimately, if not immediately, as important. Not only have rich lands lain fallow and canals fallen into disuse owing to the unsettled state of the country; in the disturbed zones of concentration crops have been laid waste by the Turks, and stores of grain unearthed and wantonly destroyed. Now, while we are feeding ourselves we are enriching the cultivators and bringing in settlement and content where neither existed before.

The Arabs are an eminently sensible people. The Turks when they evacuated the district were for destroying the Hindieh barrage, but the tribesmen preserved it.

They removed the woodwork from the bungalows, and all the brass and copper; they cut out the belting of the engines and looted everything that was handy; but they left the barrage and the regulator of the Hilleh channel intact. There was potential virtue in it, and their prudence has been justified.

The Arab knew the Turk would do nothing for him, and he would not pay him revenue if he could help it; but the collection of revenue on the Euphrates no longer calls for an armed force. Paying taxes has become an investment. For there is no cultivator in the world who will not lend a hand at getting water on to his own fields. The Arabs appreciate the art of irrigation, though they do not excel in it; and we have come to them on the Euphrates as fertilisers of the soil. The old Sheikh was speaking from his heart when he said to one of our politicals, "No other Government but the British would take the trouble to bother about our water while they were fighting."

In February I went down the Hilleh branch as far at Samawa, and the Hindieh as far as Kifl and Kufa. The armies of men we met were busy with spades—the scoop on the long six-foot pole by which the Arab is eternally adjusting his irrigation channels and coaxing the water on to the fields. The rich belts of cultivation on the edge of the desert were refreshingly green. Everywhere the Sheikhs insisted that we should dine or drink coffee with them; and they dragged us into their mud towers and spread carpets for us by the hearth while they roasted and pounded and distilled the coffee, pouring it from one beaked pot to another with all the unction of a rite. Old memories of the Arabs were revived, their eagerness to entertain the stranger, and to sit and gossip with him, and the docility of their ponies, which will jump in and out of a boat like a cat or a dog and are just as much members of the family. We travelled by *bellum*, sailing when the wind was favourable, or on horseback, or by motor where there was a track, switchbacking over the innumerable bridges of the watercuts. It was a pleasant change after the desolate country through which we had slowly fought our way up the Tigris, and the best part of it was the visible and audible happiness of the Arabs. Our ponymen sang joyously as we rode over the uninspiring plain; and the chant of our boatmen at night was answered by the fellaheen singing to their buffaloes at the water lifts which had been creaking for months like drunken violins.

CHAPTER XXXVIII

THE BIBLE AND BABEL

THERE was abundant interest in the country we were occupying on the Euphrates, and whenever there was a lull in operations I generally found myself there. During the hot weather we held Feluja, and the Turks Ramadi. South of this we penetrated without opposition to Hilleh and Museyib and the Hindieh barrage, and our Politicals were established in Kerbela and Najaf. But we did not join up communications and occupy the country between Hilleh and Nasiriyeh until the cold weather. This district was almost clear of Turks. Only one small detachment, which had been left behind at Diwaniyeh in charge of the stores and the sick during the Turks' retirement from Samawa to Ramadi, still held out at the end of the summer.

In July a number of the garrison surrendered to the townspeople and were handed over to us, but a single officer and thirty men—most of them Tartars from the Caucasus—refused to yield. Mahomet Effendi, the leader of these die-hards, was a man sufficiently out of the ordinary to merit attention; in the human catalogue he would come under the genus "character." A lieutenant of the age of forty, he had risen from the ranks and had seen twenty years' service and three campaigns. He was a junior officer in the detachment at Diwaniyeh, but when he saw the garrison were melting away he took over command, arrested his superior officer and hanged him, shot two other officers with his revolver, and wounded three others, who made their escape. I had the story first from the political officer to whom in the end he surrendered and made his statement. My friend described Mahomet Effendi as "a jaunty fellow, his cap a little on one side, a bit of a swashbuckler." The man was a fire-eater. He had also the reputation of being something of a Don Juan. He had shot his brother officers, he explained, because they were like women, and traitors to the country and to military honour. It was disgraceful, he said, for a Turk to surrender to Arabs and civilians, and he ended his statement with "God is great."

Diwaniyeh was too far from any of our posts, and we had too much on our hands between March and September to open up communications and to send troops there. It was not until our aeroplanes came and bombed the serai which Mahomet Effendi and his Tartars were holding against the Arabs that he reconciled surrender with honour. When he gave himself up he prayed that he might be allowed to fight anywhere and in any capacity, with the Sherif of Mecca for choice, or in one of our Indian battalions. He was an old soldier, he explained, and a strong man, and he would always be found in the forefront of the battle.

Such was Mahomet Effendi's presentment of himself, and such he appeared to the Political—a subject worthy of Scott or Dumas, a Turk of the old school, standing head and shoulders above his associates. But one always likes to hear two or more sides to a story, and I wondered how he appeared to the Arabs and the people of Diwaniyeh. A few months after his surrender I was in this remote, and in those days unfrequented, town on the Hilleh branch of the Euphrates, and I met a Syrian who had been there when the detachment held the serai in a state of siege, and who had seen the erstwhile commandant dangling over the gate one morning attached by a rope to the end of a protruding beam. Mahomet Effendi, as may be imagined, provided much matter for gossip in the cafés and bazaar of this little backwater.

The Syrian showed me over the serai and pointed out the hole in the bricked floor where the other two officers had been buried, the well which Mahomet Effendi had dug when there was no longer a safe approach to the river, and the bullet marks in the sun-dried brick wherever the wall faced an aperture through which the casual besiegers could lodge a bullet. And he showed me the little room, one of a thousand such cubicles familiar in every serai, opening on to the veranda over the courtyard, a small whitewashed oblong room with alcoves in the wall —a bare fourteen feet by nine. Mahomet Effendi had acted with decision. He suddenly flung open the door of the little room, his revolver in his hand, his forty followers at his back, and opened fire on the group of officers as they sat on mattresses leaning back against the wall, chatting or playing cards. Two succumbed on the spot. The commandant jumped up and cried, holding up his hands: "Don't shoot me!" To which Mahomet Effendi answered ironically: "No. I will not shoot you." They caught him and tied him up and hanged him by a rope from the parapet of the roof, and when the Arabs passed in the morning they saw him dangling there.

The walls and floor of the room were discoloured with dried blood; the walls were pitted with bullet holes. Outside, in the veranda, there were more bullet holes, but this was mostly the work of the besiegers. The Arabs sat outside and fired in. When the garrison were hungry and supplies were running out they exchanged rifles and ammunition for food. Mahomet Effendi held out until the aeroplanes came and dropped bombs in the serai. He said in his statement that, being isolated, with his supplies cut off, he deemed it not dishonourable to surrender to the British; but to Arabs and civilians, never!

The Bible and Babel

Wishing to hear the local point of view, I asked the Syrian why Mahomet Effendi had shot his commandant. The man had no subtle argument to offer. He said quite simply: "Mahomet Effendi wanted to get on. He shot the commandant that he might have the command." And he added that it was not the first time that this fire-eating Turk had taken it on himself to shoot a superior officer on the charge of treason.

I suggested the more honourable motive. But the Syrian evidently thought the idea far-fetched. Mahomet Effendi would not surrender to Arabs, not because he thought it dishonourable, but because he thought it unsafe. He did not believe the Arabs would spare the garrison.

Another inhabitant of Diwaniyeh took the view that Mahomet Effendi shot his superior officer to gain distinction, to stand well in the eyes of the higher command. His estimate of the Effendi was very much the same as the Syrian's, and I discovered that this view was generally accepted in the town, though there were one or two who maintained that Mahomet was unquestionably mad. Honour or chivalry or patriotism as a motive never entered anyone's head.

Mahomet Effendi has disappeared from our ken. He is probably now in some prisoners' camp, and I often wonder what manner of man he was. Sometimes I think of him as a genuine, hard-bitten patriot, determined to fight to the last; at other times as a swashbuckling adventurer, posing as the man of honour and iron discipline, with his eye on the main chance all the while. Whatever his motives, Mahomet Effendi was a man of action, probably neither the hero, nor the boasting, unscrupulous blackguard he was painted. Whether it was that he thought surrender dishonourable or unsafe does not greatly matter. The point is that he made a clean sweep of deserters. One likes to think that there was something of the old Plevna spirit in him, that he was a game fighter, the kind of man who would spend his last cartridge in the last ditch.

The serai at Diwaniyeh was haunted by the ghosts of the unhappy Turks whom Mahomet Effendi had put out of the way. We were in the heart of Babylonia, and if the drama had been enacted four thousand years earlier it would no doubt have been given a chapter to itself in Holy Writ; the personality of Mahomet Effendi would have been painted in no doubtful colours, and his name would have been familiar to everyone in the force as the branded assassin or the divinely-appointed scourge. But as the Diwaniyeh incident happened only the other day it is doubtful if one in a thousand of us ever heard of his existence. There was drama enough for a second Pentateuch in one crowded week of Armageddon.

Nevertheless, our eyes were often on the past. The arid tracts where our own troops and General Allenby's were fighting, and the desert between, spanned the whole land of Holy Writ, from Jerusalem to Babylon, and from Babylon to Shush, the ancient Susa or the Shushan of the Bible. Our cavalry were camped by the tomb of Daniel in Persia, and our motors plied along the old Babylon-Ecbatana road. At Kufa on the Euphrates we had a supply dump not a hundred yards from the mosque which is built on the spot where Jonah was cast up by the whale.

I passed this historic spot when motoring from Najaf to Hilleh, and half an hour after leaving it behind we came upon another Biblical feature, a relic of Babylonian Jewry. The spire in the palm clump at Kifl beside the leaning and crumbling minaret is the tomb of Ezekiel, a shrine reverenced by Moslem and Jew alike. It is one of the few shrines in Mesopotamia that Christians may visit. The custodians invite you to enter, and clamour for backsheesh. The next relics one passes on the road belong to a dynasty and faith that have left no guardians to encourage or repel visitors. Bers Nimrud, the mound of debris on the left, with the rock-like brick foundations surmounting it, is, according to Arab tradition, all that remains of the Tower of Babel.

But here the archæologist comes in again with his disappointing researches and tells us that it is some newfangled modern erection built by Nebuchadnezzar on the site. The tower remains in view until one enters Hilleh. Here we are on surer ground. Scientific research and local tradition agree. Hilleh is an offshoot of Babylon, and Nebuchadnezzar's bricks stiffen the foundations. The excavations of the ancient city lie some five miles north of the town, and German savants will, or would if they were at large, point you out the pillars that supported the hanging gardens, and the identical chamber in which Belshazzar saw the writing on the wall.

One can motor from Babylon to Najaf before lunch and see all these concrete strata of history on the way. The Sumerian plain of Shinar and the Islamic plain of Kufa merge. Here the tragic drama of Mahomet's successors was played; and if the driver of the Ford van does not bother his head much about Jonah, Nebuchadnezzar, and Ezekiel, you may be sure the Moslem sepoy —especially if he is a Shiah—is gladdened by the sight of the authentic holy ground where Ali was slain, and the golden mosque at Najaf that marks his tomb.

The British soldier never developed the historic sense in Mesopotamia, or the romantic spirit. The land is not so rich in Biblical associations as Canaan, where Allenby's men were fighting the Turk a few hundred miles away on our flank. Students may discover traces of the Captivity when the Jews were carried away into Babylonia; and in the mounds of Ur of the Chaldees and Erech they may unearth bricks of the hoariest antiquity which have been submerged in more than one flood. The

Flood is a story easily credible in Mesopotamia. It so nearly repeated itself in the first two years of our struggle towards Baghdad. One can imagine the dove vainly seeking a perching-place between Kut and Ali Gharbi, and one feels it is only natural that the survivor who had the wit to save himself in the prototype of the craft we see on the Tigris to-day should imagine that he was divinely counselled, and hand down to posterity the legend of his rewarded merit. But the Flood is an older story than Noah. There are independent Sumerian and Babylonian legends preserved from a date long before the Hebrew legend of the Ark.

Those who survived the heat of July, 1917, can believe the story of Shadrach, Meshach, and Abednego; or if there is any doubt in their minds it must be about the artificial origin of the furnace. The Qurna-Eden legend is less credible. The scepticism of the private as to the genuineness of the myth is borne out by historical research. It appears that Qurna, the reputed site, had not emerged from the sea in the days of Nebuchadnezzar. Under the circumstances one cannot blame the trooper who made the remark about "the flaming sword" and who would not sacrifice the end of a "fag" to see the "Tree of the Knowledge of Good and Evil." Another disillusionment is that Ezra's Tomb is not really Ezra's tomb after all. Or, if the bones of the scribe lie beneath the plinth, they have been moved from the place where they were originally buried, for the tomb stood on the banks of the Tigris a thousand years ago, and since those days the river has changed its course. One's enthusiasm for antiquity was always being damped by the Higher Criticism.

Babel, if not true, is the best-found tale in Genesis, and one had witness of it every day. A new tongue is arising, to increase the original confusion, compact of English, Arabic, and French. An Arab asked me at Roumethwa where the new "shemin duffer" (*chemin de fer*) was going to be. The man of the desert calls our motors "stronbills" or "terumbils" (automobile), a truly onomatopœic word. The urchin who holds out a faked curio at Babylon asks you to buy an "antiqua." The contractor is the contratchi ("contrat" and -chi, the Turkish termination that implies "agent"). Abu, father, used as a prefix, conveys a hundred new designations. A gunboat is abu-sella, "father of a basket (conning tower)." A Staff officer is abu-ahmar, "father of red (tabs)"; a political officer, abu-abyadh, "father of white (tabs)"; just as a fat man is called "father of a belly," and a certain missionary in Beirut "father of a saucepan," by reason of his habitual top-hat.

At Aden, I hear, the Arabs have coined a verb from an English expletive, "damful-ni" to abuse, which is conjugated in all its moods and tenses, "I damfuled you," "he damfuled me," etc., with the Arab inflections. Similarly the Arabs of Mesopotamia have adapted our verb "to finish." It has spread from Basra to Samarrah and to the remotest villages of the desert. A familiar greeting from the Arab as we went up the Tigris was, "Turk finished," and it was always accompanied by an eloquent gesture of finality.

The British soldier, too, was broadening his vocabulary. Two of the commonest Arab words, "*imchi*," "go," and "*makoo*," "there is none—not to be had," were the first to be adopted. There was a small post on the Euphrates where the villagers were called "imchis" by the British rank and file. The word, with its djinn-like suggestion of disappearance, is very apt. I only know one instance in which the word *makoo* was applied to an individual, and that was Makoo Effendi of Ramadi, a picturesque, dignified old gentleman, a sort of general factotum, contractor and agent, whom we inherited from the Turk. He stands with the palms of his hands turned outwards and resting on his hips, his eye fixed on a far horizon, empty of hope, the personification of *makoo*. "If you talk about work," a subaltern said to me, "he falls all of a tremble and spins out *makoos* by the yard." In Basra you hear soldiers calling for a "bill-bellum." *Bellum* in Arabic is a boat, and *bill* the preposition "in"; but Thomas Atkins was never a purist, even in his own language, and I have heard a corporal of the Manchesters talking about "the domes and marionettes of Baghdad."

A popular misconception about this country has been dispelled. More than a year ago, as I lay on a truck in Sinn railway station, I heard a soldier explaining to his mates that Mesopotamia used to be the granary of the world, and that wheat and oats and barley and rye used to grow everywhere, and the cattle stood knee-deep in the grass. His companions were sceptical. "This here the granary of the world!" one of them said, "then why the —— 'ell ain't it the —— granary now?" But the praiser of past times was equal to this thrust. "Don't you know," he asked scornfully, "as how Judas ate the apple and Gawd cursed the —— land?"

There was, however, a wiser than he in the truck, for a third voice in the darkness explained, "Tworn't Judas, it was Eve as ate the —— apple, and don't you forget it, Mr. Know-all."

That was before we had taken Kut. Now, I think, if any of the three soldiers who discussed the origin of desolation in the railway truck at Sinn ever sees the country between Hindieh and Samawa he will admit that the curse brought upon the land by Judas or Eve, or whoever the malefactor may have been, is only partial in its blight. Mesopotamia is by way of becoming a very considerable granary yet.

But we found the country a land of death. The dead hand of the Turk is visible everywhere. The embankments of the ancient irrigation channels stand above the level of the country, high broken mounds some fifty yards apart, and beyond them generally a third mound where a new canal was dug when it was found easier to dig afresh than to go on scouring out the silt in the old channel. But the Turk, good hand as he is at a trench, neither digs nor causes others to dig with energy enough to fertilise the land; and these mounds on the desert horizon are witness of his wasted inheritance.

By the Tigris and Euphrates mortality is the most obvious thing that meets the eye as one rides abroad, but the deadest of dead things in this Mesopotamian waste is Babylon. I visited the place in September, 1917, with a local produce man, and even this officer, whose business it is to discover life in places ostensibly dead, could produce nothing living out of the ruins. The excavations lie on the left bank of the Shatt-el-Hilleh, the westerly of the two channels of the Euphrates which bifurcates at Hindieh. It is fifty-six miles from Baghdad. The old nursery rhyme that gives the distance to Babylon as three score miles and ten is only out by a bare four leagues, and one can get there between breakfast and lunch, if not "by candlelight."

Twenty years ago when I visited the site the ground was barely scratched by the professional excavator, though the robbers of bricks had been busy quarrying there for centuries. Modern Hilleh owes much to the kilns of Nebuchadnezzar, and the unstable Turkish barrage at Hindieh was built out of Babylonian debris. The excavations were begun by the German archæologists in March, 1899, and from 200 to 250 workmen were employed daily, winter and summer, until the war put an end to the work. The house of the mission stands on the banks of the Euphrates, and contains a museum which we have placed under an Arab guard. A concise summary of the work has been compiled by Professor Koldewey in "The Excavations of Babylon" (Macmillan, 1914). With the help of this volume with its illustrations and plans we were able to identify the main sites. The greater part of the city which the Germans have brought to light belongs to the comparatively modern period of Nebuchadnezzar (561-504 B.C.); but there are traces in the ruins left by the first Babylonian kings (*circa* 2500 B.C.), and successive strata reveal the streets and houses built by succeeding dynasties of the Assyrian, Neo-Babylonian, Persian and Græco-Parthian periods. Also there are relics that prove a pre-historic Babylon, but it is impossible to carry excavations down to this depth owing to the rise in the water level.

The city walls of Nebuchadnezzar, a triple rampart, the outer and inner walls including the wall of the fosse at the foot, are from 17 to 22 metres thick. Two teams of four horses abreast could pass each other on the outer barrier, and the walls were towered. The whole circuit, according to the evidence of the excavations, was 18 kilometres, but Ctesias gives four times and Herodotus nearly five times this circumference, and apart from these measurements the general description of the historians is accurate. The two flanks of the wall rested on the Euphrates and were extended on the other side, so that the city formed a triangle through which the river flowed diagonally. But so far no traces of Babylon have been found on the right bank; the excavations are all on the left bank of the stream.

It is only a few hundred yards from the Germans' house to the Kasr, or Acropolis, the centre of the city, and the most renowned of the three great eminences of Babylon. It is here that the excavators have been most active. They followed the line of the Kasr roadway, a broad street which leads to the Ishtar Gate, made by Nebuchadnezzar as a processional road for the great god Marduk, to whose temple of Esagila it leads. The walls of the Ishtar Gate stand 40 feet above the foundations, and are covered with figures of bulls and dragons in brick relief. From the summit one can command a view of the whole city as far as the outer walls. Part of the brick pavement still exists, covered with asphalt, which formed the substratum of the immense limestone flags of the roadway. The double gate of Ishtar is by far the most striking feature of Babylon that has been revealed, and it figures in the foreground of most of the bird's-eye views one sees of the excavations. The nine horizontal rows of bulls and dragons are alternate, and the representations are never mixed. The bull is the sacred animal of Ramman; the dragon, of Marduk and of Nabu. He is a scaled beast with the neck and head and forked tongue of a serpent, the leg of a leopard, the clawed foot of a vulture, and the tail ending in a small curved sting.

There is little else that is decorative to catch the uninitiated eye at Babylon. The silver and gold and precious stones with which Sardanapalus filled the temple of Esagila are forgotten. The images have been removed, the double doors of cedarwood overlaid with copper, the bulls of bronze, the cedar roofs, the thresholds and hinges of brass. There is the famous headless lion standing over its human prey, raised high above the roof-tops since my last visit owing to the delving all round. It and the brick reliefs of the bulls and dragons on the Gate of Ishtar are the only pictures likely to remain in the mind of the hasty uninstructed visitor. For the rest there is the vista of dead brick walls with no windows or steps and few doors. It is hard to tell if one is standing on the roof or the floor at Babylon. The roofs of one period became the foundations of the next, yet out of this confusion the archæologists have reconstructed the ancient city. They have discovered what they are convinced is Belshazzar's banqueting chamber and the vaulted roofs which, they argue with much erudite reasoning, supported the hanging gardens. In a general way, in spite of the superimposed strata of the hungry generations that have trodden one another down, the identification of sites in Babylon is easier than in most buried cities. And this is due to the inscriptions on the bricks and flagstones. For the Kings of Babylonia were providentially vain. They left their stamp everywhere in no uncertain characters. Sardanapalus invoked curses on the head of whosoever should destroy the records of his name: " Him may Marduk the King of All behold with wrath and destroy his name and his seed in the land." Nebuchadnezzar caused a legend to be inscribed on every brick, glorifying his works. He and all his line were jealous of the record of their names. Many of his stones and bricks were inscribed with the names of the street or building for which they were destined. On the edge of each slab under the Ishtar Gate was an inscription which was destined to remain hidden and invisible until turned over by the curious excavator after twenty-five centuries had gone by: "Nebuchadnezzar, King of Babylon, son of Nabopolassar, King of Babylon, am I. The Babel Street I paved with blocks of Shadu stone for the procession of the great Lord Marduk. Marduk, Lord, grant eternal life." He described the nature of his repairs, his motive in building, and the material he employed. "The Gateway of Ishtar I made glorious for the amazement of the people." "Aibuz-Shabu, the roadway of Babylon, I filled up with a high filling for the procession of the great Lord Marduk." Neriglissar records on the bricks of his canal how "I led beneficent and inexhaustible water to the land." Nebuchadnezzar, speaking in the bricks of a protective wall he built in the Euphrates, says: " I raised its foundations on the depth of the water, its top I exalted like the wooded mountains."

The millions of stamped bricks and the thousands of

inscribed ones have preserved the name of the great king as enduringly as he could have wished. But he is forgotten by the people of the land. A particular mound of ruins to the north, known to the Arabs as Babil, Bab Ilani, the Gateway of the Gods, alone preserves the ancient name of the city. It is the one tradition of the kingdom of Nebuchadnezzar that has survived locally; and I think the name is coming to be used by the Arabs in the more general sense in which we use it, signifying the widespread strata of dead cities which once were Babylon. Standing by the Gate of Ishtar, I asked two of my escort independently to point me out Babil, and each made the same wide, sweeping gesture with his hand, pointing north and east and south, and indicating all the mounds that lay in between. But the great King Nebuchadnezzar is forgotten by the generation that has inherited the waste he used to adorn. All his bricks and memorials are in vain. Even the Lord Marduk is as dead as his royal suppliant and protector. With neither name could one conjure up the humblest local spirit or awaken a shadow of reverence or awe. Persia, Parthia, Greece and Rome have passed since, and are barely remembered. In the bazaars of Hilleh and Kerbela and Najaf, when men talk of the movers of kingdoms, one hears now the names of the all-conquering Maude, and of Supposi Kokus, to give the Civil Commissioner[1] the almost Babylonian name by which he is known to the desert tribes.

[1] Sir Percy Cox.

CHAPTER XXXIX

NAJAF

THE great Shiah shrines of Kerbela, Najaf and Kadhimain, the resting-place of Ali, Hussein, and the seventh and ninth Imams, lie on the edge of the desert in the country we occupy.

Kadhimain, the burial-place of Musa-bin-Tafar, the seventh Imam, and of Mohammed-bin-Ali, the ninth Imam, is on the Tigris, four miles upstream of Baghdad, and there is passenger traffic to the shrines from Baghdad by tram, suburban fashion. The line has been in existence for many years, and the top-heavy coaches are drawn by four skinny Arab ponies, the sorriest of drudges, which in the dust and sun never look as if they could finish the journey. Pilgrims from north-west Persia, crossing the frontier at Khanikin, and those from southern Persia, India and the Gulf, arriving at Basra by sea and coming up the Tigris to Baghdad, ordinarily pay their first *ziyaret*[1] at Kadhimain. Thence they journey on to Kerbela and Najaf, whence those in whom the flame burns strongest continue over the desert to Mecca.

Kerbela, the shrine of the martyred Hussein, the son of Ali, the holiest of all holy Shiah places, lies in the desert some twenty miles west of Museyib. The town stands on the Huseiniyeh canal, which flows from the Euphrates. The field of battle in which Hussein was slain by the Omayyed army has stirred the Shiah imagination to the farthest corners of the East. The

[1] *Ziyaret* = visit of pilgrimage.

frenzied beating of the breast in the Mohurrum is inspired by the memory of it; the spears which are carried on the eighth day represent the javelin on the point of which Hussein's head was carried; the horseshoe is the emblem of his charger; the *tazias*, covered with tinsel and coloured paper, which are borne in the procession on the ninth day, are the emblems of the martyr's tomb at Kerbela. The religious sentiment of the fervent Shiah clings more to the Hussein tradition than to the memory of Mahomet himself. The shrine at Kerbela is visualised more often in his pious dreams than the Kaaba at Mecca.

Najaf, the tomb of Ali, is the most important centre of Shiah culture and learning. It is the richest of the shrines, and vies in sanctity with Kerbela. It is also the most remote and picturesque of the three cathedral cities of the desert. A thousand years ago it probably stood on the banks of the Euphrates, but the river has changed its course, and the golden dome and minarets dominate a stretch of upland desert six miles from Kufa, which is the river port of the city. Najaf and Kufa, according to tradition, are "a piece of heaven." If you point out to the Moslem the very terrestrial nakedness of this plot of earth he will reply that God is all-powerful and will make gardens there. The mosque at Kufa, with the walls like a fortress, was built on the spot where Ali was slain. Here, too, the Prophet Mahomet and his guide, the Angel Gabriel, stayed to pray on their way to Heaven; the *maqam* in the mosque marks the position.

Kadhimain, Najaf and Kerbela, as may easily be believed, are centres of intrigue. Here the student of Eastern lore may be initiated into the arcana of Moslem social and religious life. There are the old-world ecclesiastical interests to study, and the relations of the mullahs with the desert tribes, and, more fascinating still, the human drama of the pilgrim traffic. The faithful are drawn from all the corners of the East. Many of them are not indifferent to temporal affairs, and one has to look for the reaction on internal politics of Hun intrigue. Among the pious you will find suspects on the political black list, men long known in the Gulf as gun-runners, jehadists and spies, and men who come with strange, unconvincing tales, leaving suspicion behind them but no evidence for arrest. There are the Malang fakirs who roam between the Baghdad shrine and Kandahar and the shrine of Lal Shah Baz at Sehwan in Sind. They wear a long black robe with open sleeves, a steel rod with rings, a skull-cap, and a tremendous rosary. They dominate the fanatical element in Kandahar, and things are generally more restful where they are not.

In Mesopotamia I often envied the Political Officer whose life was passed in intimate relation with these mysteries; many of them were very young, with just a smattering of Arabic. The gradual mastery of the language would come, and with it an insight into the Arab mind, possibly in time the habit of oblique thought, so that one could sit and moralise with a Bedou Sheikh or talk theology with an *alim* of the mosque and understand a great deal that is hidden and implied and never passes the lips. There were one or two men, notably Colonel Leachman, "the O.C. of the desert," who could pass as Arabs and read what was in their minds as one turns over the pages of a book. Leachman gained an extraordinary ascendancy over the desert tribes; he had a rough and ready way with them, a sense of humour which they understood, and when displeased a very angry eye, which they feared. Very rarely would he talk of his adventures, but they covered a wide field. He knew the desert from Mesopotamia to Syria and the Hedjaz; and he was familiar with the purlieus of Kerbela, where he had slipped through the hands of the suspicious Turk long before the khaki tunic was seen on the Euphrates.

I saw him in one dramatic scene early in the morning of March 8th (1916), when he and two of his brother "Buddoos"—he was disguised as one—emerged almost from under the Turkish position at the Dujaila Redoubt as we were deploying for the attack. He drew a lot of fire, and one of us put a bullet through his turban. As the three rode straight at us, as though to surrender, we ceased fire and let them come up. When Leachman dismounted, and we asked him what he had been doing in the Turkish lines, he said, "Oh, only scratching round to see if there was any water." It was a little stunt of his own, and he had been out on it all night.

Leachman was a man of stratagems and surprises. He was a pioneer among Politicals, and he was generally to be found in some unorthodox zone, preferably hostile. I saw him again at Kerbela, where he was engaged in a peculiarly delicate piece of business. The town was quiet at the time, but he had been fired at the day before by some low-class Arab skulking behind a palm tree. Leachman dragged the man from his hiding-place, thrashed him, gave him some fatherly advice, and let him go. I was surprised to meet him a few months afterwards in Bombay. He had trekked across the desert from Kerbela to the Red Sea, and the Taj Hotel was a casual caravanserai on the way back between Jeddah and Baghdad.

Najaf, being more remote than Kadhimain or Kerbela, is perhaps less affected by outside currents. The face of the city, save for the pilgrims' tramway, which has its terminus at a decent distance from the gate, is unspoilt by progress, and the remarkable serenity of its old age gives it the appearance of being at least a thousand years more ancient than Baghdad. But serenity is only on the surface. There had been trouble in Najaf when I was there in February, 1918, and there was to be trouble again. It began with the Anizeh, who depend on the city for their corn. They came in unarmed to purchase it, but the local Sheikhs and their following opened fire on the tribe and looted them and carried off their camels. The Anizeh were under our protection, and it was necessary for us as upholders of the law to see them righted. The virtual rulers of Najaf at the time were the four Sheikhs, each of them head of one of the four quarters, and each dwelling with his tribal followers in the town. The Sheikhs were summoned and the restitution of the looted property was demanded of them. All four professed submission to the decree; two of them restored their share, but the contribution of the other two was not forthcoming. They were again summoned by the Political Officer, who demanded that they should make collective payment. Again they professed willingness, but during the discussion afterwards, while certain points were being settled, one of them, Sheikh Atiyeh, who had been the irreconcilable element all along, slipped out and harangued the mob, who rushed in and destroyed the offices and records. The Political Officer was saved from the rioters by the Arab Government Agent.

While we were debating the punishment of Najaf our cavalry were fired at from the walls of the town, and a sowar of the 10th Lancers—by the irony of fate a Shiah—was killed. Soon afterwards the Najafis fired at one of our aeroplanes. The fine demanded for all these iniquities was 50,000 rupees and 500 rifles. Happily, there was no need to send a large military force to the scene. The wells in the town are brackish, and drinking water has to be brought in from a channel two miles outside the walls; in the dry season it has to be carried all the way from Kufa. By cutting off the water supply the place can be easily invested and brought to submission. Before the end of January all was quiet. The rifles had been handed in, and Sheikh Atiyeh, the irreconcilable, had absconded. He was proclaimed an outlaw, and his spacious house and compound outside the city gate had been confiscated in lieu of the fine. Here in February I stayed with the Political Officer, Captain W. M. Marshall, who a month afterwards was most foully murdered.

This was on March 21st, very early in the morning. There was a great uproar at the gate and a volley of rifle fire from the band of assassins outside. Marshall was shot in the passage just as he left his room and was making for the gate, which had been flung open. The other officer in the house arrived on the scene almost at the same moment and was severely wounded. From a corner of a room opening into the hall, where he had cover from fire directed from the window and door, he kept the assailants from entering the passage. Then in a lull, when the gang were hesitating and undecided, he managed to escape to the roof, and with the help of the guard there dispersed the mob with rifle and machine-gun fire.

Marshall was a young officer of promise. Before he had been long in Najaf he had established friendly relations with the people. I visited the Kiliddar[1] with him, and the Bokhara College, and some of the ecclesiastical dignitaries. His official and political capacity was enough to ensure him a welcome as a bringer of peace and settlement and a healer of old wounds. Apart from this, his personality and genuine Arab sympathies had won him many friends, and it does not require a detective to discover in what hostile faction the instigation to the crime was nursed. Retribution was swift. Najaf was immediately placed under a blockade until all those implicated in the murder were given up.

Najaf, like Kadhimain, is approached by a horse tram. The line runs from the river bank at Kufa to within a

[1] Kiliddar, in Arabic, the Keeper of the Keys, i.e. the Guardian of the Mosque.

few yards of the city walls, and ends as it begins in a very Hunnish-looking terminus with a sloping roof. The trams are of the same pattern as those that formerly plied in London, with the half-spiral stairs fore and aft, and the back-to-back seat on the roof. I believe the few British soldiers who have seen them rank them with the clock tower in the mosque as first among the lions of Mesopotamia, in spite of the proximity of Ezekiel's Tomb, Babylon, the Tower of Babel, and the mosque at Kufa, which is built on the spot where Jonah was cast up by the whale. To the romantic minded, perhaps, they may appear too homely and banal. But the tramway, which makes the last stage of the pilgrim's journey easy, probably serves a more spiritual use than most lines, whether they are laid in the East or the West.

The tide of war had not altogether swept back the pilgrim traffic, though some of the main communications were closed. One often met a corpse on the road packed in a long crate or bundle of palm leaves and slung across the back of an ass. The pilgrim behind was taking his relative to swell the population of the cities of the dead, by which these sanctuaries are surrounded.

While the living, as a rule, approach by the permanent way, the dead arrive on donkey-back from all points of the desert. The dearest wish of the Shiah's heart is to be near Ali or Hussein on the day of resurrection, and the nearer the shrine the more blessed the state of the pilgrim. In peace-time the dead come into Najaf from a wide radius. The donkey with the bundle like a cricket bag on its back, wrapped in wattle or rich silk according to the means of the pilgrim, may have come all the way from Damascus or Bokhara. A few years ago a corpse arrived from the Persian Embassy at Paris. Every fold in the desert outside Najaf is a cemetery of crumbling monuments or humble slabs, and the melancholy dun colour of the earth is relieved by little domes of bluish-green or greeny-blue that stand up like inverted hedge-sparrows' eggs. There is always a small group of mourners in these graveyards digging or mortaring, and always donkeys passing to and fro carrying corpses or baskets of lime.

The rich, as a rule, are buried in the shrine itself. The fee for interment in the mosque itself is £50, which is very moderate when one considers the sanctity of the place. For burial outside the walls of the city the pilgrim pays anything from four to ten rupees, according to the distance he has come. But here, too, are tombs of rich men who prefer privacy in death to being heaped one on the other within the shrine. Many pilgrims buy houses in Najaf. Either they come to end their days in the city and are buried on their own property, or agents are sent ahead of the corpse to purchase a house to bury it in. Thus the place is gradually becoming a city of the dead. Nine houses out of ten have graves in them. Wherever you pass in the narrow streets you come upon iron gratings and the tessellated front which marks a tomb. Peeping into the dim interior, one sees a slab of marble or glazed tiles, or both, richly inscribed, with a lamp standing on it. Sometimes the building is nothing else than a tomb. More often the pilgrim is buried in a single chamber set apart for the occupant, not differing in any way from the rooms where the rest of the household dwell.

The passion for burial in holy ground is peculiar to the Shiahs. It is not a Sunni custom; and there are Moslems who maintain that these pilgrimages of the dead are *haram*, or forbidden by tradition. The Wahhabi, of course, is intensely anti-Shiah. His puritanical intolerance of saints and sanctuaries and of any monument or ritual that presumes divinity in human shape made Kerbela and Najaf peculiarly unsafe. The sect looted the shrine of Hussein at Kerbela late in the eighteenth century, and even made coffee on the tomb. They would have plundered its rich treasure if it had not been carried away for safety to Baghdad. The Wahhabi menace explains the massive walls of Najaf, which are 80 feet high with circular bastions 50 feet in diameter at intervals of a hundred yards. It also explains the fortress walls of the shrine at Kufa. Najaf has proved impregnable to Wahhabi and Bedouin. It is believed to be fabulously rich. There are two stores of treasure. The old treasury has not been opened since the visit of Shah Nasir-ud-din fifty years ago. It is buried in a vault and built over with brick and lime, with no door or key or window by way of entrance. The new treasure is in the keeping of the Kiliddar, gold and silver and jewels, and precious stones, silks and shawls and pearled curtains. Not only land, but shops and houses, and gardens and baths, and even boats are bequeathed as religious endowments (*Waqf*), and the inheritors pay their tithes to the church; and besides the offerings that are brought to the shrine or sent by the pious from a distance, there are charitable endowments, such as the Oudh Bequest for Indian pilgrims, which has always been distributed through the British Resident at Baghdad. One of the first gifts for the shrines to reach Baghdad after we entered the city were four carved swords of gold, with diamonds on the sheath and hilt, one for Kadhimain, one for Najaf, and two for the shrines of Hussein and Abbas at Kerbela. They were dispatched from Constantinople to Baghdad when the British menace was regarded as a madman's dream, and bore the inscription: "From the servant of all pious Moslems, Enver Bey."

The first thing one sees when one enters the gate near the tram terminus is an ugly little obelisk which commemorates the birth of the Committee of Union and Progress. The ruined houses facing it were the Turkish Club and Municipal Offices. They were destroyed by the citizens in the spring of 1916 when the Turks fell out with the people of Najaf and Kerbela. Owing to heavy war taxes, compulsory military service, the seizure of women, and the house-searching for deserters who were dragged out and shot, Najaf rebelled and arrested the Turkish garrison. At the same time Kerbela ejected the Turks. In the fight that ensued the holy places were shelled—a sacrilege that will never be forgiven. The defenders of the town flooded the approach, and the enemy's reinforcements were held back. Turkey had other preoccupations on the Tigris and Euphrates just then, and Najaf and Kerbela held their own. Najaf had always been a thorn in the Turk's side and an asylum for deserters and political refugees. The subterranean windings of the vaults under the city make it almost impossible to unearth a man whose friends remain faithful.

The shrine, like those of Kadhimain and Kerbela, is so built round that one cannot get a view of it from near by. One approaches the east gate of the mosque through the covered bazaar, which is long and straight and at least 80 feet high. One cannot take one's eye from the rich mosaic of blue and green and gold which glitters at the end of this clear perspective. The Najafis are more fanatical than the people of Kadhimain and Kerbela, where one may admire what may be seen of the interior from the gate. Here a near approach by the Christian is resented. So one turns aside at 50 yards, right or left, into the honeycombed bazaars. These are more irregular and intricate than in Baghdad, a warren of courtyards and alleys under one roof, and they preserve more of the ancient East. One descends steps into spacious quadrangles with great scales at the corners for weighing cotton or cloth. One may buy Persian jars and carpets, and the rich silk *abas* (cloaks) for which the city is famous. But the amenities of life were becoming as scarce at Najaf as everywhere else. I saw a tin of kerosene oil, which would have cost five rupees before the war, sold for fifty. And I noticed that all the phials in the shop of the attar-seller were empty save one. There was still a little of the henna left with which the Arab ladies dye the tips of their finger-nails and hair.

I was shown over the bazaar by a Persian who took me to visit some of his friends. We went to the tomb of the great-great-grandfather of the Aga Khan, to whom Najaf owes its immense protective walls. The building is endowed as a hostelry for students of Shara, or Shiah law. Another educational establishment that we visited has lately been built out of a donation contributed by the Wazir of the Amir of Bokhara. It is a theological college in which eighty-five students are boarded. The walls of the two courtyards are richly tiled with the bright mosaic of which one or two local craftsmen alone possess the secret. The students attend the lectures by Saiyid Mohammed Kadhim, the head of the Ulema. I believe there is none of the cramming, competition, emulation, inspection, and academical whitewash that are the bane of education in progressive countries, though no doubt the system has its peculiar defects, and it is easier for a man of wealth and influence to obtain his diploma than for the obscure student who is only endowed with his native talent. When a student attains to such a proficiency of learning that he can answer any question of religion that is put to him he becomes a Mujtahid—a kind of religious lawgiver, who can grant divorces and settle disputes, quarrels, and lawsuits, religious or secular. The influence of the Najaf Mujtahid extends throughout the Shiah world.

In the theological college I was shown a typical Najaf *serdab*. These underground vaults to which the Arab or Persian retires during the hottest hours of the day are very elaborate in Najaf, and dug much deeper than in most cities. The students' *serdabs* are a repetition of the ground floor of the college 50 feet under the earth. When one descends to them in the dog-days from the grilling upper air the change in temperature is so great that one has to wear an *aba*. The interiors of some of the houses are as rich as one would expect in a prosperous "cathedral city" of the East. The courtesy of the people of Najaf, whether Arab or Persian, is of the old style. One notices it though one is in a country where courtesy is proverbial. The talk in the houses I visited was all of the war, mostly of the iniquity of the Turk and the Hun. Najaf has not forgotten the incidents of 1916. A casual remark of one of my hosts brought this home to me and suggested a parallel with Belgium. I was talking of the breaking up of families all over the world, and the separation of husband and wife, when he said: "Here not only have they taken the husband from the wife; they have taken the wife from the husband."

The Arab does not kill or molest women in war like the Turk. This is not due to chivalry so much as contempt. Woman is an inferior being—not swordworthy. In the same way a Thug would not kill a sweeper or cobbler, holding such "a sacrifice unfit for Bhawani." A primitive instinct, perhaps, but when you get to the bedrock of things, not altogether removed from the springs of chivalry. At Hilleh the Turks hanged 120 men. That was all in the day's work. But the deportation of the women to Mosul was a thing as inexplicable to the Arab as is the deportation of Belgian and French women by the Hun to clean-minded folk in the West.

One gets the best view of Najaf from the mound of debris that has accumulated outside the western gate. It is built of the scourings of the city for centuries, and has risen 80 feet above the road, and a hundred above the plain. On one side the mound commands a vast expanse of desert over which the caravans of the faithful continue their journey to Mecca. On the other side it commands the city, the most picturesque Arab city I have seen, lying compact within its walls with the great golden dome in the centre dominating the earth-coloured brick as saliently as the idea it enshrines blots out everything that is unspiritual, and merely incidental, in the mind of the pilgrim.

CHAPTER XL

THE NEW OFFENSIVE: RAMADI

The long road to Baghdad has carried us farther than our goal. It was at Samarrah that we secured our hold on the city, and the capture of the Turkish railhead is the logical conclusion to the story. The operations afterwards do not fall strictly into the account, and we must conclude our narrative, as we began it, with something in the nature of an abstract.

At the beginning of the cold weather, 1917, the Turkish forces opposing us on the north-east were holding Jebel Hamrin; in the centre, on the Tigris, they were entrenched at Daur, eighteen miles north of our position at Samarrah; and on the Euphrates they held Ramadi.

There had been great talk of a Turkish thrust in the autumn. The Hun boasted that a German army was coming down the Tigris or Euphrates to stiffen the Turk, recapture Baghdad, and drive the British into the sea. We did not seriously believe in the offensive, though we were quite ready for it and devoutly prayed that it might materialise, feeling confident that if the Hun came down on us at the end of his long desert communications he would be delivered into our hands. Without a railway at its back the thrust would have little power behind it, and the Berlin-Baghdad line was moving very slowly; railhead was still in the desert somewhere in the neighbourhood of Nisibin, and the tunnel was not yet bored through the Amanus.

At a later stage it became clear that the enemy had contemplated an offensive on the Euphrates, yet in the months of waiting before Allenby's stroke had deprived him of the initiative most of us were expecting the next clash at Samarrah. There was no reason, of course, why the Turk should confine himself to one river, but we had given and taken so many hard knocks on the Tigris that one instinctively looked for the next act there, if not the fall of the curtain and the decisive issue. The Higher Command perhaps foresaw the change of arena, but the average regimental officer probably felt that he had spent the greater part of his life on the Tigris and was likely to end his days there. And bearing in mind the trick history has of enacting new scenes on old stages, it seemed natural that Samarrah should come into focus again. The small desert town had witnessed the death of an Empire and the disappearance of the last of the Imams. Its strange corkscrew tower of fabulous origin looked expectantly into the desert. The mosque, as golden as the Shwe Dagon, Julian's tomb, that bare, flat-topped, striated mound, in imagery as well as configuration recalling an erupted volcano, left an impression that it was the kind of place where things happen; and most of us felt that Samarrah would be awakened once more by the shock of the new crisis in the East. The arena, however, unexpectedly shifted. It is true that in November we were fighting on the Tigris again and drove the Turk back beyond Tekrit; but it was not here that history was to be made during the next few months. Initiative was diverted from the centre to the flanks. Events in Palestine and Russia created new spheres of interest, and it was on the Euphrates and in Persia that we parried the Huns' next thrust.

Our sphere of operations became immensely widened. Before the spring of 1918 we had troops on the Caspian; we had been fighting in southern Turkestan and pursued the Turks as far as Altun Kupri on the Lesser Zab. We had brought peace and order to the desert cities of pilgrimage, Kerbela and Najaf; we had settled the land between Nasiriyeh and Samawa on the Euphrates, and north again as far as our arms extended. We had twice defeated the Turk on the Euphrates at Ramadi and Khan Baghdadi, each time capturing nearly the whole of his force, with generals, staff, and guns, penetrating far beyond his line with our cavalry and armoured cars, destroying his supply bases and paralysing his power of offensive for an indefinite time to come.

The fortunes of Force D had changed a great deal since the early days. Mesopotamia was probably at this time the best of all fronts. The Turk played into our hands. He had only to evaporate into the desert and our sphere of usefulness was at an end; but he obligingly hung on our skirts, giving us chance after chance, which we never missed, of rounding him up; and with our armoured cars, motor convoys, and cavalry we had the legs of him every time. Our mobility increased a hundredfold. We were always penetrating new country. And these sideshows carried us into fascinating scenes which offered large recompense for the dismal year we had spent on the mud flat ourside Kut.

From September to May it was a full and crowded life. I saw a letter from a Norfolk labourer in which he said that he had seen sights every day that he had "never dreamed of seeing on this erth." The tragic muse had deserted the stage, and the other muses came on in turn. Dates and place names jotted down in one's diary give one an idea of the quick change and variety of scene— Hilleh, Babylon, Kerbela, Najaf, Samawa, Diwaniyeh, Ramadi, Hit, Khan Baghdadi, Ana, six distinct journeys on the Euphrates side, mere trekking sometimes, the kind of thing one looks forward to in an uncertain spell of leave when one has put by the wherewithal to travel; at other times "the real thing," war as it should be waged, with the spirit of movement in it, the new scenes a background to the drama of battle, and waiting to be explored when the hostile elements in them have been placated or dispersed. On the Tigris, Samarrah and Tekrit; Mendali with the Cossacks on the borders of Luristan where the desert meets the hills; Kasri Shirin, Kerind, and Kermanshah in Persia, the flowery Zagros range, camping under the snow peaks of Perau and Bisotun, or by the rock carvings of Tâq-i-Bustan; Kifri and Tuz and Taza Kharmatli and Kirkuk and Altun Kupri in Kurdistan, a land of streams and rolling downs, and wide horizons bounded by the hills. One day with the infantry, another with the cavalry, a lift in an aeroplane sometimes, more often in a mobile column of Ford vans with machine guns and armoured cars, shepherding the Turks into our net with few casualties to ourselves. The Turk did not stay for much execution; the bloody, remorseless trench fighting of the last two years and a half was a thing of the past. He showed some doggedness in the beginning, notably at Ramadi and Tekrit, but as we broke down his moral, operations developed into a kind of glorified staff ride, and the events of each day witnessed that the staff work was good, everything according to the manual, each page cut out clean with no raw edges to it.

Our object now was not to advance but to inflict all possible damage on the Turk. There was no point in further penetration into the desert; our posts were flung far enough on the Tigris, Euphrates and Diala to secure our hold on Baghdad. If we advanced beyond them it was for political and administrative reasons, to strengthen our control of the Arab tribes, and to secure the canal heads. From a purely military point of view an extension of our gains beyond the Baghdad wilayat would be a disadvantage. An advance up the Tigris or Euphrates would be playing the enemy's game, shortening his communications and lengthening ours, which were already strained to the utmost. It would mean that the Hun would have a feebler antagonist when his railway was built, and that, when he was ready to strike, he would not have to stretch his arm so far. It must be remembered that for hundreds of miles in the line of our advance there was nothing ahead of us but desert, and no objective worth the cost of a single casualty until we reached Aleppo. To have held Aleppo would have been to cut the spinal cord of the Turks' communications in the East, for the single line connecting it with Haidar Pasha opposite Constantinople supplied all the Turkish garrisons in Syria, Palestine, Armenia, Kurdistan, Asia Minor, the Hedjaz, as well as the troops operating on the Tigris and Euphrates. If we could have landed at Alexandretta and seized Aleppo early in the war a division would have served our purpose in Palestine or Mesopotamia; but to strike at it from Baghdad, whether by the Euphrates road or across the desert from Mosul, was, of course, impossible without a railway. Sufficient rails and rolling-stock might have reached us in the fullness of time if Mesopotamia had been the only theatre of war. As it was we were hard put to it to feed and equip the forces already in the field in the positions they were holding. In November there were 406,000 mouths to feed in the country, and over 90,000 animals. In addition to this, in Baghdad and elsewhere we were feeding the civil population with grain sent from India. All the railway plant we could get into the country was needed for interior communications.

It was clear, then, that every yard we advanced, unless the new position was to serve as a jumping-off point for a thrust on Aleppo, was, in the military account, a yard given to the Turk and lost to ourselves. Only in the Baghdad area a certain extension of our zone of occupation was justifiable for local considerations. Ramadi was a case in point. In the first place, our occupation of the town would complete our blockade of the enemy from the south, as it would cut off the desert road from Kerbela by which supplies from the Lower Euphrates were getting through to the Turks. Also the town was a convenient centre for the control of the desert tribes, and an important point to hold in connection with the Euphrates irrigation scheme. For it is at this point on the river that the Habbaniyeh escape takes off by which the flood water of the Euphrates is diverted into the Habbaniyeh depression, designed to serve as a storage reservoir. These three advantages justified us in establishing a post at Ramadi; but we should have gone there in any case, whether we intended to stay or withdraw, for our immediate business in Mesopotamia was to destroy the Turk.

It was not until September 26th that a column of adequate size could be concentrated within striking distance of Ramadi. The railway from Baghdad to Feluja was not completed until a month or two afterwards—we depended for transport mainly on lorries and Ford vans. The track across the desert was as sticky and bumpy as it could be, a succession of sand-drifts and pits; and there was not a stone in the country for metalling. Yet our motor transport always arrived. Convoys passed each other in the darkness of a London fog, and the white dust which covered the faces of the *drabies* gave them the complexion of Indian faqirs. On the right bank of the Euphrates the flat alluvial soil of the delta is left behind, and one comes to low dunes and pebbly ridges where the going is better. Here, too, there are long stretches of dried mud and sand, but when the white sails of the Euphrates come into view, and the minaret of Feluja, and the poplars elongated and bunched at the top like palms in the mirage, one knows that the worst part of the journey is over.

The 15th Division, commanded by General Brooking, was holding the line of the Euphrates. This river had come to be regarded as their peculiar sphere. They had held the Nasiriyeh district from an early date in 1916;

The New Offensive: Ramadi

and in the spring of 1917 they had been moved up the Tigris to Baghdad shortly after its fall, whence they crossed to Feluja, and once more held the Euphrates line. When operations began in December their outposts were in advance of Madhij, eighteen miles west of Feluja. The Turks held an advanced position four miles east of Ramadi on Mushaid Ridge, a low line of dunes running north and south from the Euphrates to the Habbaniyeh lake. Their main position, semicircular in outline, lay about one mile to the east, and to the south of Ramadi. Our plan was to drive in our attack with the infantry on the enemy's position from the south, while the Cavalry Brigade made a wide enveloping movement on the west, cutting his communications along the Aleppo road—the only line of retreat open to him, as the Euphrates at Ramadi was unbridged and he had the river at his back. The Turk was not prepared for this move. He expected us to attack his left on the Euphrates, and all our dispositions lent colour to this idea—the bridge we threw across the river at Madhij, the supplies we were collecting on the left bank, and the movements of our troops up to the night before the attack.

Our force moved out of Madhij on the night of the 27th; the 12th Brigade (General Dunsford) on the right, the 42nd Brigade (General Lucas) on the left, and at dawn they attacked Mushaid Ridge. To clear the ridge and cross the canal was our first objective, and here we met with very little opposition. The line of knolls was quickly occupied, the enemy's patrols were brushed aside, and by 8 A.M. the dam of the canal, which was essential to our plan, fell into our hands and was made passable for all arms. At dawn we bombarded the main crest of the ridge, but the Turks had evacuated and replied with a counter-bombardment a few minutes afterwards, expecting us to follow up our barrage with an assault. We, however, as soon as it became clear that the Turks were evacuating Mushaid Ridge, changed the direction of our attack. The 12th Brigade on the right was withdrawn, and, swinging round west behind the 42nd Brigade, became the left wing of the force. Our front, three and a half miles in breadth, now lay between the Habbaniyeh Canal on the right, the water of which is undrinkable, and the Aziziyeh Canal on the left, at a point nine miles from the Euphrates.

The Turks, apparently, had not anticipated this wide turning movement. They reckoned the waterless nature of the track on which we were operating a sufficient safeguard against an advance on so extended a front. It was owing to this miscalculation that we were able to complete our ring round them before they had taken the measure of the new situation. Our system of water supply by Ford vans gave us a mobility on which they had not counted; without it we could never have brought off the manœuvre. The organisation was perfect. Twelve thousand gallons were conveyed by motor convoy from the Euphrates to our troops; the vans travelled 75 miles between the river and the front in a day, and in some cases carried water up to the firing line.

As soon as the infantry had carried Mushaid Ridge the Cavalry Brigade made a wide sweeping movement across the desert round the right flank of the Turks. They left the battle area at 7 A.M., and by four o'clock they were established astride the Aleppo road on a regular line of hills running at right angles with the river five miles west of Ramadi. By this move the Turks were cornered. The net we were flinging round them was complete. They had no bridge behind them and were cut off from all hope of reinforcements or supplies. Their only chance was to drive in a determined counter-attack and break through before we drew the ring in closer and pounded them out of their trenches with our guns.

In the meanwhile our infantry were closing in. At

The New Offensive: Ramadi

one o'clock, after a bombardment, the 42nd Brigade attacked Ramadi Ridge on the right while the 12th Brigade were working round to Aziziyeh Ridge on the left. The capture and holding of Ramadi Ridge by the 5th and 6th Gurkhas and Dorsets was a most gallant affair. This low, pebbly rise is perfectly smooth, a long and gentle gradient, a bare seventeen feet above plain level. It offered no cover of any kind, and our infantry became visible to the Turks a full two hundred yards before they reached the top of the rise. As soon as they came into view the enemy opened a concentrated rifle and machine-gun fire on our front and from our right flank, while their guns, which were perfectly registered, opened intense enfilade fire from the batteries on our left. The Gurkhas and Dorsets hung on to the position, and at night dug themselves in. Their action so occupied the Turks that the 12th Brigade, which had been withdrawn from our right and was working round in our rear, was able to launch an attack which secured a firm footing on the Aziziyeh Ridge before dark. Thus by nightfall our infantry were holding the enemy on the south-east and south between the two canals, while our cavalry, astride the Aleppo road five miles west of Ramadi, completely cut off their retreat.

It was fully expected that the Turks would attempt to break through the cavalry to the west; this was not only the direction of their line of retreat, it was also the point where the ring was thinnest. So far the Cavalry Brigade had not been seriously engaged. In the morning they had had a light skirmish with snipers on the Aziziyeh Canal, and in the evening they had come under shell fire from guns and pompoms on two barges on the river. The Turks made good shooting, but our horse gunners had the best of the duel, and eventually the two barges were fired or sunk. At night the cavalry, who occupied strong points on a front of three miles along the ridge, prepared for a desperate struggle. The expected attack began a little after three in the morning. The first alarm was given by a standing patrol of the 14th Hussars, which, falling back, closely followed by a column of Turkish infantry, led the enemy on to a prepared machine-gun position. The fire of forty machine guns and Hotchkiss guns was brought to bear on the Turks. Finding the road in front of them impracticable, they attempted to push forward through the crops between the 14th Hussars and the Euphrates close under the river bank. Only a few were able to slip through, and these were rounded up in the morning by a column of cavalry and armoured cars in a reconnaissance along the Aleppo road. The action continued two hours until dawn, when it degenerated into casual sniping. The nearest Turkish dead were found within fifty yards of the Hussars' trenches. It was now daylight, and the cavalry, whose gallant defence had rendered the Turks' case well nigh hopeless, had the rare experience of watching a battle from the rear of the enemy. One small detachment of Turkish cavalry had swum the river and escaped with a score or so of infantry, but the main army, with all the guns, was trapped. Their one hope of salvation lay in a determined counter-attack against the cavalry who held the road to the west.

On the morning of the 29th the 12th Brigade resumed the attack on the Aziziyeh Ridge. Very gallantly, in the face of well-directed fire and against repeated counter-attacks, the 89th Garhwalis, the 90th Punjabis, and the Queens carried the last outlying defences of the Turks on our left. The 90th Punjabis, after a hot engagement, drove back the Turks on our right from Unjana Hill. The rest of the brigade swept on and cleared Sheikh Faraja Ridge. This was our objective, but the bridge of the Aziziyeh Canal lay beyond, a point of vantage, for over it all guns and wheeled transport that escaped from Ramadi would have to pass. Feeling that they had rattled the Turk, that his tail was down, and that it was a moment when initiative might turn the scale, the Garhwalis pushed on another thousand yards over open ground "as bald as a coot," crossed a deep nullah, seized the bridge, scuppered the teams of three Turkish guns, captured them, and accepted the surrender of a Turkish general and two thousand men.

Ramadi was a great day for the Garhwalis. It was their début in Mesopotamia. In France they had leaped into fame at Festubert and Neuve Chapelle and secured for a little-known race of hillmen on the Nepal border a reputation in the very front ranks of the Indian Army. At Ramadi they reaped the rich field by the bridge alone. Other regiments did splendid work that day, and the officer who showed me over the ground was afraid that I should forget them in "booming his show." "It was just our luck," he explained, "that we happened to be there." Most of the 90th Punjabis had side-tracked to the right to take Unjana Hill, while the rest of the brigade swept on and cleared the Sheikh Faraja Ridge. To gain the Aziziyeh Canal the Garhwalis changed direction and bore off to the left. Other companies came up afterwards, but when the Garhwalis reached the bridge they were unsupported. They took the bridge, the guns, the two thousand prisoners, the Turkish general,[1] alone. As for the prisoners, "it was not so much a capture," the officer explained to me modestly, "as a surrender to the nearest troops, and we happened to be there."

I had watched them in the distance, black specks on the sand, but it was not until I went over the field with them the next day, and they fought the battle again, that I realised what they had done. As the Garhwalis charged over the open from Sheikh Faraja Ridge, the three guns in front of them, firing point-blank over their sights, poured in shrapnel, raking the ground, churning up the

[1] The Commander, Ahmed Bey, surrendered to the 90th Punjabis.

sand in a deadly spray. Half-way across there was a deep, dry nullah with steep banks and a few scattered palms on the other side. It was an ideal place to hold, but the enemy were slipping away. In a moment the Garhwalis were in the nullah, clambered up the opposite bank, and had their Lewis gun trained on the gun teams at 400 yards. The Turkish gunners died game, and in the Garhwalis' last burst over the flat not a man fell. They rushed the palm clump to the right of the guns, and the guns, which were undefended, with their dead all around. The three pieces were intact. The Turks had no time to damage them. The horses were all saddled up in the palms with the ammunition limbers, officers' chargers, mules, and camels. Very quickly the Garhwalis dug a pot-hook trench round the guns and palm clump, watched eagerly for the supports, and waited for the counter-attack which surely must come. The three assaulting companies were a bare hundred strong now, and behind the mud walls five hundred yards in front of them, though they did not know it, lay a Turkish general and two thousand of his men. But the silencing of the guns was the beginning of the collapse. The Turks knew the game was up. The iron ring we were drawing round them, their unsuccessful sortie against the cavalry in the night, had taken the heart out of them. No doubt they thought the Garhwalis the advance guard of a mighty host.

White flags appeared on the mud wall in front. A small group of Turks came out unarmed. Eight men were sent to bring them in. Then a "crocodile" emerged from the nullah. "I've seen some crocodiles," a very junior subaltern said to me, "but I have never seen one which bucked me like that." The monster grew and swelled until it assumed enormous proportions. One could not see whence each new fold of the beast proceeded. It was like dragon seed conjured up out of invisibility in the desert by a djinn. But it was a very tame dragon, and glad of its captivity. And there was really something of a miracle in it, the kind of miracle that happens in a legend or at the end of a fairy tale where the moral is pointed of the extraordinary rewards that befall the young who are single-minded and unafraid.

While the Garhwalis were clearing this drugged hornets' nest on the left, an intense bombardment was opened on the main Turkish trenches. Our thin line of cavalry far away to the west saw dark masses of the enemy approaching, and stiffened themselves for a bloody battle. They watched this advance, as they thought it, for over an hour, but there came a moment when to their astonishment they saw the Turks collect and walk in massed formation towards the British. The Turkish guns were silent. White flags went up all along the line. It was a general surrender. The crocodile had surrendered its folds. Ahmed Bey, the Turkish commander, who had been on the Euphrates all through the campaign from the battle of Shaiba in March, 1915, and whose troops had confronted General Brooking's at Nasiriyeh all through the summer and autumn of 1916, came out and surrendered with his whole force to his old antagonist.

Soon our tired troops were marching on Ramadi through a blinding dust storm. When I entered the village from the east with the 5th Gurkhas we could not see fifty yards in front of us, and we were involved in a scrap with the 12th Brigade who were coming in from the west. Each thought the other a body of Turks. Happily, there were few casualties. On the battlefield we passed the dead of the Dorsets and the Gurkhas who had given their lives in the gallant action of the day before. A line of the fallen marked the spot up to which the wave had rolled resistlessly, leaving a firm line which threatened the Turks with an investment from which there was no escape. A few hundred yards beyond we were carelessly jumping the formidable maze of trenches, the assault of which must have cost us thousands of casualties had it not been for the rapid and brilliant nature of the operations, the quick seizure of opportunity, and that ready concert of brain and arm which alone materialises the dreams of tacticians.

We captured practically the whole garrison at Ramadi, 8,545 prisoners, of whom 145 were officers, 18 guns, machine guns, ammunition, equipment, barges, and all the usual paraphernalia of war. The deep nullah to the west of the town was strewn with litter for half a mile—pack-saddles, furniture, boots, suit cases, office files, in addition to arms and a great herd of sorry-looking horses and baggage animals; everything, in fact, which had been left behind at the last moment when the attempt to break through the cavalry failed. The blow was a complete surprise to the enemy. The news of the capture of the garrison cannot have reached the Turks on the Tigris until nearly twenty-four hours after the event. Early on the morning of the 30th an enemy aeroplane, flying very low over our camp, was on the point of alighting when the pilot discovered the change in occupation and made off.

There is no doubt that our ineffectual advance on Ramadi in July, when we were defeated by the heat, diminished our prestige. The Dulaim and other tribes north of Feluja became openly hostile. But the clean sweep we made of the enemy's Euphrates force altered the face of things. After Ramadi the old pensioners in Baghdad began to come in for their dole. Before the fall of the town they held aloof and were afraid to apply to the British, fearing reprisals should the Ottoman appear on the stage again. But in the Baghdad wilayat Ramadi was recognised as the drop curtain for the Turk. He was never more to appear on the boards except as a prisoner. In this part he was often seen, and the whole population used to turn out and line the streets to witness the melancholy spectacle. We became quite sorry for the Turkish soldier. It is the official class that has earned the Osmanli a bad name. We found the " Askeri " a good fighter until the paralysis set in, and generally a pleasant fellow to meet, in spite of all the unkind things that were said about him in the newspapers.

CHAPTER XLI

JEBEL HAMRIN AND TEKRIT

THE shyness of the Turk after Ramadi was the natural consequence of General Brooking's *coup*. He had had experience enough of our mobility to put him on his guard, and his orders now were not to stand, but to retire at as great a cost to the enemy as possible. Under the circumstances we could not expect as big a bag on the Diala and Tigris as we had made at Ramadi. Our difficulty in getting near him increased; it was all the difference between walking up partridges in the first week of September and at the end of the season.

In spite of our efforts at secrecy the Turk must have been aware of the direction of our next move. No doubt from his eyrie in Jebel Hamrin he had been observing the dust of convoys and the smoke of trains. His entrenchments lay astride the Khanikin road and the Diala River, which was at this time of year fordable in several places, and he had a bridge behind him at Kizil Robat. It was necessary to dislodge him; not only because the position was strategically important, but because it commanded the control of the Diala canal heads. Our plan was an elaborate converging movement by which we hoped to throw our net round his Diala force and to occupy the position he held on Jebel Hamrin astride the river. In the second of these objectives we were completely successful; in the first we failed.

The 13th and 14th Divisions and the Cavalry Brigade were engaged in these operations, and the columns moved from bases as far distant as Mendali, Shahraban, Beled

Jebel Hamrin and Tekrit

Ruz, and Sindiyeh on the Tigris. On October 18th the 40th Brigade occupied Deli Abbas; on the morning of the 19th the 88th Brigade were in Mansuriyeh, and by noon they were in contact with the enemy force on the right bank of the Diala, which withdrew after dusk. Our right crossed the Ruz Canal some miles east of its intake from the Diala, and after a night march worked along the northern slope of the ridge on to the flank of the enemy's position. On the night of the 18th the patrols of our centre column, the 85th Brigade, rushed the enemy's picket where the Khanikin road crosses the Ruz Canal. On the morning of the 19th the brigade advanced on the Turkish front in concert with our right column, the 86th and 87th Brigades, which were working along the Jebel Hamrin range on the enemy's flank. By 7.80 A.M. the cavalry had got round in the rear of the position and were blocking the Khanikin road. The operations were carried through without a hitch. Everything went off like clockwork; everybody was in the right place at the right time; only our converging columns closed on emptiness. We had set a Nasmyth hammer in motion to crush a grasshopper. The Turk had slipped away in the night, crossed the Diala, and was reported by our airmen in the morning to be in retreat along the Kara Tappah road, having burnt the Kizil Robat bridge behind him.

Nevertheless, as far as terrain went, we had dislodged the enemy from a very strong position and secured our objective at an extraordinarily small cost to ourselves. I think our casualties on the left bank of the Diala were three. As we had learnt to our cost in the action of March 25th, the ground over which we advanced offers every facility to a garrison in the hills defending the position from an attack from the south. The same conditions of level approach to a honeycombed warren of mounds exists on the north side of the ridge; and this is one reason that made it important that the position should change hands. Also Jebel Hamrin no longer afforded the Turks a screen for a flanking movement. The capture of the ridge made it impossible for the enemy to operate on the Diala side unobserved. But apart from its strategical importance it was necessary to hold Jebel Hamrin, as it enabled us to control the headworks of the canals which water the fertile tracts of country on both banks of the Diala under our occupation.

It was pleasant to escape from the deltaic mud and to explore Jebel Hamrin in peace. The rocky gorge through which the clear broken stream of the Diala cuts its way in alternating rapids and pools, with rocks under which the great mahseer lie, was a refreshing change after the drab, featureless flat around Baghdad. Jebel Hamrin seemed homely to most of the force, because the scenery was the very antithesis of the land in which they had laboured and fought. A Highlander described it as "a bit of old Scotland"; a South African veteran was reminded of the Basuto frontier, and an Anzac of some antipodean haunt in which he had fished and shot in college days. It was too late in the season to expect flowers; yet, as if to prove the catholic virtue of the soil, the ground at the foot of the range was starred with the lovely blossom of the autumn crocus.[1] And there was abundant colour in the hills. The sandstone rock varied in the changing light from the dark red[2] of an old brick fortress to the rosy pink of a shell cast up by the tide. There was plenty of small-game shooting to be had, duck and geese and snipe, partridge, sand-grouse and quail, and some excellent mahseer-fishing. We envied the garrison who were left behind on the Diala. But there was a great deal of spadework to be put in. Seventy-five bridges were built over the canals which take

---

[1] *Colchicum autumnale.*
[2] Jebel Hamrin, Red Hills. *Hamrin*, in Arabic, is the feminine plural of the adjective *ahmar*, red.

off from the stream near its exit from the gorge, and the range was pierced in three places by good roads available for all arms. Early in the summer of 1918 the railway was carried through to Khanikin.

I was enjoying the peace of Jebel Hamrin when news reached us of a Turkish demonstration on the Tigris. In the middle of October the enemy advanced to El Huweslat, eight miles north of Samarrah, and were entrenching themselves when General Maude ordered an attack before they had time to consolidate the position. On the night of October 24th the 7th Division captured El Huweslat. The Turks had abandoned the position and fallen back on Maashad-ad-Daur, eighteen miles up stream of Samarrah. On November 8rd, after a night march, the 28th Brigade drove in an attack at daybreak and captured the position. The Turks, finding their right turned, abandoned their trench system extending three miles between the point where we attacked and the river, and fell back in the direction of Tekrit, heavily shelled by our artillery. Our infantry maintained a running fight with the enemy's rearguard until 10 A.M., by which time they were in possession of the Turks' main line of trenches. The guns supporting their advance found excellent targets, finally shelling the enemy as they evacuated their position, at 1,200 yards. In the meanwhile the 21st Brigade, operating on the left bank, occupied Daur village.

We gained an easy victory at Daur, but we had hoped for bigger things. The cavalry had concentrated very secretly, moving by night and taking cover by day in the innumerable nullahs and beds of dry canals. They made a night march well out in the desert on the flank of our infantry, and were to work round in the rear of the Turks at dawn and cut off their retreat when we had dislodged them from their trenches. Unhappily, the plan did not materialise. Their failure, I think, was due to loss of direction and to exposure in consequence in broad daylight to the heavy artillery fire under which the enemy made good his retreat. The Turk was as shy on the Tigris as on the Diala; he was not going to suffer another Ramadi. The position from which we evicted him was a very strong one. The southern slope, forming a natural glacis with gentle gradients, contained three fire trenches all commanding the open approach to the position. The trenches were narrow, with well-sited machine-gun emplacements. The gun emplacements were well camouflaged against ground and aeroplane observation. The complicated system of roofed dug-outs behind indicated the enemy's intention of extending and consolidating the position. The capture of the Daur position at such small cost to ourselves was due to the rapid and secret nature of our concentration, and above all to the splendid endurance of the infantry. No movement was possible until after dusk, yet the whole force debouched through the narrow exits of our complicated defences at Samarrah, concentrated and marched some twenty miles to their objective by 4 A.M. The greater part of the ground was unknown, and there were no natural landmarks. By 10 A.M., marching and fighting, they had covered every bit of thirty miles.

The next morning, November 3rd, we followed the enemy up and shelled them in their trenches at Tekrit. I was with the cavalry who were operating on the flank to the north-west of the town. We were to work round by the river and "mop them up" if they left their trenches. But this time the Turks did not budge. They had registered most of the ground we were covering, and the cavalry came under a good deal of artillery fire, especially at the point of crossing the Hit-Tekrit road.

We pressed on our advance on November 5th. Tekrit, where the Turks lay entrenched, had been their riverhead

Jebel Hamrin and Tekrit

on the Tigris since our capture of Samarrah in March. They had built an elaborate trench system here, seven miles in circumference, with both ends on the river, and with strong rearguard positions thrown back several miles to the north. We attacked this position on the morning of November 5th. The first assault was delivered by the 8th Brigade on the enemy's centre at 11.80 A.M. The 59th Rifles on the right, the 47th Sikhs on the left, with the 124th Baluchis in support, advanced with great dash over a distance of 1,200 yards and captured the enemy's trenches on the front of attack. The Manchesters went in at 1 P.M. There was some sticky fighting in a complicated warren of trenches for the next three and a half hours. Twice the enemy counter-attacked in force and were driven off. The ground was broken, the trench system irregular, and it was very difficult to know exactly where the Turks were. I found Henderson with a small group of Manchesters holding a forward salient, enfiladed on both sides, with his right flank apparently in the air. He had just driven off a counter-attack, and soon after I came up he received a telephone message that the Seaforths and 125th Rifles were going to attack. The Staff, of course, knew the line we held, and our gunners made no mistakes, but an idea of the complicated nature of the ground in front may be gathered from the fact that the Manchesters were expecting the advance of the Seaforths on their right. Henderson put up a blue flag to indicate the end of the line he held in this direction, but while we were waiting for the Seaforths to come up on our right a heavy barrage opened on an area three-quarters of a mile to the south-west, well behind us on our left at a point we thought clear of the enemy. We saw our line rise from their trenches and walk slowly over the ground, an advance of about 700 yards, while our artillery put in a most effective bombardment. With our glasses we could recognise the men's kilts, and we realised that this was the attack of the Seaforths, very far from the point where we expected it.

At seventy yards from the trench the Highlanders were halting for the barrage to lift, but the Turks, seeing the familiar tartan, did not wait for the bayonet. The glimpse of the enemy through the dust and smoke as they scrambled over the parados was too tempting for the Seaforths, who risked the last few seconds of the barrage. Just as they reached the enemy's line the barrage lifted, and the Turks in the trench threw up their hands. Those who had bolted were thinned by our artillery and machine-gun fire. The second line fell to us immediately afterwards.

The Turkish 51st, 52nd, and 14th Divisions had been opposed to our 7th Division all along. The sight of the advancing tartan of the Black Watch and Seaforths made their hearts tired. It was associated now with blank foreboding and the bitterness of reverse. It was as if the spirits of the Scots who had fallen in the earlier battles marched beside their inheritors. Certainly the old drafts had handed down to the new not only their irresistible Highland *élan*, but a tradition of awesomeness which unnerved the Turk before the impact of the steel. Abu Reish, Father of the Feather (heckle), was the Arabs' name for the Highlanders, and we learnt from them of the Turk's fear of the Scot.

At this point the Seaforths and the 125th Rifles, who had carried the trenches on the Turkish right, came under enfilade fire from a new position opposite the dismounted patrols of the 18th Hussars. All through the day our cavalry patrols had contained the Turks in the trenches on the left of our infantry. During the morning attack they had kept down the enemy's fire on this flank. The moment now had come for mounted action, and the order every cavalryman dreams of, but so seldom hears, for the charge and the drawn sword. The 18th Hussars and a squadron of the 18th Lancers were ordered to charge and complete the demoralisation of the enemy. They went in with the point, jumping the trenches, and scattered the Turks, who were fleeing in confusion from the position where the assault of the Seaforths and 125th Rifles had been driven in. The charge was carried through a thousand yards beyond the trench held by our infantry when machine-gun and field-gun fire was encountered at close range. The cavalry wheeled about and covered their withdrawal by dismounted action. The affair called to mind the action of the 18th Hussars at Lajj, and of the 82nd Cavalry at Istabulat. The *élan* of these charges offers the most splendid example of the military spirit; but the wisdom of the command which launches them will always be disputed. There is no severer test of leadership than the decision, demanded on the instant, whether the certain and considerable cost in casualties involved in a charge on an entrenched position, even where the enemy is demoralised, is worth the impetus given to his retreat.

The Turks' right was now broken, and they were in danger of being rolled back on the river over the area covered by the fire of our troops in the centre. Mingled with the smoke of our bursting shells, columns of denser smoke were now seen rising from the ammunition and ordnance dumps around Tekrit which the Turks had fired. This and the relative cessation of gun-fire were sufficient indication that the enemy were preparing to retire. At 5 P.M., when the 92nd Punjabis delivered another attack on our right, they got in with slight loss and little opposition. A few snipers and a single machine gun alone remained to hold this portion of the line. After dark our patrols pushed forward, and at 4 A.M. we were in possession of the town.

Early in the morning I was exploring the place with the patrols of the 92nd Punjabis. It is a picturesque old walled town built on a bluff. The houses stand on the sheer edge of the cliff which rises abruptly a hundred feet from the shingly bed of the river. Inland the town is almost islanded by a deep nullah which surrounds it like a moat, and the desert beyond is unrelieved by any patch of cultivation.

We found the place very quiet. The customary white flag was fluttering on every roof. The townspeople, loitering in the streets, received us with assurances of good will. A few Arabs were pilfering wood. But the Turk had left very little behind. He had burnt his aerodrome and his ammunition and ordnance dumps. The prisoners taken in the action and pursuit did not exceed 820. Of supplies there was no evidence, though Tekrit had been the enemy's riverhead on the Tigris all through the summer and autumn. The Turk was living from hand to mouth, and he has a genius for spiriting stuff away. In no place that we occupied, however sudden and rapid the operations may have been, did we find enough food to keep a brigade for half a day.

During the following night the enemy withdrew the whole of their force to Shoreimiya. The chance of a real *coup* on the Tigris was lost when the Turks escaped our net at Daur. In their retirement on Tekrit the advantage was, if anything, on their side. In the skilful little rear-guard actions they put up on their own ground, with every nullah registered by their artillery, they thinned our battalions without great loss to themselves. During the operations the news reached us of the fall of Beersheba, and there was an idea that our advance was ordered in the hope of drawing away troops from Allenby. But it is doubtful if such a consideration weighed with General Maude at the time. The Turk was not to be bluffed. He knew our limitations too well. Our troops in the forward area could only be fed by Ford vans, and an advance up either of the two rivers beyond a point which could be effectively served by our transport would be playing into the enemy's hands. We withdrew from Tekrit a few days after the Turkish retirement, though at a later date we occupied the town without opposition.

In the meanwhile we had surveyed the ground over which we should have to fight if at any time our advance up the Tigris was continued, and we had made sure that the Turk had no leaping-off place for months, not even the beginning of the great advance depot which must be accumulated before a serious offensive.

CHAPTER XLII

THE DEATH OF GENERAL MAUDE

THE one stroke of ill-fortune that overtook the Expeditionary Force in these days of continual victory was the loss of the Commander whose character and genius had changed the whole aspect of the campaign. On November 18th General Maude died of cholera in Baghdad. Our only consolation, a thought that must have brought him peace in his last hours, was that Maude's work was almost complete—more complete than we realised at the time, for the Turks never rallied from the hammer strokes he had dealt them. He rests now in the desert cemetery beyond the North Gate, among the dead to whose splendid resolution, courage, and endurance he has borne such generous witness, and to whom he was a constant stimulus.

General Maude arrived in Mesopotamia from Egypt in command of the 18th Division in March, 1916. He had commanded them in Gallipoli, where he superintended the evacuation first of Suvla, then of Helles. On August 28th he was appointed Army Commander in succession to Sir Percy Lake. We have seen how, with his remarkable gift for organisation, he built up the fighting machine. He had at his back a Government awakened at last to the full cost of the undertaking to which they were committed, and determined to make good, though in the light of recent disaster anything in the nature of adventure was discouraged, and it was never stated what ultimate hope may have been in their minds. The troops Maude commanded had for months known only reverse;

he had to acquaint them with victory and inspire them with a confidence which nothing in their past relations with the Turk warranted. And the Turk, now swollen with success, he had to acquaint with defeat. It was a task that called for not merely a clear and alert brain but a great heart, and a great personality, and a single-mindedness which eliminated every conceivable issue that did not contribute to the one end. The modest certainty with which he set about to encompass the destruction of the Turk can only be realised by his Staff and the men who were near him at the time. Kut, though visible on the physical horizon, was a very long way off, and Baghdad, in the minds of most of us, an impossible dream. And yet, I believe, General Maude saw Baghdad in his grasp all the while, his own personal objective, for he had no orders from home in which the city was written large as a definite goal. It was Maude's reasoned daring and his caution, tempered with a fearlessness in responsibility and decision, when at last he saw the opening he had created, that pulled us through.

The operations that led to the capture and securing of Baghdad were a series of masterly strokes so brilliant in conception that the Turks never seriously contemplated their success. But Maude was always confident of breaking through. In the long, costly, and laborious business of evicting the Turk yard by yard from his elaborate trench system about Kut he was satisfied all the while that things were going well. And his confidence was infectious. It was communicated by his eye and voice, though in the early days of the fighting on the Hai we had little ground for optimism.

The most marked thing about General Maude was his modesty. He made it appear on the surface that his confidence proceeded not so much from the sense of his own powers as from his complete reliance on his machine. And when one was with him one could not help feeling that he believed this, in spite of his habit of controlling details of Staff work that are generally left to subordinates. He would never take for himself the credit for any successful operation, or stroke of genius, or sound piece of organisation. He never listened to congratulations without minimising his own part in the affair. "Don't congratulate me," he would say in a tone of injured brusquerie and good-natured impatience, "it was the men who did it." And he was as genuinely uncomfortable as if he were wearing borrowed plumes. He had probably conceived every detail of the operations, even to the handling of a single battalion; yet when the *coup* was accomplished he would reflect the whole credit on the subordinate command. He detested flattery, fulsomeness, hyperbole of any kind. I believe, if it had been possible, he would have liked to carry on the campaign anonymously. No personal reference to himself was permitted in any public communiqué, and his modesty may be read in every line of his dispatches. Pomps, ceremonies, appearances, the unessential trappings of war, did not appeal to him. He derided the idea of a triumphal entry into Baghdad. He was never out to impress the people; and for this reason, on account of his very neglect of the arts by which the Oriental mind is supposed to be subjugated, he probably impressed them all the more. The evidence of power was visible everywhere; only the man behind it, who quietly destroyed an army, dispossessed the Turk, and unmade an Empire, did not often appear.

He was very simple, natural, and direct in all his relations, and as disciplined in his routine as a clock. He would start work at five in the morning. Breakfast was at seven, and it was finished at 7.15. Then office, and the full day's work until his ride in the evening. He travelled light with a valise and a small kit-bag containing everything he possessed. An 80-lb. kit is an officer's allowance, and he was the last man in the world to entertain the idea of privilege. "Time in war is everything," was one of his favourite quotations. "Every officer," he said, "ought to have it inscribed on his shaving glass." Maude was never late. From the day he left Sandhurst his profession always came first, and nothing was ever allowed to interfere with his work. All this gives one rather the idea of a stern, sunless nature. It is a catalogue of virtues one reads in the epitaphs of smaller men. Yet the precise and methodical side of him must not be overlooked, as it explains a great deal of his inevitability and success. But in emphasising it too much one might give a very misleading picture of the Army Commander, an image of stiffness and pedantry that would be very wide of the mark. One would expect a man who was so eminently a precisian to be lacking in human qualities, but General Maude was a lovable as well as a great man. He was very warm-hearted and affectionate, and he keenly enjoyed sport and pleasure of all kinds. He was always ready to take endless trouble to do a kindness for anyone, and he never spared himself. Absolutely good-tempered and with perfect health, nothing ever came amiss to him, and the more work he had to do the happier he was and the more thoroughly he threw himself into it. He always gave his best and utmost, and expected others to do the same, though he was more ready to make allowances than most disciplinarians, perhaps too ready sometimes.

In Mesopotamia everyone who met him felt his personal magnetism, and those who best knew him best loved him. His sympathy and consideration were well known to his troops. On the eve of any operations he would send them encouraging messages, and he made a point of presenting medal ribbons immediately after the action to those who had distinguished themselves. Delay in this respect, he considered, defeated the object aimed at. He would travel long distances by aeroplane for this purpose. As soon as any wounded officers or men arrived at a hospital from the front, his first thought was to go and visit them. If there was an officer whom he knew ill in hospital, he would pay him constant visits. He never failed in kindnesses of this nature, however pressed he might be with work.

Men who knew him in the old days as Adjutant of the Coldstreams, or in South Africa, Canada, or the Curragh, speak of his unselfishness, and his invariable habit of putting himself aside. "What one remembers most of him," one of them wrote, "is his sunny temperament, and the tonic he was to everyone." Simple, openhearted, open-handed, with a horror of all meanness and lack of straightness, he was a very gallant gentleman, and a soldier in the best sense of the word.

In the confused perspective of the moment one cannot form a just estimate of the place history will give him. *Ex officio* he will have a niche among the immortals merely as the conqueror of Baghdad. But none realise better than the Army he led how individual his successes were. He was the heart and brain of the machine. Though he would be first to deny it, it is doubtful if in the whole of our military history before the capture of Baghdad there is a parallel instance in which a series of victories can be more exclusively attributed to the personality of a single man. This is likely to be recognised more and more as our perspective becomes clearer. Coming generations, perhaps, will class General Maude as a great leader with Alexander and Julian, who conquered the ungrateful soil and became its victims. He fixed a memorable link in the continuity of history when he entered Baghdad; and one may safely predict that his name will be associated with a more lasting and beneficent change in the fortunes of the country than can be credited to the score of Roman, Persian, or Greek. But at the moment the men who helped him to make history were not concerned with posterity. The thought that troubled them, recurring at all hours, was that of the two or three new graves in the British cemetery, one covered the bones of the man they could least spare, of the Commander whose quiet and confident smile was an assurance that no sacrifice he demanded of them was in vain.

CHAPTER XLIII

KARA TAPPAH

IT was becoming more and more difficult to get in a blow at the Turk. He receded like the mirage, and left us in possession of the sand and the dust. As a pugilistic sergeant put it, we had "bitten off his left ear and his right, and broken his nose, and knocked him over the ropes, and it didn't seem as if he was going to stand up to us any more." And this meant, to change the metaphor, that, pull as hard as we could, we were not pulling our weight. Geographically and strategically the Hun had the advantage of us. He was at the apex, the Allies scattered at different points along the broad base, of the triangle. With his interior lines, he could contain with a small force numerically superior armies, and he consoled himself for the loss of a province by talking about "the British army of internment in Mesopotamia."

There may have been a certain sting in the jibe, though we were far from being interned. Our sphere of influence widened every week; the work that was being done for the development and settlement of the country would bear fruit after the war, and with respect to the military issue, there were surprises in store for the Turk yet.

Soon after Tekrit I found myself with the Cossacks at Mendali. On September 29th, while the battle of Ramadi was being fought, our cavalry occupied the town. The small Turkish garrison fled into the hills, abandoning their camels and a large quantity of grain.

The arrival of the Cossack Partizanski on the scene a few weeks afterwards was one of the many secrets in

GENERALS BICHARAKOFF (left) AND BARATOFF (right).

Mesopotamia which the Official Eye-witness was not permitted to divulge. The reason of this secrecy is difficult to understand. The Turks must have been aware of the coming of the Russians, as the road was open to the north; and the news could only have been inspiriting to the public at home. The detachment was made up of picked regulars who had volunteered from the different regiments of the Caucasian Army on the Persian front. The fighting spirit of these Cossacks was unbroken by the Revolution. Waiving their rights as free citizens to desert their Allies and return to their homes, they preferred to keep in touch with the enemy and carry on with the war. The old relations existed between officers and men. They had volunteered in the same spirit as the Battalions of Death on the European Front, and they had sworn to follow their officers and to preserve the traditions of the old Russian Army. The skull and crossbones on the pennants of the squadron commanders, white on a black field with maroon edges, symbolised their determination to fight to a finish. General Bicharakoff, the commandant of the Partizanski, was a hard-bitten soldier of the old school. He was the only man I met who, after three and a half years of war, still loved fighting for its own sake, though he had received six wounds in six different engagements, carried a bullet near his spine, limped on one foot, had lost the use of his right arm, and only retained the partial use of his left. The Partizanski were with us in the operations on the right bank of the Diala in the first week of December, and Bicharakoff, who was a sick man at the time, commanded the detachment from his stretcher.

On the Tigris and Euphrates the Turks had retreated out of rapid striking distance, and our next stroke, in which the Cossacks joined, was directed against the enemy force, part of the Turkish 18th Army Corps, which was holding the Diala above Mansuriyeh, the passes over Jebel

Hamrin on the right bank of the river, and Kara Tappah. Four converging columns were engaged in these operations, while the cavalry demonstrated up the Adhaim River to the west in order to prevent reinforcements being brought down against our attacking force from Tuz Kharmatli and Kirkuk.

On our far right to the north-east the 87th Brigade forced the crossing of the Diala at night in the neighbourhood of Kizil Robat, while the 85th Brigade were holding the enemy at a point farther south. The 87th Brigade, having cleared the ground on the right bank, withdrew, and on the night of the 2nd—3rd the 85th Brigade crossed and started their advance. The Russian Partizanski crossed at the same time a few miles farther north near Kishuk. At dawn on December 3rd, after a night march, the 38th and 40th Brigades surprised the enemy at different points in the extended position they were holding on the foothills west of Deli Abbas. The 38th Brigade worked along the crest of the ridge from the Diala River; the 40th Brigade attacked frontally; both columns had penetrated the hills before daybreak.

The Turks' main line of communications lies along the Kifri road which winds with many twists and zigzags through Jebel Hamrin. The entrance from the south is by the Suhaniyeh Pass; from the north by the Sakal Tutan Pass. The direction of the road is roughly north and south; but certain stretches of it lie parallel with the bases of the hills. Thus our column which attacked on the front well to the west of the opening of the Suhaniyeh Pass were able by rapid marching to strike a point in the track which cut off a section of the enemy's rearguard before they could reach the gap where the Sakal Tutan Pass debouches into the plain to the north.

The result of the drive was that we had manœuvred the enemy out of the first lines of his position and captured two field guns and 170 prisoners before midday. The field pieces, which were captured with gun teams and horses, passed our artillery as they were going into action, and a Turkish gunner told us that his seventy-fives had opposed us in Gallipoli.

Driven from their forward positions, the Turks had fallen back and were holding the Sakal Tutan Pass, a formidable natural line of defence. They had entrenched along the crest of the ridge, and their machine-gun and gun emplacements dominated successive defiles of the road. Here, if they had not been afraid of envelopment, they might have put up a rearguard action very costly to the attack; but they had reason to know that the manoeuvre by which they were being forced out of Jebel Hamrin was only part of a more extended converging movement, and that they were in danger of having a wider circle drawn behind them. One cavalry column was active on the Shatt-el-Adhaim to the west, while another cavalry column, including the Cossack Partizanski, was working round from the Diala to the north-east, and the 85th Infantry Brigade was approaching Kara Tappah from the direction of Kizil Robat. Under this threat the Turks withdrew after dark, and our patrols, pushing forward, found the position abandoned.

The next morning at dawn, standing on the Sakal Tutan Pass, we had an extensive view of the Kara Tappah plain to the north, and of the low range of hills beyond, but no sign of the Turk save a few white wisps of dust like the smoke of fires. An aeroplane reconnaissance reported the enemy entrenched in the hills north of the village of Kara Tappah. Soon afterwards the flash of a helio some eighteen miles away to the north-east revealed the Cavalry Column advancing from the Diala River, and farther east still, but nearer in to Jebel Hamrin, a long grey caterpillar of dust told us that the 85th Brigade from the direction of Kizil Robat were on their way. This column was to play an important part in the next day's fighting, but during the remainder of the 4th we were fully occupied in bringing up ammunition and supplies over the pass and building ramps for the fording of the Nahrin Kupri River, where the Turks had blown up the centre arch of the fine old brick bridge in their retreat.

On the morning of the 5th we joined battle again. Our cavalry patrols reported Kara Tappah unoccupied; and from the highest roof in the village, with a gunner F.O.O. and a crowd of interested Arabs, I had a clear view of the action on our left and centre, and watched the enemy slowly driven back over the hills, fighting a rearguard action as they retired. The general scheme of the action of the 3rd was repeated, but without the element of surprise. The blow was delivered on both flanks simultaneously. The 40th Brigade, which had cleared the Sakal Tutan Pass, extending on our left, attacked the enemy's right, while the 85th Brigade, which had come up from the Diala, attacked his left. By three o'clock in the afternoon our infantry were on the crest of the ridge and our guns shelling the retreating Turks. Judging by the rifle fire on our right, the resistance here was more stubborn, but the progress of the action on this flank was hidden in the folds of the hills. When the two columns met after dusk I learnt from the 85th Brigade that the 37th Dogras and the 2/4th Gurkhas had struck a strong point. The Turks opposite the Dogras had waited for the bayonet. The casualties in the two battalions were 24 killed and 98 wounded. This was not heavy, but our total casualties during the operations did not exceed 280. The small cost with which we gained our objectives was due to good Staff work. We went into the attack on a wide front with a thin, extended line —the wisest tactics when the enemy is fighting a rearguard action with machine guns. Had we attacked on a narrow front at any great depth our casualties must have been heavy. As it was, our losses fell far short of the total of the Turks' prisoners and dead.

The doggedness displayed by small batches of Turks during the Kara Tappah action was the exception. Our general impression of the enemy was of a tired, hungry, ragged, and ill-equipped force. There had been a marked tendency to surrender. Small bodies of deserters had been coming in daily during the last month. After the action of the 5th prisoners stated that their officers left them when our first shells burst over their trenches. From this date onwards there were increasing signs of the enemy's demoralisation. From the German prisoners on the Euphrates side we had a picture of the chaos prevailing on the lines of communication. Dishonesty and peculation were rife, and thefts of grain and ammunition on an extensive scale were of common occurrence. The friction between the Turks and their would-be masters was increasing; and the German Staff complained that they were almost helpless against the dead weight of Turkish apathy and incompetence.

On the morning of December 6th our airmen reported that the enemy were melting away along the Mosul road after firing their coalmines at Kifri. Our line was stretched too far to admit of pursuit, and on the 8th we withdrew to Jebel Hamrin, leaving posts on the Sakal Tutan and Abu Zenabil passes and at Nahrin Kupri, and establishing a bridgehead at Kizil Robat. On the 9th we occupied Khanikin on the Kermanshah road, and for the next few months we were busy improving our communications with a view to parrying the enemy's designs in Persia.

On the way back from Kara Tappah we came in for an abnormal spell of cold weather. Snow had fallen in the hills. The water in the canvas basin outside my tent froze to a solid block of ice. Our troops, marching on the Samarrah road, had ice in their water-bottles. It was lucky that the cold spell did not begin a week earlier, for during the advance the 40th Brigade, which I had joined, had to spend two nights without their first or second line transport, and one or two of us who were without overcoats or blankets believe we saved our lives by rolling up in the leaded aeroplane signal sheets. Twelve degrees of frost were registered at Samarrah; 6.6 at Baghdad; nothing very severe when judged by ordinary standards, but after the abnormally hot weather we were more sensitive to cold, our blood thinner, and the pores of our skin more penetrable. In five months there had been a difference of 100 degrees between the maximum and minimum readings. The air was keen and dry. Since a week or two before our entry into Baghdad on March 11th there had not been a shower sufficient to lay the dust. The total rainfall in Baghdad in the last ten months had been 0.09 inches.

CHAPTER XLIV

HIT—KHAN BAGHDADI—KIRKUK

THE next fighting was on the Euphrates. After Ramadi the Turks received reinforcements on this front. They were holding Hit, with their outposts thrown as far downstream as Uqbah; their main forward position was above Hit, behind the Broad Wadi, two miles north of the town, while the bulk of their forces were at Salahiyeh, fifteen miles further upstream. General Marshall decided to capture Hit and, if possible, its garrison. "There would be no difficulty," he thought, "in capturing the town and driving the Turks out of their positions; but the capture of the Turkish force would be a matter of extreme difficulty, in consequence of their previous experience at Ramadi."[1] This forecast was exactly fulfilled. On February 19th our troops entered Uqbah, which was found unoccupied. During the next three weeks we maintained touch with the Turk by patrols and reconnaissances, but he was in no mind to try conclusions with us. On the night of March 8th our patrols discovered that Hit was evacuated, and the Broad Wadi position behind the town. We entered Hit on March 9th, and Salahiyeh on the 10th. The Turks fell back on Khan Baghdadi. Our aeroplanes precipitated their retreat, harassing the enemy's infantry and transport with bombs and machine-gun fire all day.

Hit occupies the same position on the Euphrates as Tekrit on the Tigris seventy miles to the east. A desert road connected the towns, and by it the Turks maintained

[1] General Marshall's dispatch, dated April 15th, 1918.

communications between their forces on the two rivers. This route, which on account of water and transport difficulties never admitted the passage of a large force, was now closed to them, and as they retired north and west communications over the widening stretch of desert between the Euphrates and the Tigris became increasingly difficult, if not impossible.

At Hit we entered a new country, a land of limestone and gypseous clay, where the river winds in a valley between low hills. Viewed from a mile or two downstream Hit reminds one of a town in Italy. It is built of grey limestone as compact as a castle within its walls; the small minaret stands out like a campanile; the palms below the walls appear in the distance as black as cypresses, and the arched aqueducts running out into the Euphrates, or standing broken and isolated in the middle of the river, are very Roman-looking. The waterwheels stand in the openings of the stone piers, 85 ft. high, and receive the full force of the current, which is concentrated into a narrow channel by the weirs built wedgewise in midstream. As the wheels revolve the earthen vessels bound roughly to the rims spill the water into the conduit, whence it is carried on to the crops and palm gardens. I have seen waterwheels in Cambodia constructed on the same plan. Hit marks a dividing point on the Euphrates. Here the river leaves its rocky bed and emerges into the alluvial plain of Mesopotamia. One does not meet with these water lifts downstream; the current loses its power, and the ox and the buffalo are called in to work the Persian wheel.

As one enters the town the enchantment that distance lends disappears, and the resemblance to Tekrit becomes more marked. The houses are tightly packed on the circular hill like one huge honeycombed dwelling falling away into a moat inland from the river. The shell of the town is formed of the conterminous walls, many of which are crumbling and expose ruined interiors, alcoves and divans. The moat-like depression is not really a moat, but the dip which has formed between the foundations of the town and the mound of refuse that has risen round it—the scourings of centuries. One cannot escape from refuse in these small, ancient Biblical cities. It is the salient thing. They are built on refuse. The Hit of to-day is built on strata of Hits dating back to the Ava of the Bible. The debris without grows until it threatens to dominate the walls of the town; yet the debris within never decreases, and being more recent is more offensive. One would think that bitumen must have a purging effect. The steep, narrow alleys were once paved with it, but they have become drains. The refuse thrown into the street, assisted by the rain, has worn a passage, and one has to walk like a crab edging along the walls of the houses to prevent slipping down into it. These open sewers poison the air the year through until an occasional winter shower washes the noisome filth and offal into the river, where the women go to fill their pitchers. Inside the town the dogs are the municipal scavengers, and outside mangy little donkeys forage in the offal in lieu of grass. The incense that arises one has sniffed in a lesser degree elsewhere on the Tigris, Euphrates and Karun. But, unsavoury as their town is, our airman probably wronged the Hitites when he implied that the smell which offended his nostrils as he flew over in his machine 800 ft. above the earth, travelling at ninety miles an hour, proceeded from the streets. He must have struck an emission of sulphuretted hydrogen from the bitumen wells. Whiffs of it are carried into the town sometimes when the wind is in the west, and the change of smell is, if anything, a relief.

The Arabs used to call these bitumen wells, which are scattered all over the desert, " the mouths of hell." There is one within half a mile of Hit, and it lives up to its reputed origin. One need not ask the way to it, one is guided by the smell; and when one reaches the spring, one is held there watching it with a horrid fascination. The foul gas spouts up in intermittent gushes, raising the scum in bubbles like gigantic black boils, which distend and burst with a hissing sound. The pitch discharges itself down a slope, where it is collected and carried away by the Arabs in panniers on their donkeys. One finds it on the roofs and stairs and streets of Hit. Boats are caulked with it. It is invaluable for boat bridges. Basketwork coated with bitumen is used as a substitute for wood in the *gufars*, and for metal in the pitchers the women carry down to the Euphrates—a different type of vessel to any I have seen elsewhere. The pitch is the bituminous residue of the asphaltic base oil distilled by the sun. The nature of the surface discharges in the neighbourhood varies a great deal according to age and locality. One finds congealed lakes of asphalt smooth and flat and hard as pavement, standing a foot above ground, and one finds imperfectly solidified stretches, as at Ain Marich, where the surface rocks as you walk on it like a quaking bog. The springs of this dried patch are the crude oil from which petrol, kerosene, fuel and lubricating oil are prepared. But there is an essential difference between the asphaltic base oil of Hit and the paraffin base oil of Maidun-i-Naftun in the Persian oilfields; the asphaltic variety does not yield the same quantity of pure oil on distillation as can be got from the paraffin.

Bitumen, waterwheels and dirt are likely to be the abiding impressions that the Euphrates Force will carry away from Hit. These are the things that have stuck in my mind since I visited the place twenty years ago, and these are the things that everybody was talking about on the day of our entry. Until I visited Shuster I had always thought of Hit as the dirtiest little town in Asia, and in this judgment the sentiment of the Mesopotamian Expeditionary Force was with me.

A more attractive feature of the place is its gardens. Hit is famous for its mulberries, and the palm gardens have an undergrowth of peaches, apricots and figs. What was left of the peaches and apricots were in blossom when we entered the town, but most of the trees had been cut down by the Turk to revet his trenches and roof his dug-outs, which he did not hold against us after all. The people of Hit have not forgiven, and are not likely to forget, the crime. The wrecking of orchards in fat and fruitful lands is sad enough, but the spoliation of these walled gardens, wrested from the desert at such pains, suggests a melancholy fable on the wastage of war.

In my earlier visit to Hit, in the first week of January, 1898, I was crossing the desert with the camel post to Damascus. The journey, four hundred miles as the crow flies, used to be made by the post in seven or eight days. The caravan route by Tadmor, the ancient Palmyra, leaves the Euphrates at Deir-el-Zor. The journey takes on an average twenty-four days in summer, and sometimes as many as thirty in winter. There are wells between Deir and Damascus which are never dry throughout the year. A quicker route is by Kerbela and Shifafeh, where one strikes a well every day or every second day. The Sheikhs of the Bedouin tribes are given *khauvah*, or safe-conduct toll, by the caravans. In the old days of the camel post from Hit to Damascus the mail contract was auctioned. A postman was sent across with the letters every week. The contractor kept a stable of thirty fast riding camels of special breed, and these beasts were put to a severe test. From Hit to Damascus they were ridden eighteen hours a day with two short halts for food; after the journey they were given nearly seven weeks' rest. The speed of the post was not due to urgency in getting the letters through, but to lack of water. There are two wells between Kubeisa, twenty miles from Hit, and the outskirts of Damascus, but one could not be certain of striking them. Sometimes the postman lost his way, followed the wrong star, as the expression is, and wandered in the desert until he and his camel died of thirst and exhaustion. Some twelve or fourteen years ago the desert service by camel to Damascus was abandoned for the *arabana* (carriage) service to Aleppo. The Baghdad-Aleppo route is twenty long stages, averaging thirty miles each, but with relays of horses the mails can be carried through in ten days.

At Hit I made inquiries for Haji Musa, the old postman who had taken me across. There was a man in the town who had been employed in the camel post in those days. Oddly enough, he remembered meeting Musa with an Englishman in the village of Dumeir outside Damascus about the time I crossed with him. He came into our mess and told us the story of Haji Musa with the inimitable histrionic gestures with which the Arab unfolds his tale. It was a sad history. The old Haji had been killed by the Dulaim five years after we made the journey together.

"Was it a quarrel?" I asked.

"No, it was avarice. The motive was greed."

They had not intended to kill Musa, but the merchant who was travelling with him had taken a large convoy of camels to Damascus and sold them there. It was believed that he was returning with the money on his person. So they shot him as he sat by his fire of camel thorn brewing his coffee in his beaked pot. Then they said, "Haji Musa knows and will tell." So they shot Haji Musa too.

I could not find the house where Musa and I put up. There were many like it—a low door opening into a courtyard under one of the innumerable arches that span the streets—streets so narrow that one's camel bags rub the walls on either side, walls of mud and limestone, the colour of a speckled grey hen—a lodging inland from the river, but within sound of the eternal drone of the waterwheels that are chanting day and night. Hit does not change much. It must have worn the same look of arrested decay for centuries. I have no doubt that the temples of the Gods of Ava were in continual disrepair, and the walls and floors innocent of whitewash and pitch. Now masons and scavengers are busy, immemorial smells are being exorcised, and the work of purgation has begun.

A repetition of Ramadi seemed too much to hope. The shyness of the Turk increased as the months went by. He had slipped away from us at Hit, and no one believed for a moment that he would make a stand at Khan Baghdadi. There was, however, a psychological factor which counted in his decision. Subri Bey, the General Commanding the Turkish force which had evacuated Hit without opposing our advance, had been deprived of his command. This, as we understood from deserters, was on account of his failure to risk an action. A greater temerity might be predicted in his successor Nazmi Bey, who would naturally expect to be superseded in his turn if he showed the same readiness to quit. General Brooking, in his estimate of the chances that might contribute to success, set great hopes on this, and he was not disappointed.

The Turk had suffered by underestimating the length of our arm at Ramadi, but we had increased our mobility since then. The Cavalry Brigade and armoured cars and Ford van convoys had come up very secretly, moving by night and concealing themselves by day. Our force advanced fourteen miles from Salahiyeh on the night of November 25th. The enemy held two positions at Khan

Baghdadi, the first a mile and a half south-east of the Khan astride the Aleppo road, the second a mile upstream of the Khan, where the road follows the Euphrates bank and is commanded by steep cliffs. Other trenches were thrown out to meet attacks on the flank and rear from the desert. Instead of retiring, as we feared, the Turks moved troops to their forward position and held it in force. I was following with the mobile column of armoured cars and Ford vans which were to come in on the flank or the rear of the enemy as the battle developed. At 2.25 A.M. we heard the welcome bark of guns, which told us that the enemy were still in their trenches. Our one prayer was that they might stand. If our infantry could pin them to the position long enough, we hoped to make a ring round them, as at Ramadi. The element of uncertainty lay in the nature of the country inland from the river, which was intersected by steep and rocky nullahs. If this ground proved practicable for cavalry and armoured cars the enemy's chance of extricating himself was small. The general lines of the Ramadi action were repeated at Khan Baghdadi, our infantry attacking the enemy's front and flank while our cavalry and armoured cars worked behind and cut off their retreat, holding a line extending inland from the river. The Turkish first line of trenches, which we attacked at 2.80 in the morning, was a formidable position splayed out among the low crests of the ridge on both sides of a defile through which the road passes. As soon as the Turks sighted our infantry in the bright moonlight they sent up flares, and in a few moments their guns opened on us. Our men rushed the first two lines with slight losses, but as the approach to the third line was enfiladed on both sides by machine guns our further advance was delayed until we had brought up our artillery.

At 11 A.M., after a bombardment, our infantry went

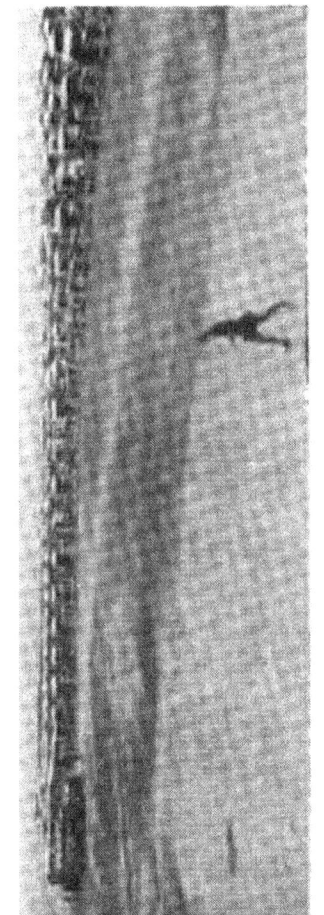

MOBILE MOTOR COLUMN WAITING FOR THE ORDER TO PURSUE.

SIKHS LAUNCHING RAFTS ON THE TIGRIS.

in and captured the position with slight casualties, taking some prisoners. The advance was then continued, and the leading troops took up the line half a mile north-north-west of Khan Baghdadi, with their right flank on the river, pinning the Turks to their positions.

In the afternoon orders were received to attack the enemy's northern position. By this time our guns had come up and registered. The advance began by 5.80 P.M. and was covered by a barrage of artillery and machine-gun fire which enabled the infantry to get right on to the enemy with trifling loss. The clouds of dust that were raised must have been blinding to the Turks, and had much the same effect as a smoke barrage. The intensity of our bombardment was doubled by machine-gun fire. In this broken country the Turks could occupy no ground which was not commanded at cross range by hills, and the low ridges to the south enabled our machine-gun companies to keep up a terrific fire on the enemy trenches.

All this while our mobile motor column (Colonel Hogge) lay out in the desert impatiently awaiting the order for the enveloping movement. But the cavalry had made good progress on the right of the Turkish position, and in the afternoon it was decided to send Colonel Hogge's column along the Aleppo road to assist the infantry by enfilading the enemy from the Euphrates side. Light was failing when we reached the scene, and the work was almost finished.

At 6 P.M. the first line was captured and four guns and many prisoners were taken. As it grew dark the remainder of the position fell to us without heavy fighting, and we bivouacked on the ground captured. The advance was continued between two and three o'clock in the morning. Those of the Turks who had escaped had to reckon with our cavalry, who had made a wide circuit and were closing in on Wadi Hauran, seven miles to the north-west, barring their retreat. During the night they made efforts to break through, but were everywhere repulsed.

The scene of the surrender the next morning was more dramatic even than that at Ramadi. At Ramadi the men emerged from the trenches in a dust storm and delivered themselves up to different units all along the line. The collapse was more sudden and the surrender more compact, but I did not see anything in the earlier action so dramatic as the scene we witnessed soon after daybreak on the 27th. The same undulating country extends beyond Khan Baghdadi in a succession of wide plateaux, intersected by ravines with steep cliffs. We scaled one of these and saw in front of us black masses of the enemy's transport and infantry, dotted like ants on the face of the ridge beyond. There was some show of movement among them, but no sound of firing. A white flag fluttered on the top of the hill under which they were gathered, and beyond, in the far distance, there rose a scarf of black smoke, the signal of destruction of the material of war abandoned in the flight. We found these troops with their transport under a small guard of Indian cavalry. The armed motor convoy, which I accompanied, passed through them in pursuit, and all day we were rounding up more prisoners. The enemy made no attempt at delaying the action, and it was the most complete rout imaginable. The Turks, overtaken by our armoured cars, would throw up their hands or fling themselves flat on the ground, thinking this position safer.

We passed the same litter on the road as in the pursuit before Baghdad; not so much impedimenta and ammunition, but more prisoners and a great deal more live transport. There were ambulances, field kitchens, water-carts and convoys of lagging bullock wagons, with their bullocks yoked and the drivers standing by their side; wounded men, dead men and sick men, who had fallen out, and others whom we left for the column which followed to rope in; also bombs and live shells, boxes of ammunition, portmanteaux and office paraphernalia, and books and papers.

At Haditha I saw a farrier's forge in a cave, with the embers still burning. Another cave held a dump of equipment which had been fired and emitted a smell of burnt leather, but the Turks had not had time to destroy much. We passed an island in the river where some fugitives were hesitating between concealment and surrender. They waded across to us and gave themselves up.

Ten miles farther on a British aeroplane, scouring the ridges parallel with the road, was machine-gunning the few stragglers who still hoped to escape, and shepherding them into a queue. Soon the whole road became a procession of prisoners. In the evening Khan Feheme was reached. On the 29th we were in Ana, and the pursuit was continued by armoured cars 78 miles along the Aleppo road. The Turks were exhausted and demoralised, and in most cases surrendering freely. But the O.C. of the column had an object nearer at heart than the rounding up of more prisoners. It was known that somewhere not very far ahead, carried along in the confusion of the retreat, were two British Staff officers. Lieut.-Colonel Tennant, Director of Aviation, and Major Hobart, who had made a forced landing in the enemy's lines at Khan Baghdadi on the evening of the 25th, were prisoners in the hands of the Turks, who were making every effort to get them away. They were travelling all night on the 25th, and on the evening of the 26th they were at Haditha when news of the Turkish defeat reached the post. In the confusion that prevailed the guard over them was not relaxed. They were pushed off in an Arab chaise at a gallop, and, travelling through the night, reached Ana early in the morning. Here they stayed only two hours, and were sent on by camel with a Tartar guard. In the afternoon four of our aeroplanes passed over, flying low. Hobart waved at them, whereat one of the guard tried to shoot him, but his rifle missed fire at point-blank range. The next stage, Nahiyeh, was reached on the night of the 27th. Here they met a number of German officers and men, including a wireless company. The order stood that they were to be sent through to Aleppo without delay, and they left by camel the next morning. Soon after noon our aeroplanes passed them again and turned back. They had almost given up hope of release when our armoured cars arrived on the scene. The road running between the hill and the river was full of corners, and the appearance of the cars was sudden and dramatic. They came up stealthily on top gear with very little noise. The first intimation of them was the machine-gun fire they opened on the guard. Happily, the two Englishmen were separated by twenty-five yards from their escort at the moment, and as the Tartars dived for cover Tennant and Hobart ran for the car, which kept up a hot barrage over them all the time. I met them at Khan Baghdadi the next morning, the happiest men in Mesopotamia, and Hobart, who told me the story, said that the stage-management was perfect, and that the officer standing over the machine gun in the car was literally and figuratively the best illustration of a *deus ex machina* he had met.

Our prisoners, 213 officers and 5,082 other ranks, including the Commander and Staff of the 50th Turkish Division, exceeded the estimate we had formed of the enemy's whole force. But it must be remembered that we had raided his line of communications to a depth of 130 miles behind his battle front. Our own casualties were only 157, including killed, wounded and missing.

The endurance and rapidity of movement of the troops were extraordinary. The infantry were marching two days and two nights with little or no sleep, and fighting all day and part of two nights. The cavalry covered something like ninety miles in the first two days, and the armoured cars 170 miles, apart from detours, between Hit and the farthest point of pursuit beyond Ana. The success of the pursuit and the raid on Ana, by which we completed the demolition of the enemy's war material on the Euphrates front, was largely due to our airmen. By the intelligence they brought in we knew exactly what we had to meet.

Khan Baghdadi was a crushing blow to the Turk. Both in plan and execution it was as brilliant an achievement as Ramadi, and the collapse of the enemy was more complete. His Euphrates force had ceased to exist, and the destruction of his depots precluded any opportunity of initiative for an indefinite period on this front. His ammunition depots at Ana and Haditha had been slowly accumulated during the summer to meet the needs of the Turco-German army which was to have descended from Aleppo to recapture Baghdad. Four million rounds of small-arm ammunition and 50,000 shells were destroyed at Ana alone. Preparations on this scale, coupled with the uncompleted engineering work on the road, proved that the big offensive had been intended. Also we learnt that the German naval personnel in charge of the *shaktur*[1] fleet on the Euphrates had been increased by several hundred, though after the offensive was abandoned it had dwindled down to a few score, many of whom we captured. The Falkenhayn

---

[1] The *shakturs*, despite their primitive character, proved themselves better adapted than any other craft for work on the Euphrates. They are of two kinds, and always lashed together in pairs. The larger, German-made *shakturs* were built at the German shipyard at Jerablus. From Jerablus they were navigated downstream, and broken up for firewood on arrival at their destination, as it was not worth while towing them back many hundreds of miles up river for a second trip.

Kulawund action, rather than face the tribesmen returned and surrendered to our cavalry.

On April 28th our cavalry were reconnoitring all day. By the evening the 18th Infantry Division under General Cayley had come up, and the attack was planned for the 29th. The enemy, reinforced by a battalion from Tauq, were holding a seven-mile front on the far bank of the Aq Su River, stretching east from Yanijah Buyuk to Tuz Kharmatli. At Tuz they held a position on the near bank covering the road and extending into the hills. The river is fordable here at all points. The infantry deployed at dawn in two main attacks on Yanijah from the south-west and on Tuz from the south. At Tuz the Turks had to be cleared from the hills commanding the road before the assault could be pressed home frontally. They were already falling back when the position was carried on our left at Yanijah by the 88th Brigade advancing with great steadiness under machine-gun and artillery fire right up to the guns, which continued in action until they were within 200 yards' range. This advance on the Turks' right flank made Tuz untenable by the enemy, for to have held it would have meant envelopment. As the infantry pressed through the abandoned position, the cavalry who had crossed the Aq Su in the dark were heading for the Tuz-Kirkuk road to cut off the retiring enemy. The Turks, however, maintained a steady machine-gun fire, and for some time held up the pursuit. The key to this resistance was a knoll on our right. This was brilliantly turned by Lieutenant Macdonald, of the 18th Hussars, who with his troop galloped the hill and charged the machine gunners in the flank and reverse, and in less than five minutes had the whole party of Turks killed or marching as prisoners to the rear. After this the fire from the other hills died away. By nine o'clock all opposition had collapsed, and it was only a case of mopping up parties in retreat. The position had fallen to us in three hours with very slight loss; 1,200 prisoners were taken, 20 machine guns, and the 12 field guns that were in the position.

There was no serious fighting after Tuz Kharmatli. We occupied Tauq on May 5th without opposition, and Taza Kharmatli on the 6th. Our cavalry pushed on. The same evening they were in contact with the Turks on the western of the two main roads leading from Kirkuk to Altun Kupri, but the nature of the ground and the enemy's dispositions in the hills made it impossible to reach the eastern road before nightfall. It was along this road that the enemy effected their retirement.

The 38th Infantry Brigade, after a long and arduous march of twenty-five miles, reached a point five miles south of Kirkuk with the intention of attacking the next morning. At eight o'clock it began to rain, and it poured steadily all night. Our bivouac was soon a flood. The pitch darkness was lightened at intervals by flares and explosions, and we knew that the Turks were burning their ammunition with the intention to quit. By midnight they were all away. We had more heavy rain on the 7th; the fords behind us became impassable, and the heavy going greatly hampered the pursuit.

When we entered Kirkuk on the morning of the 7th we found the place given over to loot. There was a procession in the streets of men, women and children carrying furniture like a crowd leaving an auction. We put a guard over the bridge by which the stuff was being carried from the Turkish administrative quarter on the right bank to the Kurdish quarter on the left bank of the Hasa Su. In the bazaar we were in time to save some of the fittings of the shops, looms, anvils, forges, doors, and benches, but everything of value had been taken. The last act of the Turk before leaving was to blow up the Christian church. It was a mere shell of a building without a roof, and it had been used as a ceme-

CHAPTER XLV

CONCLUSION

I

OUR narrative in these two volumes has been mainly concentrated on the wearing down of the enemy. In closing it a brief summary is necessary of the wider political issues of the campaign. The operations in Mesopotamia served two purposes, the safeguarding of India and the destruction of the Turk. The first objective, even if the second had not been incidental to it, must be regarded as the more vital of the two. In the perspective of history the issues will not be confused, but it is doubtful if it is even now realised that the Mesopotamian Expedition was, in its inception, one of the few brilliant strategical strokes of the war, and that it was our promptness in occupying Basra that dissipated the Hun's dream of domination in the East. The tragedy of those disastrous months after the retirement from Ctesiphon, the long series of reverses culminating in the fall of Kut, the blunders of strategy and command, have left such a dark impression that we cannot clearly see the light behind it, and we are apt to forget that the small force which anchored off Bahrein in October, 1914, pending Turkey's decision to enter the war, probably saved India.

So far as our interests in the Gulf were concerned—and on these depended the safety of India—the outbreak of war with Germany in 1914 was a positive blessing. The Hun had made no secret of his designs in the East. Bernhardi openly proclaimed them before the war. He counted on the union of Pan-Islamic forces with the revolutionary elements in Bengal, seeing in the combination "a very grave danger capable of shaking the foundations of England's high position in the world." Turkey, as a weapon of Germany, was to be a two-edged sword; for it was fully believed that the ranging of the Caliph with the Central Powers would raise Islam against us throughout the East.

Every month of delay before hostilities must have strengthened Germany's grip on Mesopotamia, which was to be the base of her flank attack on India. For years the agents of Germany had been nursing and developing her political and commercial interests in the Gulf. Our politicals on the spot were alive to the strategical danger ahead, but the Foreign Office, pursuing a policy of conciliation at all costs, played into the hands of the Hun and the Turk. Just before the outbreak of war we granted a concession for the continuation of the German Baghdad railway as far as Basra. We have it from Prince Lichnowsky that an International Commission was to regulate navigation on the Shatt-el-Arab. "We were also," he states in his pamphlet, "My Mission to London, 1912-1914," "to have a share in the harbour works at Basra and receive rights for the navigation of the Tigris, which hitherto had been a monopoly of the firm of Lynch. By this treaty the whole of Mesopotamia as far as Basra was to be included in our sphere of influence."

Had there been any delay or indecision in the dispatch of the expedition to Mesopotamia in October, 1914, we should have left the field open to the Hun. With Basra in the hands of the enemy our line of communications to the East would have been threatened by flank attack from the sea; we should have lost the oilfields in Southern Persia (invaluable to the Navy); the Arab would have been thrown into the arms of the Turk instead of looking to us for liberation from his yoke; Persia, Afghanistan, and the tribes on the Indian border would have been exposed to fanatical influences which we should have been unable to check; and the result would no doubt have been a general Pan-Islamic conflagration spreading to our frontiers and a dangerous internal situation in India at the same time. So far from sending troops to fill the gap in France, India would have been compelled to call for help from home, which, of course, in that grave crisis, when our thin line was stretched almost to the breaking point, could not have been spared. Our position in Egypt would have been most precarious, and we should have lost an ally in the Sherif of Mecca, who could not have turned to us for support in his struggle for independence against the Turk.

Such was the coil the Hun hoped to wind round us by intrigue in Mesopotamia, Persia, Afghanistan and India. We have been faced by some grave crises, but the menace would have been immeasurably more serious if we had played into his hand by delay. It is admitted that the Mesopotamian Expedition was a necessary, and even vital, move. At Qurna and Amara Force D held back the Hun from the gate. Criticism of the expedition as a waste of energy and a dissipation of resources is only justifiable in so far as it applies to expenditure in man-power and material over and above what was necessary for the safeguarding of the Gulf, the protection of the oilfields, and the closing of the avenue of approach to India. The first adventurous advance, in which Nixon's small force was drawn on towards Baghdad with insufficient transport and no reserves to fall back on, was a blunder for which we paid dearly. The second advance, under Maude, in which we made good, was a glorious achievement. Whether the gain was worth the cost in the man-power and material so vitally needed nearer home is open to dispute.

The strategy that determined the advance on Baghdad in the winter of 1916-17 was peculiarly British. The spirit of the nation was deeply stirred, and it was contrary to tradition and precedent to sit down under a reverse. To most Englishmen the all-important thing at the moment seemed to be our prestige on the Tigris. We should have been wiser, perhaps, if we had cut our losses in Mesopotamia and delivered the counter-blow to Kut, which honour demanded, nearer the heart of the Turkish system; if we had been content with holding the delta of the Shatt-el-Arab while we concentrated our main strength, as we did later, against the Turk in Palestine, for the drive up north towards Aleppo. The first axiom of strategy in Asiatic Turkey, as elsewhere, is that one should strike as near the spinal cord as possible. With Aleppo in our hands the Turks would have been starved and impotent on the Tigris and Euphrates, whereas the extension of our gains about Baghdad did not materially help our army in Palestine, or draw off enemy forces from in front of it proportionate to our own troops locked up in Mesopotamia.

But from the purely local point of view, in which the immediate safety of our Eastern Empire loomed larger than the ultimate defeat of the Hun, Baghdad was a tremendous asset. Our command of the railhead at Samarrah, of the approach to Baghdad by the Aleppo road along the Euphrates, and, more important still, of the communications by the Kermanshah-Hamadan road between Baghdad and the Caspian, put us in a much stronger position to parry a thrust on India.

It was, as we have seen, mainly the Palestine menace that averted the Turco-German offensive on Baghdad in the autumn of 1917. There was, however, another consideration which weighed with the Hun. The defection of Russia, opening out an easier and less costly line of penetration through Persia and the Caucasus, completely altered the situation on the Mesopotamian front. A new strategy was dictated. The Hun, while containing our considerable forces on the Tigris and Euphrates, now aimed at a political offensive by way of the Caucasus. The door seemed open again, and the old hope of raising the land between the Caspian and the Indian frontier was revived.

The virtual annexation of the Ukraine gave Germany the control of the great trunk railway through Rostoff and the northern foothills of the Caucasus to Baku. Another avenue leading to the very borders of Afghanistan lay open to her in the branch line of the Siberian railway from Orenberg to Tashkend where it joins up with the Trans-Caspian line. Here we were faced with menace of trouble whether she came as an ally of Bolshevism or as a Power promising peace and settlement to a land exhausted by Bolshevik excesses. The danger of Germany's Central Asian designs would have been more formidable had the war been protracted; but Merv, Bokhara and Tashkend were too far distant for the Teutonic wave to reach them, and what with Bolshevism, Menshevism and Pan-Turanianism, Germany had so many conflicting interests to reconcile that she never gained a footing in this disturbed zone. A more immediate danger lay in her penetration of the Caucasus. The treaty of Brest-Litovsk had restored to Turkey not only the Armenian provinces of Erzerum and Bitlis, wrested from her in the Russian offensive in the spring of 1916, but the provinces of Kars, Ardahan, and Batum, ceded to Turkey by Russia in 1878. Thus converging lines were open to her north and south, and there was nothing to prevent an advance of the Turks on Baku, the bridgehead of the Caspian, or into Persia by Batum and Tabriz.

The new situation, though it seemed dark at first, contained elements of promise for the Allies. In the first place, Ottoman ambitions in the Caucasus drew off the greater part of the reserves that opposed Allenby, and it was to this that General Liman von Sanders mainly attributed the Turkish collapse in Palestine. But, apart from the military issue, the extension of the war into the Caucasus meant a clash of imperialistic aims between Turkey and Germany. The Hun was trafficking with Christian and Moslem elements at the same time, and his intrigues threatened to dissolve into thin air the dream of a Moslem domination of Trans-Caucasia on which the Turk had set his heart. A Georgian Mission was received in Berlin. Tiflis was to become the capital of a Georgian State. And to the Turk this independent Georgian Republic was not merely so much territory unfairly filched by his ally from the spoils of a dismembered Russia; its existence was a reflection upon his pretensions as a civilising agent, a point upon which the Osmanli is always sore.

In the race for the Caspian the Turk won by a short head; there were six German battalions in Tiflis soon after he reached the coast. Germany's intrigues with Georgia, coupled with her attitude in the Crimea and her seizure of the Russian Black Sea fleet, exasperated the Ottoman Government. At the time of the military debacle, after Bulgaria had signed the armistice, the relations between the two Powers had become so strained that no bribe Germany could offer could dissuade Turkey from a separate peace.[1]

The defection and dismemberment of Russia did not open the road to an enemy offensive on a European scale. The movement of large bodies of troops through Persia is a military impossibility. The danger on our frontiers lay in political penetration. But there was no ground for pessimism. So long as we held our own in the West these diversions of high politics in the Caucasus and Persia were more in the nature of an embarrassment than a

[1] The Germans promised Talaat not only Baku, but the satisfaction of the Turkish claims against Bulgaria, if only he would restrain the Ottoman Government from making a separate peace.

menace to our security. They made big headlines, but one forgot the relative insignificance of the forces engaged as compared with the Western Front. Dearth of supplies, the absence of good roads, insufficiency of transport make the concentration of troops a difficult matter. A brigade is a very large force in Persia. It is true that the Black Sea was a German lake sailed by German shipping, and that the Caucasus railways were in German hands, that the Georgians had ranged themselves with the enemy, and that Turkish forces were pressing on to the Caspian; but it is a long cry from the Black Sea to the railhead at Tabriz, and the terminus of the Caucasian railway is the Caspian. Baku was to fall, but friendly forces were holding Krasnovodsk, the bridgehead on the eastern shore in Turkestan. Enzeli, too, the only port on the Caspian with communications into the interior of Persia, was in our hands. And the invasion of Persia by the Turk from the north-west involved almost insuperable difficulties. A hostile force detrained at Tabriz would have a stretch of over 200 miles to march before they ran into our outposts at Kazvin. And it must be remembered that roads in the north and west of Persia pass through mountainous country, that an invading force cannot depend on other lines of communication than these ancient and unaccommodating tracks, that its flanks may be exposed to attack in a succession of defiles, that there is no scope for any wide turning movement, and that the odds are always in favour of a smaller force sitting tight on the defensive.

South of the Tabriz road there are tracks leading into Persia through Suleimania and Mosul, but these are so difficult that they need not be regarded as a serious menace to our flank. The only other practicable road into Persia from the west is the old Baghdad-Kermanshah road to Hamadan, the ancient road from Babylon to Ecbatana trodden by Cyrus and Hystaspes. It was along this road that General Dunsterville's small force made its adventurous march from Baghdad to the Caspian.

It was about Christmas time, 1917, that one began to hear of the incubation of another mysterious " sideshow " in Mesopotamia. Volunteers were called for, and officers, nominated from different regiments, were collected in a camp, not without the suspicion of segregation, a few miles from Baghdad. This was the nucleus of the " Hush-Hush Push." The force consisted entirely of officers and a few picked N.C.O.s, and its numbers were gradually augmented by recruits from overseas. These men hung together mysteriously in groups, and kept their own counsel about their future plans, of which, as a matter of fact, they knew very little indeed. But it was noted that they provided themselves with warm poshteens against an Arctic cold, that they had forsaken the study of Arabic for Persian, and that a procession of them might be met at the Field Treasury Office any day of the week changing rupees for the Persian kran. In the middle of January, to complete the mystification, General Dunsterville, the original of Kipling's Stalky, arrived in Baghdad to lead his band of adventurers into the unknown.

It was common talk now that the destination of the " Hush-Hush Push " was Persia; and it was generally believed that they were going to found a kingdom somewhere in the north. Armenia was the whispered goal. And here for once rumour was not very wide of the mark, though the garment of romance with which she invested the figure of Stalky was embroidered with some picturesque and unorthodox additions. Stalky was not to be king—there was no design of territorial aggrandisement; but he was to found a kingdom, or, if not a kingdom, at least a republic. Armenia was to become a buffer State; the remnants of her population were to be saved from the Turk, and such as were capable of bearing arms were to be drilled and disciplined into an organised force. Thus the little expedition combined the attractions of a military adventure and a crusade.

The "Dunster Force" knew very little of the material they would have to work on if ever they reached the Caucasus. Up Tiflis way and in the country between Tiflis and Erzerum, and between Tiflis and Tabriz, there are bands of hardy mountaineers, comitadjis as they would be called in Europe, Georgians and Armenians and Tartars, generally at strife among themselves, yet most of them hostile to the Ottoman and Bolshevik alike. The Georgians and Armenians were already disputing as to who was going to possess the land before they had begun to dispossess the Turk. Whether any nucleus of cohesion could be found among these warring elements was very doubtful, but it was generally agreed that if anyone could form any sort of organism out of them, or call into being a body with related front and flanks, capable of interdependent action, it was General Dunsterville. But the political situation in the Caucasus was constantly changing. One day the Bolsheviks would be in power; another the so-called Trans-Caucasian Government friendly to the Entente. The general trend was to anarchy—tempered with Bolshevism.

General Dunsterville left Baghdad on January 27th. In a few days he was in Hamadan, whither most of his staff had preceded him.

Between Baghdad and Kermanshah he had 230 miles of road to traverse, much of it execrable, and four passes of over 5,000 feet. The villainous stiff, rocky gradients were not the chief obstacle. Our pioneers and sappers could cope with these. The thing which immobilised the party for days at a time was the friable black cotton soil, which after one heavy shower became impassable to wheels. From Kermanshah the road winds round Bisotun to Kangavar and Hamadan, another 108 miles, with a pass of 6,750 feet to climb or circumvent. Between Hamadan and Kazvin, a stretch of 145 miles, there is a 7,500 feet pass on the road. From Kazvin to Enzeli there are another thirteen horse stages. This last stretch of the road is the best. The transport difficulties in the early stages prohibited the movement of any but small bodies of troops.

Even when the gradients had been made easier and a great deal of the boggy ground metalled, it took a convoy of 750 Ford vans, plying daily in stages from Khanikin, to feed a force, less than a battalion strong, at Hamadan. And so far from depending on local supplies we had to feed, as far as we were able, the people of the country. There was famine in Persia. Five armies had passed through in eighteen months, Cossack and Turk, living on the country, and leaving desolation behind them. Trees had been felled, standing crops burnt, granaries destroyed; there was no seed grain left for the next harvest. On the top of this came the drought. Our relief works at Kerind, Kermanshah, and Hamadan saved thousands from starving, though one could only command corn enough to affect the margin of distress.

When General Dunsterville reached Enzeli on the Caspian he found the Bolsheviks in possession. He received a summons to their tribunal on the night of his arrival, but he wisely invited the Committee to call on him at the house where he lodged. He and his small party of officers had no escort beyond the drivers of the Ford vans in which they had come from Hamadan. They found themselves in a hornets' nest of angry, hostile, and suspicious Bolsheviks, who demanded Dunsterville's name, the nature of his errand, and his destination. He told them that he was going to Tiflis. Russia, he explained, by standing out of the war had left his flank exposed to invasion by the Turk, and the British Government had deputed him to go to the Caucasus and report and advise on the situation.

The Bolsheviks declaimed angrily. They told Dunsterville that they would not permit him to go to Baku. They had a gunboat watching the ship that was to take his party. Their guns were trained on it, and if he sailed they would sink it. The Germans and Turks, they said, would take it as an unfriendly act if they gave him a passage. They ended every new argument with " And the Germans and Turks are our friends."

All this was a little trying to the temper, coming from our allies of a month or two ago, for whom we had originally taken up arms. Bolshevism, it must be remembered, was then a reptile newly hatched. She had not yet raised her ugly head. In Mesopotamia we thought of the Bolshevik as a poor creature who wanted to save his skin at the expense of his friends. We also gave him credit for a desire to save his face, as we were aware that he had imported a new political philosophy from the Hun to this end. But we had no suspicion of his real iniquity. It must have been difficult for Stalky to keep his hands off the men, or to spare them the lash of his tongue. His sang-froid and tact, however, did not desert him.

"Of course," he agreed, smiling pleasantly. " I quite understand. Naturally you would be their friends. You could not possibly be anything else. And now, what about a little light refreshment?"

There were 8,500 hostile Bolsheviks in the town, the remnants of the Russian Army of the Caucasus; but, instead of interning him, the Committee gave him petrol for his cars to take him back to Hamadan.

II

General Dunsterville was too late to make a buttress of Armenia against the Turk, though the liberation of that unhappy land was nearer than the most sanguine of us could have anticipated.

Conclusion

The Armenian scheme had fallen through, but the presence of the "Dunster Force" with Bicharakoff and his now reduced Partizanski on the Enzeli-Kermanshah road effectually barred the way to the Turk on the north and the west. An enemy column was coming down from Tabriz, and there were skirmishes between our outposts and their patrols, but they never penetrated the line we held, thinly garrisoned as it was, between the Caspian and Baghdad. The hostile Jungalis in the hills south of the Caspian, who had joined the Bolsheviks earlier in the year, threw in their lot with ours.

Enzeli is the strategical key to the north of Persia. It is the only port on the Persian shore of the Caspian which offers a base for troops with a line of communications into the interior. On the eastern shore Krasnovodsk, the terminus of the Russian line running parallel with the north Persian border, is the vital point. A hostile power holding this line could concentrate a force at Kakhka, less than eighty miles from Meshed, for the invasion of Persia. But here Germany's design of penetration had failed. Early in the war her agents had been trafficking in Russian Turkestan, playing upon the anti-Muscovite sentiments of the Turcomans; then, when Russia ceased to be a nation, she won over the Bolsheviks in Merv and Tashkend; and in the last phase we had reason to fear that she might be called in to reconstruct Central Asia by a population weary of Bolshevism, and thus, if she were not entirely broken in the war, establish herself as a formidable menace to our Indian Empire. But the Russians and Turcomans along the all-important stretch of the line from the Caspian north of the Persian border were anti-Bolshevik. Krasnovodsk and Astrabad were in friendly hands. We were extending the Nushki line into Persia from Quetta. In the summer of 1918 it had reached Mirjawi. The Russians and Turcomans over the border were with the Allies, and they called on us for assistance.

Indian troops passed up through Meshed to Astrabad. We had also a small garrison at Krasnovodsk. So long as Germany was fighting for her existence on the Western Front a serious invasion of Central Asia was out of the question.

In July, 1918, Baku became the storm centre. In three months the town had seen more than one revolution. Two-thirds of the population are Tartars, the other third Armenians with a sprinkling of Russians. In April the Russian Bolsheviks and Armenians bombarded the Tartar quarter, and drove out the Tartar National Council, who retired to Elizabetpol. The combined Bolshevik and Armenian regime existed until July 25th, when it was overthrown by an Armenian and Russian bourgeois regime, also anti-Tartar. The new Government sent a request for British aid to repel the Turks. Dunsterville by this time was established at Enzeli with the greater part of the 39th Brigade. The Bolshevik troops who had held him back on his earlier visit had melted away to their homes. The shipping on the Caspian was not under our control, but the Baku Government had in their possession a few transports and sent them down to Enzeli, and it was in these that our force embarked on their adventurous journey. The detachment we could send was necessarily small; it comprised parts of three battalions, the Worcesters, Warwicks, and North Staffords, one of which was certainly not more than half strength. The concentration of a column this size at the end of over a thousand miles of communications between Basra and the Caspian was a remarkable achievement, and anyone familiar with the difficulties of the road and the scarcity of local supplies would have thought it impossible. Unfortunately events proved that it was not large enough for the task to which it was committed, though it might have been sufficient as a stiffening if the troops it supported had remained staunch. The local force at Baku, work-

Conclusion

men with no military training, most of them volunteers organised in defence of the town, numbered about 7,500 Armenians and 8,000 Russians. By the time we arrived their fighting spirit was exhausted; they were greatly outnumbered; the Turks, who had command of the railway, were in a position to throw in constant reinforcements; there was a considerable hostile element in the town; and part of the garrison were negotiating with the enemy.

On August 26th a determined Turkish attack was beaten off by men of the North Staffords and Worcesters, who had, however, to give ground, though fighting gallantly. By the end of August it was realised that the co-operation of the local government and forces would not be sufficiently effective to justify the retention of our small detachment in Baku in the face of the numbers which the enemy would be able to collect with his superior communications, and on September 1st definite orders were issued for the evacuation of the British troops. But on the same day the Turks again attacked, and our allies again failed to co-operate, with the result that the Royal Warwickshire Regiment had to cover the Armenian and Russian retirement, and lost heavily.

On September 2nd the Russian General Bicharakoff occupied Petrovsk, on the shores of the Caspian, 200 miles to the north, and promised to send reinforcements to Baku. Ships were sent from Baku to bring them. The first small detachment of Bicharakoff's troops actually arrived at Baku on September 9th. The comparative inactivity of the enemy and this promise of reinforcements gave new heart to our allies, and for a time there seemed a chance of saving Baku; this hope, however, was soon dispelled by the vacillating attitude of the garrison, some of whom were negotiating with the enemy to hand over the town.

On September 14th the Turks made a determined

attack in force, and after a fight lasting over sixteen hours, the brunt of which was borne by the British, our troops withdrew. The evacuation was very skilfully carried out under circumstances of the greatest difficulty. We got away all our guns and the 1,200 survivors of the detachment. Baku remained in the hands of the enemy until some time after the conclusion of the armistice.

The dispersal and defection of a number of the Armenian garrison under the menace of Turkish frightfulness without, combined with the presence of the enemy within, the gates was the immediate cause of our failure at Baku. They had organised the defence of the town and held it against the Turks for two or three months, only to disperse when we arrived in answer to their appeal. Reading of their action far away from the scene of anarchy and confusion, and ignorant of the influences that decided it, one was naturally incensed; but it must be remembered that they were an isolated band, exhausted and famished, and threatened with terrible reprisals. The stigma that attaches to them must not make us forgetful of the services of their nation as a whole. In the early years of the war the Armenian regiments were among the best troops of the Russian Army of the Caucasus, and chiefly contributed to the capture of Erzerum. In France the Armenian detachment of the Foreign Legion were almost exterminated in their gallant defence of Verdun, and nearly every one of them, before he fell, received a decoration. In Palestine, with Allenby, they bore their part. After the collapse of Russia the Armenians were left alone to hold the gate in the Caucasus against the Turk. They fought stubbornly from February to June, and the Turkish communiqués paid grudging tribute to the gallantry of their defence. For five months they delayed the enemy's occupation of the Caucasus and Northern Persia; and at the end of the war Andranik and his gallant band, the scourge of the Turk from the beginning, were still carrying on a guerrilla warfare in the mountains.

The news of our gallant and tragic intervention at Baku was the first official intimation of the existence of the " Dunster Force," and it provoked a great deal of uninformed criticism as regards the wisdom of our presence in Persia at all. It was objected that these far-flung expeditions meant an unwarrantable dissipation of resources, and it was not generally realised what small means were employed to secure large ends. A common misconception was in respect to numbers. The arm-chair critic thought in the terms of armies or divisions when it was a question of brigades or battalions or even of half-battalions. In Persia the minimum military outlay obtained the maximum political results.

The dispatch of the Dunsterville Force to Baku was condemned in certain quarters as a quixotic adventure. This attitude was most ungenerous. It also pointed to a complete ignorance of the situation. We had to take these risks and lend all the support we could muster to the friendly elements which were still ranged with us in the struggle to the death against Bolshevism. Had the Caucasian Government made good, the dispatch of Dunsterville's force to their aid would have been proclaimed a brilliant strategical move.

And the same critics who talked gloomily of a German menace to India directed from the Caspian made capital, in their indictment of the Baku incident, out of the precarious nature of our communications. It should be remembered that this argument of the impotence of a force at the end of a long and difficult line of communications applied conversely to the other side, and it knocked the bottom out of the threat of an armed invasion of India.

But no sane person who had given a thought to the subject contemplated an invasion of the kind. Any soldier who understands the conditions of the East will smile at the picture of a Turco-Germanic-Bolshevik force, self-supplied, with communications behind it, and a sufficiency of artillery and ammunition, descending from the Trans-Caspian line by way of Meshed to attack India. Such a stroke was not in the Hun's mind. Germany's hopes still centred in political penetration. Her dream was to stir up Afghanistan and the Pathan tribes on the border, and at the same time to engineer a mutiny among the people of India against the British Raj. In these hopes she was consistently disappointed. Some of the wild Persian tribesmen touched her gold, but they did little for her in return, and were curiously unresponsive to the incitement to murder civilians in their beds.

The Amir of Afghanistan throughout proved our staunch friend. He turned a deaf ear to the political missionaries and jehadists, and he controlled the fanatical elements in his State like the strong ruler that he is.

But the most unfruitful branch of the Hun's propaganda was the department that aimed at the seduction of the sepoy. With the one exception of the trans-frontier tribesman, who is not a subject of the King, his missionary efforts met with poor response. The Indian soldier soon learnt to detest the Boche, and the strong ties that bind him to his British officer have been strengthened by the disgust each feels for an unclean fighter. And Kultur is as abhorrent to the intelligentsia as to the sepoy. The educated Indian of the middle classes is through the nature of his education and circumstances a Liberal. Militarism and bureaucracy are his bugbears; the voice of articulate India was heard early in the war when a member of the Viceroy's Legislative Council declared that no sacrifice of men or money would be grudged "in order that the success of British arms should establish the triumph of right over might, of civilisation over the military barbarism of Germany, of ordered freedom over military slavery."

Conclusion

To this ideal India proved true. In Palestine and Mesopotamia she contributed two-thirds of the force which evicted the Turk. The Ottoman Empire, as a province of Germany, appealed to her in vain for sympathy or support. Our Mohammedan sepoys were not deceived by the pretext of a religious war; and nearly every page in this story has borne witness to the courage, devotion, and endurance with which the Indian soldier, Moslem or Hindu, has played his part. It was through his constancy that we were able to beat down the Turk. When at Aleppo and Qalah Shergat the last remnants of the broken Ottoman Army laid down their arms and saw all round them the resolute dark faces of the sepoy and sowar, they knew in what proportion the Indian Army had contributed to their defeat.

The end was sudden and dramatic. Those of us who left Mesopotamia in the summer of 1918 only missed one week's fighting. It was Allenby who unlocked the door at Aleppo, but by this time the Turk was beaten to a standstill on both fields, in Palestine and in Mesopotamia. Had General Marshall delayed his stroke a week the road to the Mediterranean would have lain open to him; he might have gained the Turkish railhead at Nisibin without a casualty. But so tame a conclusion to the epic of Mesopotamia was incompatible with his own daring initiative and with the offensive spirit of his troops. By his action at Qalah Shergat he precipitated catastrophe, cutting away the last prop from under the tottering fabric of the Ottoman Empire. On October 81st, the day before the armistice was signed between the Allies and Turkey at Mudros, he enveloped and captured the entire Turkish force opposed to him on the Tigris.[1]

[1] The cost in casualties of victory in Mesopotamia was—Officers, 4,335 (killed or died from wounds or disease, 1,340); other ranks, 93,244 (killed or died, 29,769).

"Operations [1] commenced on October 24th with an attack on the strong Turkish position at Fathah, where the Tigris flows through the Jebel Hamrin. This was carried out by the 17th and 18th Indian Divisions west and east of the Tigris respectively, assisted by the 7th Indian Cavalry Brigade on the east bank of the Tigris, and the 11th Indian Cavalry Brigade on the west bank. The latter by a march of over 50 miles forced a crossing over the Lesser Zab in face of opposition, and by a further march of about 50 miles got right round the Turks and astride their lines of communication at Hurwaish, where they were joined by our Armoured Car Brigade.

"Outmanœuvred on the east bank and driven back on the west bank, the Turks fell back to their second line at the confluence of the Lesser Zab, a position of great natural strength. On October 25th the 18th Indian Division forced a crossing over the Lesser Zab and drove back to the west bank of the Tigris all Turks who were east of that river, while the 17th Indian Division closed up to the enemy, who were now all on the west bank.'

"The fighting which ensued was of a very severe nature. The hilly ground, indented with ravines and previously prepared for defence, was all in favour of the Turks, who fought with the greatest stubbornness. Our difficulties were increased by the sandy nature of the soil, which delayed transport, and by absence of water except the Tigris itself.

"After continuous fighting the 17th Indian Division forced the Turks to fall back on their third position on the hills covering Shergat on the morning of the 27th. All that day Turkish reserves tried to break through the 11th Indian Cavalry Brigade, who barred the road to Mosul, but without success, though the arrival of the Turkish reinforcements from Mosul forced that Brigade to draw back its right in order to cover its rear.

"On the night of October 27th–28th the 7th Indian Cavalry Brigade joined the 11th Indian Cavalry Brigade, and the 53rd Indian Infantry Brigade, moving up the east bank after

[1] As these operations took place after I left Mesopotamia, I quote General Marshall's own summary.

a march of 88 miles, was able to support the cavalry in preventing any Turks breaking through northwards. On October 28th the 17th Indian Division successfully assaulted the Turkish Shergat position, and on the 29th, though exhausted by their continuous fighting and marching through the rugged hills, pushed forward and attacked till nightfall the Turks, who were now hemmed in.

"On the morning of the 30th the Turkish Commander surrendered his total force, consisting of the whole of the 14th Division, the bulk of the 2nd Division, and portions of two regiments of the 5th Division, with all their artillery train and administrative services.[1]

"The fortitude and courage displayed by all the troops was beyond praise, and was the main factor in the defeat of a stubborn enemy holding carefully prepared positions in a rugged and difficult country."

And so the Expedition ended. The long road to Baghdad carried us to the shore which for years had been the utmost boundary to the kingdom of our hopes. Often in Mesopotamia, as mile by mile we fought our way slowly north and west, I remembered the emotion with which, standing on Lebanon twenty years earlier, after the passage of the desert, I looked down on the bright waves of the Mediterranean. To a tired traveller the crossing from the Shatt-el-Arab to the blue inland sea is almost allegorical. How much more moving to the survivors of the army who have buried their dead in the mud and sand of the accursed plain! To the south and east their mind's horizon was bounded by the yellow silted stream which for months merging into years had been the scene of suffering and disaster. When the pioneers of the Expedition crossed the bar at Fao on November 6th, 1914, they entered a sullen and hostile expanse of waters, an avenue as void of physical and spiritual inspiration as the land to which it admitted them. Four years

[1] The Turkish Army Commander, Ismail Hakki Pasha, surrendered with 8,000 men

almost to a day had passed since the guns of H.M.S. *Odin* silenced the Turkish battery at Fao, when General Townshend, as emissary of the Turks, carried their unconditional surrender to the Admiral of our fleet at Mudros. Those of the Force who made the great traverse, whose eyes were gladdened by the sight of the homely European sea, must have felt like Xenophon and his ten thousand when they gazed on the Euxine from Mount Theches and uttered the great cry that has resounded through the ages. Only this struggle was more protracted, and its fruits were victory.

And here this chronicle of war is ended. The historian of peace will tell how the inheritors of the Turk reaped the harvest of our sacrifice.

ROLL OF OFFICERS, NON-COMMISSIONED OFFICERS AND MEN OF THE MESOPOTAMIAN EXPEDITIONARY FORCE WHO HAVE BEEN AWARDED THE VICTORIA CROSS

No.	Rank	Name	Unit	Place and Date of Gallantry
—	Major	George Godfrey Massy WHEELER	7th Hariana Lancers	Shaiba, 12th April, 1915
—	Lieut.-Commdr. (Actg. Commdr.)	Edgar Christopher COOKSON, D.S.O.	Royal Navy	Nr. Magasis, 28th Sept., 1915
3398	Sepoy	CHATTA SINGH	9th Bhopal Infantry	Wadi, 13th Jan., 1916
501	Lce.-Naik	LALA	41st Dogras	El Orah, 21st Jan., 1916
—	Captain	John Alexander SINTON, M.B.	Indian Medical Service	Orah Ruins, 21st Jan., 1916
15818	Private	George STRINGER	1st Bn. Manchester Regt.	Es Sinn, 8th March, 1916
—	Lieutenant (temp. Captain)	Angus BUCHANAN, M.C.	4th Bn. S. Wales Bordrs.	Falahiyeh, 5th April, 1916
920	Corporal	Sidney WARE	1st Bn. Seaforth Highrs.	Sannaiyat, 6th April, 1916
—	Sec.-Lieutenant	Edgar Kinghorn MYLES, D.S.O.	9th Bn. Worcester Regt.	Sannaiyat, 9th April, 1916
—	Reverend	William Robert Fountaine ADDISON	Temp. C.F., 4th Class	Sannaiyat, 9th April, 1916
411220	Private	James Henry FYNN	4th Bn. S. Wales Bordrs.	Sannaiyat, 9th April, 1916
1605	Naik	SHAHAMAD KHAN	89th Punjabis	Beit Aieesa, 12th–13th April, 1916
—	Lieut.-Commdr. (temp.)	Charles Henry COWLEY	R.N.V.R.	Falahiyeh, 24th April, 1916
—	Lieutenant	Humphrey Osbaldeston Brooke FIRMAN	Royal Navy	Falahiyeh, 24th April, 1916
—	Major (act. Lieut.-Col.)	Edward Elers Delaval HENDERSON	2nd Bn. N. Staffs. Regt.	W. B. Hai, 25th Jan., 1917
—	Temp. Lieut.	Robert Edwin PHILLIPS	13th attd. 9th Bn. Royal Warwick. Regt.	Nr. Kut W. B. Hai, 25th Jan., 1917
811	Sergeant	Thomas STEELE	1st Bn. Seaforth Highrs.	Nr. Kut Sannaiyat, 22nd Feb., 1917
—	Captain (temp. Major)	George Campbell WHEELER	2/9th Gurkha Rifles	Shumran Bend, 23rd Feb., 1917
18233	Private	John READITT	6th Bn. S. Lancashire Regt.	Nr. Kut, 25th Feb., 1917
18105	Private	Jack WHITE	6th Bn. K.O.R. Lancs. Regt	Diala, 7th–8th March, 1917
—	Captain	Oswald Austin REID	2nd Bn. King's L'pool Regt. attd. 6th Bn. N. Lan. Regt.	Diala, 8th–9th March, 1917
871	Private	Charles MELVIN	2nd Bn. Black Watch (Royal Highrs.)	Istabulat, 21st April, 1917
—	Lieutenant	John Reginald Noble GRAHAM	9th Bn. Arg. and Suth'd Highrs. attd. 136th M.G. Co.	Istabulat, 22nd April, 1917

INDEX

ABADAN, oil works at, i. 2, 6, 9, 10, 12, 241, 248, 249
Abdul, Sultan, ii. 128
Abu Jisra, ii. 137
—— Roman, i. 122, 158
—— Zenabil Pass, ii. 257
Aerial, i. 100, 131, 132
Aeroplane supplies for Kut, i. 221, 226
Afghanistan, Amir of, ii. 294
—— and German propaganda, i. 254
Ahmed Bey, surrender of, ii. 231 (note), 233
Ahram, i. 258
Ahwaz threatened by Turks, i. 12; life in, 245
Ahwaz-Amara march of the 12th Brigade, i. 235
Ain Faris, occupied by British, ii. 273
—— Marich, asphalt lakes at, ii. 262
Ajab Khan, Subadar Major, i. 243
Aj Jali Canal, ii. 175
Akarkuf Lake, ii. 133
Aleppo, military importance of, ii. 225; arabana service to, 264; Indians at, 295
Ali Gharbi, muddle at, i. 40; order of advance from, 128; arrival of Cossack squadron at, 290
—— Hussein, i. 133
—— Sharqi, i. 39
—— tomb, of, ii. 199, 209
Al Khubn, ii. 165
Allenby, General, ii. 198, 272, 295
Altun Kupri, Turks pursued to, ii. 222
—— —— road, enemy attacked on, ii. 276
Ammianus, on the Saracens, ii. 87
Ana, ii. 269, 271
Andranik, guerrilla warfare of, ii. 292
Anglo-Persian oilfields, i. 2, 6, 9, 10, 12, 241, 248, 249

Anizeh Bedouins, ii. 125; and Najaf sheikhs, 212
Aq Su River, ii. 274
Arab cavalry, i. 110, 111
—— fugitives from Kut, i. 226
—— Khans proclaimed outlaws, i. 259
—— rising in Persia, i. 240
Arabs, riverain, i. 34; looting propensities of, 105, 106, 107, 112, ii. 24, 25, 75, 87, 100; of Hamar Lake district, i. 273; and British occupation of Mesopotamia, ii. 188; and Euphrates irrigation scheme, 191, 192
Ardahan, ii. 282
Armenians, massacre of, ii. 118, 119, 122; defection of, at Baku, 292
Armoured cars, ii. 68, 230; rescue of British prisoners by, 270
Army transport carts used to convey wounded after Sheikh Saad, i. 57
Arsenjan, Germans defeated at, i. 260
Asarabad Pass, ii. 136
Asphaltic oil springs, ii. 262
Asquith, Mr., on objectives of Mesopotamian campaign, i. 2
Astrabad, ii. 289
Atab, ii. 3, 11
Atiyeh, Sheikh, ii. 212, 213
Aylmer, General, ordered to advance on Kut, i. 42; engages enemy at Sheikh Saad, 44; responsibility of, for attack on Dujaila Redoubt, 148; recall of, 162; wire from, to Kut garrison, 227
Azerbaijan, i. 258
Aziziyeh, General Nixon's concentration at, i. 21; enemy evacuation of, ii. 77; supplies accumulated at, 79
—— Ridge, a footing secured on, ii. 229

301

Index

BABEL, ii. 199, 200
Babil (Bab Ilani), ii. 207
Babylon, excavations at, ii. 199, 203; walls of Nebuchadnezzar, 204; Acropolis of, 204; Ishtar Gate, 204, 205; Belshazzar's banqueting chamber, 205; hanging gardens, 206; Kings of, 206
Babylon-Ecbatana road, ii. 198
Baghailah, ii. 15, 18, 73; haul at, 76
Baghdad, first advance on, responsibility for, i. 4, 21; second advance on, ii. 84; British entry into, 96, 99; first days in, 97; scenes in streets of, 101, 102; wireless station at, 106; graveyards of, 112; proclamation to people of, 114; Turkish rule in, 114; Armenians in, 122; climate of, 179; improved conditions in, after British occupation, 184
—— -Aleppo mail route, ii. 264
" —— boil," i. 234
—— Railway, ii. 226; concession for continuation of, 279
Baharan, i. 15
Bahrein, i. 9, 256
Bakhtiaris, i. 246
Baku, and Turkey, ii. 283 (note); revolution in, 290; British force dispatched to, 290; evacuation of British troops from, 291; Russian reinforcements for, 291; remains in enemy hands, 292
Baldwin, General, i. 177 (note)
Baluchistan Infantry (124th), ii. 141, 143, 241
Band-i-Adhaim, battle of, ii. 160
Bani Lam, i. 37, 38
Baquba, ii. 137, 149, 182
Baratoff, General, i. 219, 220, 283, 284
Barjisiyeh, battle of, i. 14 (note)
—— Wood, i. 114
Barnsley, Seaman-Gunner, i. 292
Barrett, General Sir Arthur, i. 10, 14
Barrow, Sir Edmund, i. 22
Basra, abandoned by Turks, i. 10, 11; disembarkation of infantry and guns at, 127; scenes in, 231; river craft at, 233, ii. 5; navigation control at, 7; development of, 8, 9; climate of, 179, 181; effect of occupation of, 278
Basra, ii. 74, 75
Basrugiyeh, ii. 11
Bast, Persian system of, i. 263
Batum, ii. 282
Bawi tribe, i. 240, 241, 242, 249, ii. 93
Bedouins, Anizeh, ii. 125
Beersheba, fall of, ii. 244
Beit Aieesa, shelled by British, i. 119; battle of, 186; enemy counter-attack at, 192; Turkish casualties at, 190, 197, 198
Beled, occupation of, ii. 151, 182
—— Ruz, ii. 236
Bellum, the Arab, i. 131, 270, ii. 202
Beni Taruf Arabs, i. 14, 243
Berlin-Baghdad Railway, ii. 221
Bers Nimrud, ii. 199
Bhopal Infantry (9th), i. 48, 49, 53, 95, 164, ii. 134, 135, 167, 168
Biach, Dr., i. 260
Bicharakoff, General, ii. 253, 289, 291
Bint-el-Hassan, ii. 154
Bitlis, ii. 282
Bitumen wells, ii. 261
Black Watch, i. 27, 32, 40, 48, 49, 63, 93, 94, 95, 164, 180, 200, 202, 206, ii. 95, 96, 105, 134, 135, 167, 168, 169, 242
Blewitt, Adjutant, ii. 174
Bolsheviks, and General Dunsterville, ii. 287
Boom of Koweit, i. 233
Boota Singh, i. 80
British Red Cross Society, and garrison at Kut, i. 223
Brooke, Captain, ii. 70
Brooking, General, ii. 226, 265
Brown, Major, ii. 21
" Buddoo " Arabs, i. 51, 110, 111, 113, 114, 115, 116, ii. 13, 25
Buffs, i. 48, 94, 164, ii. 70, 104, 154
Buggalows, Arab, i. 233
Burma Infantry (93rd), i. 188, 193, ii. 20, 140, 143
Burma Sappers, ii. 54
Bushire, German intrigues in, i. 256; British administration of, and restor-

Index   303

ation to Persia, 257; Tangistani attack on, 258
Buttercup, i. 233

CAMEL post, ii. 263
Camels as second line of transport, i. 135
Campbell, General, i. 194, ii. 143
Cartwright, Sergeant, ii. 36
Caspian, British troops on, ii. 222
Cassels, Colonel, ii. 175
Cassels' Cavalry Brigade, ii. 155, 158, 159
"Catty's Express," ii. 152
Caucasus, political situation in, ii. 286
Cavalry, Colonel Henderson on, ii. 67
—— (23rd), i. 245
—— (33rd), i. 241
Cayley, General, ii. 152, 274
Censorship, and the war correspondent, i. 65, 80, 101, ii. 253
Chaab Arabs, i. 241, 242
Chaman Keupri, ii. 273
Chernobuzoff, defeats Turks at Lalgan, i. 284
Cheshires, ii. 11, 38, 93, 153, 160, 161, 163
Christian, General, i. 151
Chunuk Bair, i. 177
Clio, i. 15
Close-Brooks, Captain, ii. 21
Cobbe, General, ii. 107, 133
Comet, i. 16, 25, ii. 76
Connaught Rangers, i. 158, 159, 188, 197
Cossacks, arrival of, at Ali Gharbi, i. 290; kit of, 291 (note)
Cowley, Lieut.-Commander, i. 208, 209
Cox, Sir Percy, ii. 207 (note)
Crocker, Colonel, ii. 161
Ctesiphon, deficient medical supplies at, i. 7; battle of, 23; retreat from, 24; casualties at, 24 (note); neglect of wounded at, 60; Turkish prisoners at, 215; abandoned by Turks, ii. 84; Arch of, i. 266, ii. 87; Townshend's disastrous victory at, 87

DABBA Island, i. 9
Daghistani, Mahomed Pasha, i. 242, 243

Dahra Bend, ii. 29; offensive for, 45; Turks dislodged at, 46; wholesale surrender of Turks at, 47, 48
Dahuba, ii. 158
Damascus, camel post to, ii. 263
Daniel's tomb, ii. 198
Daur, ii. 221, 239, 240, 244
Deccan Infantry (97th), i. 48
Deir-el-Zor, Armenians at, ii. 124; camel post from, 263
Delamain, General, i. 10, 19, 256
Deli Abbas, ii. 138, 145; British occupation of, 146, 237; enemy surprised at, 254
Dennys, Colonel, i. 45
Devons, ii. 40, 41
Dhibban, ii. 183
Diala, ii. 71, 84, 88; attack on, 89; crossed by Allies, 254
Dibaiyi, fighting in, ii. 95
Diwaniyeh, i. 275, ii. 194
Dogameh, enemy defeat at, ii. 145
Dogras (37th), i. 48, 93, 95, 164, ii. 46, 47, 104, 107, 109, 256
—— (41st), i. 48, 49, 53, 93, 94, 95, 164
Dorsetshire Regiment, i. 10, 13, 19, 95, 164, 203, 241, 242, ii. 140, 141, 144, 229, 233
Drabis, i. 133, 287, ii. 102
Dryfly, i. 268
Dujaila Redoubt, attack on, i. 138 *et seq.*, ii. 167 *et seq.*; casualties in, i. 143 (note), 155
Dulaim tribes, hostility of, ii. 234
Duncan, Dr., i. 95, 164
Dunlop, Colonel, i. 243
Dunsford, General, ii. 227
Dunsterville, General, ii. 285; expedition of, 286; and Bolsheviks, 287
Dust storms, i. 234, ii. 81, 90, 94, 99, 112, 161, 162, 233

EAST LANCASHIRES, ii. 70, 90, 156, 157
Eddis, Commander, ii. 75
Eden, Garden of, i. 33, 230, 266
Edwardes, General, ii. 147
Egerton, General, ii. 152
El Hannah (*see* Umm-el-Hannah)
El Huweslat, capture of, ii. 239
El Orah, check at, i. 162 *et seq.*

Elizabetpol, ii. 290
Enver Bey, ii. 216
Enzeli, ii. 284, 287; Bolshevism in, 287; strategical importance of, 289
Erech, ii. 199
Erzerum, restored to Turkey, ii. 282; capture of, 292
Esagila, temple of, ii. 204, 205
Espiègle, i. 9, 10, 11, 15, 17
Euphrates, Turkish concentration on, i. 12; irrigation scheme, ii. 189; two branches of, 189, 190; fighting on, 259
—— Column, objectives of, ii. 132
Ezekiel's Tomb, ii. 198
Ezra's Tomb, i. 33, 266, ii. 7, 200

FALAHIYEH, Turkish reinforcements at, i. 174; the battlefield, 175; punitive expedition to, 242; ammunition barges destroyed at, 290, 292-4 (*see also* Sannaiyat)
Fao, British occupation of, i. 9
Farrukh Shah, murder of, i. 263
Feluja, occupation of, ii. 132, 133, 183, 194
Field Artillery, Royal, ii. 154, 159
Firefly, i. 25, ii. 74, 75
Firman, Lieutenant, i. 208
Flies, plagues of, in Mesopotamia, i. 235, ii. 164
Flycatcher, i. 232
Flood, the, i. 103, ii. 200
Fort Kermea, ii. 152
Frazer, Colonel, i. 11
Fry, General, i. 10, 11, 19

GARDEN OF EDEN, i. 33, 230, 266
Garhwal Rifles (39th), ii. 230, 231
Germany and the Bakhtiari Khans, i. 248; and Armenian massacres, ii. 128; at Samarrah, 178; intrigues of, i. 253, ii. 272, 278, 283, 294
Ghulab Khan, i. 80
Gloucesters, ii. 44, 45, 71, 146
Goltz, von der, i. 23, 41, ii. 57
Gordon, Lieutenant, ii. 21
Gornah (*see* Qurna)
Gorringe, General, in command on Karun river, i. 14, 242, 243; in command of Nasiriyeh force, 17; and attack on Dujaila Redoubt, 148; recall of, 162
Graham, Lieutenant, ii. 174
Grahame, Mr., i. 260, 262
Green, Sec.-Lieutenant, ii. 36
Greisinger, intrigues of, in Kerman, i. 263
Grenadiers (102nd), i. 48, 94 (note), ii. 46, 104, 107
Griffiths, Colonel, ii. 176
Gufars, i. 132, ii. 107, 262
Gunboats, pursuit of retreating Turks by, ii. 72
Gurkha Rifles (1st), ii. 18, 20, 140, 141
—— —— (2nd), i. 153, 154, 155, ii. 53
—— —— (4th), ii. 48, 70, 95, 107, 256
—— —— (5th), ii. 229, 233
—— —— (6th), ii. 229, 233
—— —— (8th), ii. 134, 135, 167, 168, 170
—— —— (9th), i. 75, 188, 193, ii. 40, 41, 53

HABBANIYEH Canal, ii. 228
Haditha, ii. 269
Hai bridgehead, ii. 29
—— salient, Turkish bravery at, ii. 30; bombardment of, 35
—— town, raid on, ii. 24
Haidar Khan, i. 254
Hamadan, Russian victory at, i. 259; Turks at, ii. 107, 148; General Dunsterville's arrival at, 286
Hamar Lake, i. 272, 273
Hamilton, Sir Ian, Gallipoli dispatches of, i. 177
Hampshire Regiment, i. 94, 95, 164, ii. 37, 47, 54, 65, 107
Harbe, ii. 151, 152
Hardinge, Lord, and Sir John Nixon, i. 21
Hardman, Sec.-Lieutenant, ii. 21
Hariana Lancers (7th), i. 114
Hay, Colonel, ii. 41
Hayer, von, assassination of, i. 262
Heat-stroke, i. 286, 289
Hehir, Colonel, i. 227
Henderson, Colonel, ii. 36

Index

Henry of Reuss, Prince, i. 253
Herts Yeomanry, ii. 70, 96, 98
Highland Light Infantry, i. 150, 288, ii. 17, 20, 26
Hilleh, ii. 194
Hinaidie, ii. 104
Hindieh barrage, ii. 189, 190 ; irrigation works, 191
Hindijan, Mirs of, i. 241
Hit, ii. 259 ; entered by British, 259 ; topography of, 260 ; filth at, 261 ; bitumen wells at, 261 ; flora of, 263 ; streets of, 265
Hobart, Major, ii. 269-70
Hogge, Colonel, motor column of, ii. 267
Horse Artillery, Royal, ii. 144
Houston, Lieutenant, ii. 95
"Huffs," the, i. 164
Hunter, Captain, ii. 285
Huseiniyeh Canal, ii. 208
"Hush-Hush Push," ii. 285
Hussars (13th), ii. 81, 242, 243, 274
—— (14th), ii. 230
Hussein, shrine of, ii. 208, 215

Ihsan Bey, ii. 146, 151, 152, 153, 162
Illah, enemy retreat to, i. 242
Imam Ali Mansur, i. 286, ii. 3, 13, 14
—— Mahdi, Turkish retreat on, ii. 66
India, safeguarding of, ii. 278 ; German designs upon, 294 ; part of, in the War, 294-5
Indian Army incited to mutiny, i. 254, 256
—— contingent embark at Marseilles, i. 27
—— Government and Mesopotamian Expedition, i. 6, 7
Infantry (97th), i. 94, 95
—— (119th), i. 13
—— (121st), i. 223
Inland Water Transport, ii. 7, 8
Irrigation work in Euphrates Valley, ii. 189
Isfahan, German wireless station at, i. 258 ; German intrigues at, 261
Islamic propaganda, i. 255
Ismail Hakki Pasha, surrender of, ii. 297 (note)

Istabulat, battles of, ii. 167
Izhaki Canal, ii. 175

Jaipur and Bharatpur Imperial Service Transport Corps, i. 134
Jarrah, Mirs of, i. 241
Jat Light Infantry, i. 49, 52, 93, 95
Jebel Hamrin, battle of, ii. 22, 137 ; evacuation of, 146 ; fauna and flora of, 238 ; British withdrawal to, 257
Jerablus, German shipyard at, ii. 271 (note)
Jews, Turkish persecution of, ii. 120
Julian's campaign, ii. 85
Julnar, i. 208, 209, 226, 228
Jumailat, reconnaissance at, i. 119
Jungalis join Bolsheviks, ii. 289

Kadhimain, ii. 95, 208
Kakhka, ii. 289
Kala Haji Fahàn, ii. 12
—— Hissar, Armenian refugees from, ii. 124
Kangavar, ii. 286
Kara Su River, ii. 136, 148
—— Tappah, ii. 254 ; battle of, 256
Kars, ii. 282
Karun River, British garrison on, i. 12, 245 ; climate of, 234, 235 ; and the oil-fields, 240
Kazim Karabekir Bey, ii. 165
Kazvin, Russian troops arrive at, i. 251, 259
Keary, General, and attack on Dujaila Redoubt, i. 142, 148 ; commands Khanikin Column, ii. 136
Kelleks, transport by, i. 129
Kemball, General, and the battle of Sheikh Saad, i. 44 ; and attack on Dujaila Redoubt, 142, 148, 153
Kerbela, rising at, i. 275 ; shrine of Hussein at, ii. 208 ; looting of, 215 ; caravan route from, 263
Kerind, ii. 287
Kerkha, crossing of, i. 242
Kerman, expulsion of Germans from, i. 259, 260
Kermanshah, i. 258, ii. 136, 286, 287

Khafajiyeh, i. 14, 243
Khalil Bey, i. 107, 108, 212, ii. 58, 65
Khamisiyeh, i. 282
Khan Baghdadi, Turkish defeat at, ii. 223; enemy retreat on, 259; battle of, 265; enemy surrender at, 268; aviators taken prisoner and rescued, 269-70; Turkish prisoners captured at, 270
—— Feheme, ii. 269
Khanikin, Baratoff's march on, i. 283; British advance on, ii. 132; occupation of, 257; supplies for Dunsterville's Expedition from, 287
—— Column, ii. 136
Khaurvah, ii. 263
Kifl, ii. 190, 191, 192, 198
Kifri, ii. 257, 273
—— road, ii. 254
Killddar, ii. 213
King's Own, i. 183, ii. 44, 70, 89, 90, 103, 104, 157
Kirkuk, ii. 254, 275
Kishm, i. 263
Kishuk, ii. 254
Kizil Robat, encounter of Allied Armies at, ii. 147; bridge burnt by enemy, 237; Diala crossed at, 254; bridgehead established at, 257
Krasnovodsk, ii. 284, 289, 290
Kubbej Village, ii. 157
Kufa, ii. 198; Plain of, 199; mosque at, 209, 214
Kulawund, charge at, ii. 273
Kum, rebels defeated at, i. 259
Kurdistan (Southern), operations in, ii. 272; flora of, 277
Kurds, looting by, ii. 100
Kurnah (see Qurna)
Kut, Turkish concentration at, i. 18; strategic value of, 18; battle of, 19; investment of, 42; Aylmer's unsuccessful attempt to relieve, 43; fall of, 210, 211, 283, 284; diary of siege of, 213; grain stores discovered at, 214, 221; aerial bombardment of, 216; armistice at, 217; privations of garrison of, 221, 226, 228; tobacco famine at, 222; amusements and games at, 223; death-rate at, 224, 227; East Mounds captured, ii. 22; liquorice factory taken, 45; Union Jack hoisted at, 72

LAJJ, British wounded removed to, i. 24; Turks withdraw to, ii. 77; action of 13th Hussars at, ii. 81
Lake, General, i. 128; and attack on Dujaila Redoubt, 148; succeeded by General Maude, ii. 246
Laigan, Turkish defeat at, i. 284
Lal Shah Baz, shrine of, ii. 210
"Lambs," ii. 68
Lancers (10th), ii. 96, 98, 212
—— (13th), ii. 143, 147, 243
—— (32nd), ii. 96, 98, 176, 243
Lawrence, i. 11, 15
Layard, Sir A. H., on riverain Arabs, i. 37
Leachman, Colonel, ii. 210
Leicestershire Regiment, i. 46, 95, 164, 180, ii. 18, 62, 151, 172, 173
Lewin, General, ii. 32, 33, 161, 163
Lewis Pelly, i. 16
Listermann, propaganda of, i. 256, 257
Loman, Lieutenant, ii. 92
Loyal North Lancashires, i. 177, 183, ii. 17, 45, 46, 70, 90, 93, 155, 159
Lucas, General, ii. 227

MAASHAD-AD-DAUR, Turkish retreat on, ii. 239
Macdonald, Lieutenant, ii. 274
—— Sergeant, i. 81, 92
Macfarlane, Piper, i. 31
MacIlwaine, Captain, i. 292
Macnabb, Sergeant, i. 178, ii. 182
Madhij, Euphrates bridged at, ii. 227
Magasis, Julnar captured at, i. 208; forward post at, ii. 3; Fort of, 5; daring stroke at, 50
Mahailas, i. 131, 233, ii. 8
Mahomed Abdul Hassan, battle of, ii. 18; fall of, 25, 29
Mahomet Effendi, ii. 194
Mahratta Light Infantry (105th), ii. 142
—— —— (110th) i. 11, 13, 223, 269, ii. 20

Index

Mahrattas (117th), i. 13, 19
Maidun-i-Naftun, oil-field at, i. 240, ii. 262
Makoo Effendi, ii. 201
Malang fakirs, ii. 210
Manchester Regiment, i. 152, 153, 154, 195, ii. 20, 21, 141, 143, 241
Mansuriyeh-el-Jebel, ii. 138, 237
Mantis, ii. 72, 73, 80
Marid, i. 241
Marshall, Captain W. M., murder of, ii. 213.
Marshall, General, ii. 107, 152, 155, 159, 259, 272, 295
Martin, Captain, i. 293
Mashhufchis, definition of, i. 273
Mashona, i. 11
Mason's Mound, i. 122
Matthews, Lieutenant, i. 215
Maude, General, ii. 2, 3, 77; death of, 246
Mazeera, Turkish defeat at, i. 11
Mecca, Sherif of, i. 256, ii. 280
Mecheriyeh Canal, ii. 7
Melliss, General, i. 13, 24
Melvin, Private, ii. 169-70
Mendali, ii. 236, 252
Merv, Bolshevism in, ii. 289
Merwara Infantry (44th), i. 235, 245
Mesopotamia, transport difficulties in, i. 6-8, 32, 40, 41, 54, 96, 126, ii. 6; amphibious actions in, i. 15, 17, 270; climate of, 18, 185, 231, 234, 237, 238, 244, 267, 270, 281, 284, ii. 15, 48, 164, 177, 178, 257; flora and fauna of, i. 38, 39, 167, 168, 230, 267, 268, 272, 273, 282, 284, ii. 140, 263; beginning of trench warfare in, i. 164; tribal system in, 273; present and past of, ii. 185; Biblical features of, 198
—— Commission, i. 4
Mesopotamian Expedition, objectives of, i. 2, 6, ii. 278; tragedy of, i. 5; casualties in, ii. 295
Miner, i. 11, 15
Mirages, i. 111, 117, 120
Mirs of Jarrah and Hindijan, i. 241
Mitchell, Major, ii. 161

Mohammedans, German propaganda among, i. 285
Mohammed-bin-Ali, shrine of, ii. 208
Mosquitoes, i. 236, 267
Moth, ii. 73, 76
Muhammad Ali, i. 133
Muhammerah, Sheikh of, i. 240, 241
Mule, the, and his driver, i. 132
Muntafik confederacy, i. 274, 277
Murphy, Major C. C. R., i. 13
Musa-bin-Tafar, shrine of, ii. 208
Musa, Haji, ii. 264
Museyib, ii. 194
Mushaid, British withdrawal, to, ii. 183
—— Ridge, attack on, ii. 227
Mushaidie, engagement at, ii. 133; casualties at, 134, 135; Turkish retreat from, 135

NAHR KELLAK, i. 26
—— —— Bend, battle at, ii. 73, 76
Nahrin Kupri River, ii. 256, 257
Nahrwan Canal, ii. 156, 157
Najaf, i. 275, ii. 199; Ali's tomb at, 199, 209; trouble at, 211; graveyards of, 214; treasure in shrine at, 216; the Mujtahid of, 218
Nakhailat, ii. 59
Nal Sikhan Pass, ii. 148
Napier's Rifles (125th), i. 49, 181, 200, ii. 241, 242, 243
Nasiriyeh, strategic value of, i. 17, 275; fall of, 17, 18, 274; floods in, 276
—— Arab Scouts, 277
Nasir-ud-din, Shah, ii. 216
Nazmi Bey, ii. 265
Neidermeyer, propaganda of, i. 260
Nisibin, ii. 22, 295
Nixon, General Sir John, censure of, i. 4; defenders of, 4; takes supreme command, 14; dispatch of, 17; confidence of, in ability to capture Baghdad, 21
Norfolk Regiment, i. 11, 13, 95, 164, 203, 224, ii. 51, 52, 65, 86
Norie, General, and Sheikh Saad battle, i. 44
"Norsets," i. 95, 164, 203
North Stafford Regiment, ii. 35, 71, 146, 290, 291

Nunn, Captain, i. 16
Nur-ud-Din, i. 18, 108, 215, 228

O'Connor, Colonel, i. 258, 259
Odin, i. 9, 11, 15, ii. 298
Oliphant, Major, i. 258
Orah, camp life at, i. 163
Oxford and Bucks L.I., i. 15, 180, 216

Palestine, Armenians in, ii. 292
Pan-Islamic movement in Persia, i. 253
Paraffin oil springs, ii. 262
Pathans, German propaganda and, i. 254
Peck, Colonel, ii. 154
Pembroke, Sec.-Lieutenant, ii. 21
Persia, rising in, i. 240, 241; German intrigue in, 247, 253, ii. 283; failure of *coup d'état* in, i. 259; famine in, ii. 287
Persian Arabistan cleared of enemy, i. 14, 243, ii. 150
Pessick, Lieut.-Colonel, ii. 174
Petrovsk, ii. 291
Pioneer, ii. 74
Pioneers (34th), ii. 141
—— (125th), i. 48
—— (128th), i. 197
Pony transport train, i. 134
Pugin, Dr., in Isfahan, i. 261; supersession of, 262
Punjabi Rifles (56th), i. 78, 180, ii. 18, 94, 134, 174
Punjabis (22nd), i. 15
—— (24th), i. 13
—— (26th), ii. 37, 65, 66
—— (27th), i. 197, ii. 50
—— (28th), i. 48, 200, ii. 167, 168
—— (62nd), i. 95, ii. 40, 45, 65
—— (67th), ii. 65
—— (82nd), ii. 37, 65
—— (89th), i. 159, 188
—— (90th), ii. 230, 231
—— (92nd), i. 44, 46, 200, 202, 206, ii. 58, 94, 167, 243
Pusht-i-Kuh, i. 166; Wali of, 240, 291

Qalah Shergat, ii. 295, 296, 297
Qasr-i-Shirin, ii. 136, 149

Queen's, ii. 230
Quetta, Nushki line from, ii. 289
Qurna, fall of, i. 11; second battle of, 15; Turkish prisoners and guns captured at, 17; reputed site of Garden of Eden, 33, 266, ii. 200

Rahda, i. 234
Rajputs (2nd), i. 153, 154, 155, 195
—— (7th), i. 11
Rajputana Infantry (120th), i. 11, 13
Ramadi, Turkish retirement on, ii. 133, 194, 223; battle of, 182; new offensive for, 221; and Euphrates irrigation scheme, 226; surrender of Turks at, 231; capture of garrison of, 234
—— Ridge, attack on, ii. 229
Ras-el-Ain, Armenian survivors at, ii. 123
Rawling, Captain, i. 258
Rice, General, i. 44, 45, 48
River transport difficulties, i. 126. (*See also* Transport)
Robinson, General, i. 241
Rotah, reconnaissance at, i. 12
Royal George, i. 27
Russell, Lieutenant, ii. 53
Russia, defection of, ii. 281, 283, 286
Russians, capture of Kermanshah by, ii. 136; join British at Kizil Robat, 147
Ruz Canal, ii. 137

Sagwand Arabs, i. 246, 247
Sahil, Turkish defeat at, i. 10
Saida, fighting in, ii. 95
Said Hashim, raid against, i. 117
Saif Ulla, taken prisoner, i. 107
Saihan, enemy attacked at, i. 10
Saiyid Mohammed Kadhim, ii. 218
Sakal Tutan Pass, ii. 254, 255, 257
Saklawie, ii. 131, 133
Salahiyeh, enemy forces at, ii. 259; entered by British, 259
Salar-i-Masud, Khan, i. 247, 248
Samarrah, capture of, i. 1, ii. 29, 130; station bell of, 105 (note); battle

Index

of, 132, 172; summer quarters of British, 177; Julian's tomb at, 178, 222
Samawa, i. 275
Sandbrook, Mr. J. A., ii. 153 (note)
Sanders, General Liman von, ii. 283
Sand-flies, i. 236
Sand-grouse, i. 54
Sandstorms, ii. 177
Saniyeh, troops disembarked at, i. 10
Sannaiyat, battles of, i. 179, 183, 199, ii. 10, 49, 57, 171
Sappers and Miners (22nd Coy.), i. 19
Scarth, Quartermaster, ii. 174
Scinde Rifles (59th), i. 152, 154, 193, 195, 196, ii. 27, 241
Scurvy, outbreaks of, i. 221, 284, 285
Seaforth Highlanders, i. 48, 49, 52, 54, 95, 164, 180, 185, 200, 202, 206, ii. 58, 61, 168, 241, 242, 243
Sehwan, shrine of Lal Shah Baz at, ii. 210
Seiller, at Isfahan, i. 262
Seleucia, ruins of, ii. 87
Serajik, ii. 155
Serdab, definition of, i. 245, ii. 109, 181
Seyyid Issa, i. 254, 260
Shahraban, ii. 137, 236
Shaiba, i. 12, 13, 135
Shaitan, i. 11, 15, 16, 17, 25
Shaktur, definition of, ii. 124; fleet on Euphrates, 271
Shamal, the, i. 231
Shatt-el-Adhaim, defeat of enemy on, i. 1; fighting on, ii. 132, 153; Turkish retreat on, 146, 151
Shatt-el-Arab, i. 9, 131, ii. 8, 9
Shatt-el-Hai, i. 275; surprise march on, ii. 10, 11
Shatt-el-Hilleh, ii. 189
Shatt-el-Hindieh, ii. 189
Shaw, Major-General, i. 177 (note)
Shawa Khan, ii. 93
Shefket Pasha, ii. 165, 173
Sheikh Faraja Ridge, ii. 230, 231
—— Saad, battle of, i. 45 *et seq.*; hospital accommodation at, 54 (note); cemetery at, 60; British encamp at, 139; clearing hospital at, 285

Sheikh Saad-Sinn-Atab railway, ii. 3, 78
Sher Khan, Jemadar, i. 205
Shiah shrines, ii. 208
Shialah, ii. 153
Shinar, Plain of, ii. 199
Shiraz, i. 257, 258, 260, 265
Shoreimiya, enemy withdrawal to, ii. 244
Shumran, i. 129, ii. 13, 48, 51, 65, 69, 70
Shush, i. 246
Shushan, i. 25, 277, ii. 198
Shuster, i. 245
Sikh Pioneers (34th), ii. 21
Sikhim, i. 213
Sikhs (36th), ii. 38
—— (45th), ii. 38
—— (47th), i. 153, 155, 193, 195, 196, ii. 22, 241
—— (51st), i. 46, 180, ii. 62, 94, 172
—— (53rd), i. 46, ii. 18, 62, 151, 174
Siloam, Pools of, i. 125, 140
Sindiyeh, ii. 237
Sinn, attack on, i. 138; defences of, 179; Turkish evacuation of, 283, ii. 3
Sirjan, German defeat at, i. 260
Somersets (4th), i. 150, 152, 154
South Lancashire Regiment, i. 195, ii. 43, 70, 156, 157
South Wales Borderers, ii. 11, 13, 14, 47, 161, 162, 163
Subhi Bey, i. 11, 270
Subri Bey, ii. 265
Sugar Loaf Hill, ii. 134, 135
Suhaniyeh Pass, ii. 254
Sultan Bulagh, Russians at, i. 284
Sumaikcha, ii. 151
Sumana, i. 15, 16, 26, 215
Suq-esh-Sheyukh, occupation of, i. 17
Suwacha Marsh, i. 166
Suwada, ii. 59
Sykes, General, i. 260

TABRIZ, i. 258
Tadmor, ii. 263
Tangistanis, i. 256 *et seq.*
Taq-i-Garra Pass, battle of, i. 283, ii. 136, 148

Tarantula, ii. 73, 75, 80, 84
Tartar National Council, ii. 290
Tashkend, ii. 289
Tauq, ii. 274, 275
Taza Kharmatli, ii. 275
Tekrit, enemy retreat on, ii. 177, 239; trench system at, 241; attack on, 241; surrender of Turks at, 242
Tel Mahomed, ii. 95, 98
Tennant, Lieut.-Colonel, ii. 269
Thirst, tortures of, i. 287
Thompson, Colonel, ii. 37
Thomson, General, ii. 172
Thorny Nullah, i. 125
Tiflis, ii. 283
Tigris, enemy defeat on, i. 1; as line of advance, 126, ii. 7; fleet for, i. 127, 129, ii. 6; in flood, i. 184, 200, ii. 6; vagaries of, 6; British advance on, 29; crossed at Shumran, 51; opened to navigation, 64; bridged at Bawi, 93; flood level of, 131
—— Arabs, i. 105-6
—— fleet, enters Baghdad, ii. 72, 75
Townshend, General, captures Amara, i. 16; outmanœuvres the enemy, 19; brilliant generalship of, 20; overconfidence of, 42; last communications from, 211; arrives at Kut, 214; addresses to garrison at Kut, 219, 225, 228; interviews Nur-ud-Din, 228; surprises Daghistani's force at Amara, 243; and the Emperor Julian: a parallel, ii. 87; at Mudros, 298
Transport difficulties, i. 6-8, 32, 40, 41, 54, 96, 126, 129, ii. 5
Trench warfare, i. 47, 76, 164, 169, ii. 26, 59, 71
Turcoman tribes, German propaganda and, i. 254, ii. 289
Turkestan (Russian), German intrigues in, ii. 289
—— (Southern), fighting in, ii. 222
Turkish Arabistan, trouble in, i. 241
Turks, courtesy of, i. 104, 108; burial of British troops by, 106; their mistrust of Arabs, 107, ii. 75; treachery of, at Hai Town, 25; bravery of, at Mahomed Abdul Hassan, 26, 27, 30; characteristics of, 117; extortion and torture of Jews by, 120; sacrilege by, 217
Tuz Kharmatli, ii. 254, 272, 274

UBALLA CANAL, Gardens of, i. 230
Ukraine, annexation of, ii. 282
Umm-el-Hannah, battle of, i. 83; sapping up to Turkish position at, 110; advance on right bank at, 110, 125; night attack at, 122; attack on, 171
Umm-el-Tubal, i. 24, 25, ii. 74
Unjana Hill, Turks driven from, ii. 230, 231
Uqbah, ii. 259
Ur of the Chaldees, i. 266, 277, ii. 199

VICTORIA CROSS awards, ii. 299

WADI, battle of the, i. 74; British losses in, 95
—— Hauran, ii. 267
Wahhabis, ii. 215, 216
Walker, Sec.-Lieutenant, ii. 21
Waqf, ii. 216
War correspondents, modern, i. 63
—— Office takes over charge of Mesopotamian Expedition, i. 7
Warwicks, i. 172, ii. 36, 71, 95, 146, 290, 291
Wassmuss, intrigues of, i. 256, 257, 258, 260, 262
Water supply by motor convoy, ii. 228
Waterwheels, Mesopotamian, ii. 260
Wellesley's Rifles (104th), i. 11, 269
Welsby, Lieutenant, ii. 161
Welsh Fusiliers, Royal, i. 183, ii. 34, 41, 47, 153, 155, 162
—— Pioneers, i. 170, 184, ii. 11
West Kents, i. 244, 282
Wheeler, Major George, ii. 53 (note)
Willcocks, Sir William, ii. 110, 189, 190
Wiltshires, i. 177, 183, ii. 27, 33, 34, 92, 146, 163

Lightning Source UK Ltd.
Milton Keynes UK
UKOW05f0911290915

259471UK00011B/357/P